ARNOLD'S
ENGLISH
TEXTS

General Editor JAMES SUTHERLAND

Emeritus Professor of Modern Literature
University College, London

ROMANTIC CRITICISM
1800-1850

edited by R. A. FOAKES
Professor of English,
University of Kent at Canterbury

EDWARD ARNOLD (PUBLISHERS) LTD.
41 Maddox Street, London W.1

First published 1968

Boards Edition SBN: 7131 5379 2
Paper Edition SBN: 7131 5380 6

Printed in Great Britain by
The Camelot Press Ltd., London and Southampton

General Preface

THE design of this series is to present fully annotated selections from English literature which will, it is hoped, prove satisfactory both in their breadth and their depth. To achieve this, some of the volumes have been planned so as to provide a varied selection from the poetry or prose of a limited period, which is both long enough to have developed a literary movement, and short enough to allow for adequate representation of the chief writers and of the various cross-currents within the movement. Examples of such periods are the late seventeenth century and the early eighteenth century. In other volumes the principle of selection is to present a literary kind (e.g. satirical poetry, the literary ballad). Here it is possible to cover a longer period without sacrificing the unified and comprehensive treatment which is the governing idea for the whole series. Other volumes, again, are designed to present a group of writers who form some kind of "school" (e.g. the Elizabethan sonneteers, the followers of Ben Jonson), or who were closely enough linked for their work to be brought together (e.g. the poetry of Johnson and Goldsmith).

Each volume has a full critical introduction. Headnotes, a special feature of this series, provide relevant background and critical comment for the individual poems and prose pieces. The footnotes are for the most part explanatory, giving as briefly as possible information about persons, places, allusions of one kind or another, the meaning of words, etc., which the twentieth-century reader is likely to require. Each selection aims at providing examples of the best work of the authors represented, but it is hoped that the inclusion of some less familiar pieces not available in any other collection will widen the reader's experience and enjoyment of the literature under review. The series is intended for use in universities and the upper forms of schools.

This volume extends the scope of the series to include selections of literary criticism; it will be followed by similar volumes presenting the criticism of the neo-classical period, the twentieth century, and other periods. In the present volume Professor Foakes has concentrated on Romantic criticism of the first half of the nineteenth century; and although the various critics represented dealt incidentally with the drama, the novel, and other forms, their main attention was given, naturally enough, to poetry. Within the limits set it has been necessary to represent such a work as Coleridge's *Biographia Literaria* in selection, but many of the pieces chosen are given in a virtually complete form. When that was not practicable, the editor has taken pains to choose passages which present the most important ideas of each critic, and to do full justice to his critical significance. Most of the writers represented here are English; but the inclusion of Kant, Chateaubriand, Schlegel and Poe has enabled the editor not only to widen the scope of his volume, but to introduce some essential documents in the development of Romantic criticism. The headnotes are designed mainly to draw attention to the most significant pronouncements of each critic, and, by cross-reference, to indicate how critical ideas were shared and gradually established in the period covered by this volume.

Contents

Acknowledgements

The texts of essays and extracts reprinted in this volume are taken from the following editions:

Blake: *Poetry & Prose of William Blake*, edited by Geoffrey Keynes, revised edition 1946: pp. 833–6, 866–7, 809, 639, 821–2. *Reprinted by courtesy of Nonesuch Press Limited.*

Wordsworth: *Lyrical Ballads*, edited by R. I. Brett and A. R. Jones, 1963: pp. 235–66. *Reprinted by courtesy of Methuen & Company, Limited.*

Schlegel: *On Dramatic Art and Literature*, translated by John Black, 1846: pp. 19–27, 340, 342–3. Bohn's Library.

Wordsworth: *The Poetical Works of William Wordsworth*, edited by E. de Selincourt: Volume II (1944), pp. 431–42. *Reprinted by courtesy of the Clarendon Press, Oxford.*

Coleridge: *Biographia Literaria*, edited by J. Shawcross, corrected edition 1954: Volume I, pp. 58–64, 163–7, 174–87, 202; Volume II, pp. 9–13. *Reprinted by courtesy of the Clarendon Press, Oxford.*

Keats: *The Letters of John Keats*, edited by Hyder Rollins, Oxford University Press, 1958 (two volumes). *Extracts reprinted by courtesy of Harvard University Press.*

Hazlitt: *The Complete Works of William Hazlitt*, edited by P. P. Howe, 1930: Volume V, pp. 1–14. *Reprinted by courtesy of J. M. Dent & Sons, Limited.*

Shelley: *The Complete Works of Shelley*, edited by Roger Ingpen and Walter E. Peck; Volume VII (1965), pp. 109–16, 117–18, 129–40. *Reprinted by courtesy of Ernest Benn Limited.*

De Quincey: *Works*, edited by David Masson, 1897: Volume X, pp. 46–9.

Carlyle: *Critical and Miscellaneous Essays*, Centenary Edition, 1899: Volume III, pp. 3–7, 22–5.

Mill: *Early Essays by John Stuart Mill*, edited by J. M. W. Gibbs, 1897: pp. 201–14, 221–36.

Smith: "The Philosophy of Poetry", *Blackwood's Edinburgh Magazine* XXXVIII, December, 1835: pp. 827–39. *Reprinted by courtesy of William Blackwood & Sons, Limited.*

Keble: *Keble's Lectures on Poetry, 1832–1841*, translated by E. K. Francis, 1912: Volume I, pp. 19–21, 22, 47–8; Volume II, pp. 201, 476–8.

Poe: *Complete Poetical Works and Essays on Poetry*, edited by J. H. Ingram, 1888; pp. 153–5, 157–61, 166, 172–4.

Kant: *Immanuel Kant's Critique of Pure Reason*, translated by Norman Kemp Smith, 1933, pp. 111, 141–7. *Reprinted by courtesy of Macmillan & Company Limited, St. Martin's Press, and The Macmillan Company of Canada Limited.*

Chateaubriand: *Œuvres Complètes*, Paris, 1852: Volume III, pp. 174–5 [Editor's translation].

Note: The texts as indicated above have been followed closely, except that eccentric spellings and punctuation have been regularised for the sake of consistency and for ease of reading.

Introduction

SOME of the best romantic critical writing remains buried in periodicals or voluminous collected editions, and only a few well-known pieces are readily found in cheap and accessible form. The selection of essays now reprinted is designed to provide a comprehensive range of material illustrating the bases and developments of Romantic critical theory. It can be used as a companion to the study of the poetry of the first half of the nineteenth century, or as a companion to the study of the critical tradition as exemplified in M. H. Abrams' *The Mirror and the Lamp* (1953). Each selection is prefaced by a brief headnote giving basic factual information and drawing attention to ideas of general importance, and to links with other selections. The volume is provided with a full index of critical terms like "imagination," "power" or "emotion", and changes in ideas may be traced by means of this.

*   *   *

Some aspects of Romantic critical thinking were anticipated in the eighteenth century, and its influence is with us still. In spite of this, and in spite of the difficulties modern critics have in defining Romanticism, the essays reprinted in this volume belong to a recognisable tradition that was dominant in the period they cover—roughly the half-century from 1800 to 1850. They represent Romantic criticism in that they begin from a rejection of the rationalism and of the neo-classicism that were prominent features of eighteenth-century literature; they tend to see art as subjective and particular, as a welling-up of emotion, as organic, and reject a view of it as objective, mirroring external reality, and seeking its "perfect form" by "leaving out particulars, and retaining only general ideas".[1] They tend to elevate the imagination at the expense of the understanding, the unconscious as opposed to the conscious powers of the mind, and the intensity of the vision rather than the artistic powers of a writer.

Many of the authors of these essays were poets whose business was to defend the kind of poetry they were writing. They mentioned the novel from time to time and John Stuart Mill gave it several pages, so that he

[1] Sir Joshua Reynolds, *Discourses on Art*: the quotation is from Discourse IV, delivered at the Royal Academy in December 1771.

could distinguish poetry as superior, but he may have been the first, in 1833, to regard fiction as a serious competitor to the higher art of poetry. The period from 1800 to 1850 was the last in which poetry meant literature; in other words, the critic took for granted as a secure basis for his arguments the idea that the poem was the supreme literary form, and paid homage to prose works only in so far as they could be regarded in some sense or other as poetry. So Mill claimed (p. 154), "Many of the finest poems are in the form of novels, and in almost all good novels there is true poetry". The critics then, when generalising about literature, talked in fact about poetry, including poetic drama, as indeed critics had always done. The age of the novel had begun by 1850, but its heyday was still to come.

Although the critics represented in this collection begin from similar premisses, they nevertheless offer a less homogeneous picture than the blanket term "Romantic" might suggest. The early critics were struggling like Wordsworth in his Preface to *Lyrical Ballads*, to formulate their ideas, and what for them was a hard-won formulation might be taken over and used much more casually later on. A notable example is Wordsworth's careful attempt in his Preface to *Lyrical Ballads* (1800-2), to elaborate an expressive theory of poetry; he defined poetry twice (pp. 27, 43) as "The spontaneous overflow of powerful feelings", but went on to qualify this notion of poetry as the expression of emotion, by adding that poems of any value could only be produced by a man "who being possessed of more than usual organic sensibility had also thought long and deeply" (p. 27). His sense of the primacy of feeling in poetic expression, and of pleasure in response to poetry, was linked with a strong didactic urge, and he was much concerned to bring home to his readers his claim that each of his poems had "a purpose" (p. 28).

Later writers tended to seize on Wordsworth's central concept of poetry as expression of feeling, and ignore his qualifications. On the one hand, the idea of the feelings welling up from some deep region of the soul seemed to establish their truth and immediacy, so that Keats could write in 1817 of the "holiness of the Heart's affections" (p. 95), and Keble's sense of the "sacred feelings" of men encouraged him to ascribe a quasi-religious function to poetry (p. 196). So to some of the critics who followed after Wordsworth, the expression of feeling came to seem a sufficient definition of poetry, and indeed J. S. Mill in 1833 reduced the formula to "Poetry is feeling" (p. 158). On the other hand, Wordsworth's concern with thought, which was elaborated in his Preface in a long passage linking the poet with the "man of science" as both seeking knowledge, tends to vanish, and there develops an increasing emphasis on the poet's concerns as distinct from and superior to those of other men. Poetry as expressing feeling is opposed to prose as concerned with information; the "man of science", a phrase used again by

J. S. Mill, or of business, deals in facts, and his mind works in different ways from that of a poet, whose aim should be to exclude "the outward and every-day world".

It would be wrong to see these departures from and revisions of Wordsworth's cautious formulations as simply a decline from, or distortion of, what was strong in Romantic criticism. Later critics seized on particular ideas and developed these because they seemed to reflect and support current poetic practice; and it could well be argued that they simply drew out the implications of Wordsworth's emphasis on emotion and ignored what was less important in his Preface. In a similar way, Coleridge's subtle discrimination between the powers of the imagination and the fancy is lost in the cruder generalising of Carlyle, who reduces Coleridge's attempt to define the process of intuition to a general association of poetic composition with the unconscious mind: "always the characteristic of right performance is a certain spontaneity, an unconsciousness" (p. 147). At the same time, the increasing emphasis on spontaneity and feeling, and the simplifying out of the complicated and difficult theorising of Wordsworth and Coleridge spring to a large extent from the need to make use of what was most immediately valuable in their analyses.

The first generation of Romantic poets attempted to use inherited forms, the ballad, the epic, the five-act poetic drama, the meditative blank-verse poem, as a basis for their art. They had some difficulty in assimilating old forms to new content, and the shape of some poems seems at first sight odd; so, for example, Wordsworth's *The Prelude* (completed in 1805) has thirteen books, or fourteen in the revised version printed in 1850. For poets like Wordsworth the supreme task appeared still to be the composition of a poem on a grand scale, as *The Prelude* was itself intended to be but the "ante-chapel" to a much grander design. Blake, Keats, Shelley and Byron all attempted poems on an epic scale, like *Hyperion* or *Don Juan*. However, in Wordsworth's critical account of poetry as the "spontaneous overflow of powerful feelings", and in Coleridge's emphasis on the intuitive nature of the creative act, there lay an idea of poetry that was to some extent at odds with their practice as poets.

They were clinging to old forms, and to old ideas about art as representative, as concerned with truth and value, and as determined by its form, "the parts of which mutually support and explain each other" (p. 91); at the same time they were experimenting in their poetry, and proposing new ideas about art as expressing feeling, and as born out of the "sacred power of self-intuition" (p. 79). As later critics drew out the implications of Wordsworth's emphasis on emotion, or Shelley's stress on unpremeditated inspiration as the immediate source of poetry, they also inevitably came to give prominence to the poetic forms which best exemplified a theory of poetry based on intensity of personal utterance. It is in the poem of meditation, the hymn, the melancholy or rapturous ode, and the personal lyric, that Romantic poetry finds its most characteristic expression, and as critics came to attach increasing importance to lyric poetry, they were reflecting to a large extent a movement in poetry itself.

At the same time, this elevation of the lyric was perhaps conditioned by a desire to defend poetry against possible encroachment or attack. So, on the one hand, J. S. Mill was anxious to distinguish poetry from fiction, seeing the novelist as concerned only with "outward things, not the inward man" (p. 155), and on the other hand De Quincey pressed home an antithesis between literature, or poetry, as communicating "power", and all other forms of discourse as communicating "knowledge" (p. 141). A price had to be paid for isolating poetry as a realm of discourse on its own, akin more to music than to other modes of writing, in a withdrawal from moral and political claims on its behalf. Some critics were content to pay this price, and to take their stand on what seemed to them the purest kind of poetry. Edgar Allan Poe summed up this trend by rejecting the idea of a "long poem" altogether, and making beauty the sole "province of the poem"; he said "Its sole arbiter is Taste. With the Intellect or with the Conscience, it has only collateral relations. Unless incidentally, it has no concern whatever either with Duty or with Truth."

This is an extreme view, but it represents a natural process of development from the expressive theory of poetry initiated by Wordsworth. His determination in his Preface to *Lyrical Ballads* to maintain an identity between poetry and other forms of discourse was exemplified in his assertion, criticised later by Coleridge in Chapter 18 of *Biographia Literaria* (1817), that there "neither is nor can be any essential difference" between "the language of prose and metrical composition" (p. 32). The desire to maintain this link withered away as critics came to make ever more rigorous distinctions between prose and poetry; and the formula of Alexander Smith, writing in 1835, "prose is the language of intelligence, poetry of emotion", anticipated the distinction between "scientific" and "emotive" language given currency in this century by I. A. Richards in his *Science and Poetry* (1926). The rejection of epic and of public forms of verse for lyric and private forms, made it difficult to hold on to that sense of moral and religious grandeur which informs the idea of poetry held by Wordsworth, Coleridge and Shelley. However, not many critics were content with Poe to make beauty the sole "province of a poem", and John Keble ably defended poetry as fostering piety, and as therapeutic in relieving the overburdened spirit. He described the art of poetry as "a kind of medicine divinely bestowed upon man"

(p. 195). This is a good deal less than earlier Romantic critics had urged, but at least poetry for him retained psychological and quasi-religious functions.

Although the critics represented in this volume start from similar assumptions about the nature of poetry, and may properly be called Romantic, they reflect, as has been shown, important changes and developments in ideas about the scope, function and effect of poetry. At the beginning of the nineteenth century, Wordsworth was at work on *The Prelude*, a major poem in blank verse written in an epic tradition derived from Milton and Spenser; at the end of the period covered in this volume, Tennyson produced his major poem, *In Memoriam*, a collection of short lyrics. The difference between these is measured by the change in critical attitude shown in the essays printed here. It is odd that, by some irony of chance, *The Prelude*, posthumously, *In Memoriam*, and Poe's *The Poetic Principle*, were all published in the same year, 1850, as if to mark the close of an era.

William Blake

1757–1827

LETTERS AND OCCASIONAL NOTES 1799–1826

WILLIAM BLAKE's vehement reaction against the prevailing climate of opinion in the late eighteenth century is illustrated in his annotations to the *Discourses* delivered by Sir Joshua Reynolds (1723–92) to students at the annual prizegiving of the Royal Academy between 1769 and 1790; Reynolds offered a neo-classic formulation of principles based on the "grand style", and on "General Ideas, the Presiding Principle which regulates every Part of Art" (Discourse IV). Blake noted in his copy of the *Discourses*, "This man was hired to Depress Art", and "To Generalise is to be an Idiot. To Particularise is the Alone Distinction of Merit." In such sharp notes, and in occasional remarks in letters, Blake heralded much that was to inform the critical writings of the Romantic movement. As against Reynolds' principles based on "General Ideas", Blake offers "Imagination & Vision" (p. 19); as against reason, he values "Spiritual Sensation", and finds a particular visionary power and capacity for spiritual sensation in children; as against "implicit obedience to the *Rules of Art*" (Discourse I) as a basis for training, Blake proclaims the need to rely on inspiration (p. 22).

Like Shelley (see p. 118), Blake was much influenced by Plato and identified the world of the imagination with the "Infinite & Eternal" (p. 21). In associating poetry, through the divine vision of the imagination, with religious experience, he proposed what was to become an important aspect of the theories of Wordsworth, Coleridge, and Keble (see pp. 38, 89, 197). Blake also emphasised the importance of the unconscious or spontaneous powers of the mind (p. 20), again pointing to what was to develop as an important theme in Romantic critical theory (see below, pp. 27, 144). At the same time, Blake equated the world of imagination with the world of eternity; for him the imagination operated in a realm of the spirit, beyond the immediate world apprehended by the senses. So, while appreciating Wordsworth, he found in his 1815 Preface (see below, p. 22) "the natural Man rising up against the Spiritual Man continually", inasmuch as Wordsworth associates his world of imagination with the world of natural objects.

The extracts printed here are from the *Poetry & Prose of William Blake*, edited by Geoffrey Keynes (Nonesuch edition, revised 1946), pp. 833–6, 866–7, 809, 639, 821–2.

TO THE REVD. DR. TRUSLER[1]

13 Hercules Buildings,
Lambeth,
August 23, 1799.

Revd. Sir,

I really am sorry that you are fall'n out with the Spiritual World, Especially if I should have to answer for it. I feel very sorry that your Ideas & Mine on Moral Painting differ so much as to have made you angry with my method of study. If I am wrong, I am wrong in good company. I had hoped your plan comprehended All Species of this Art, & Especially that you would not regret that Species which gives Existence to Every other, namely, Visions of Eternity. You say that I want somebody to Elucidate my Ideas. But you ought to know that What is Grand is necessarily obscure to Weak men. That which can be made Explicit to the Idiot is not worth my care. The wisest of the Ancients consider'd what is not too Explicit as the fittest for Instruction, because it rouses the faculties to act. I name Moses, Solomon, Esop, Homer, Plato.

But as you have favor'd me with your remarks on my Design, permit me in return to defend it against a mistaken one, which is, That I have supposed Malevolence without a Cause. Is not Merit in one a Cause of Envy in another, & Serenity & Happiness & Beauty a Cause of Malevolence? But Want of Money & the Distress of a Thief can never be alleged as the Cause of his Thieving, for many honest people endure greater hardships with Fortitude. We must therefore seek the Cause elsewhere than in want of Money, for that is the Miser's passion, not the Thief's.

I have therefore proved your Reasoning Ill proportion'd, which you can never prove my figures to be; they are those of Michael Angelo, Rafael & the Antique, & of the best living Models. I perceive that your Eye is perverted by Caricature Prints, which

[1] *Dr. Trusler:* John Trusler (1735–1820), clergyman and voluminous author.

ought not to abound so much as they do. Fun I love, but too much Fun is of all things the most loathsom. Mirth is better than Fun, & Happiness is better than Mirth. I feel that a Man may be happy in This World. And I know that This World Is a World of Imagination & Vision. I see Every thing I paint In This World, but Every body does not see alike. To the eyes of a Miser a Guinea is far more beautiful than the Sun, & and a bag worn with the use of Money has more beautiful proportions than a Vine filled with Grapes. The tree which moves some to tears of joy is in the Eyes of others only a Green thing which stands in the way. Some see Nature all Ridicule & Deformity,[2] & by these I shall not regulate my proportions; & some scarce see Nature at all. But to the Eyes of the Man of Imagination, Nature is Imagination itself. As a man is, so he sees. As the Eye is formed, such are its Powers. You certainly Mistake, when you say that the Visions of Fancy are not to be found in This World. To Me This World is all One continued Vision of Fancy or Imagination, & I feel Flatter'd when I am told so. What is it sets Homer, Virgil & Milton in so high a rank of Art? Why is the Bible more Entertaining & Instructive than any other book? Is it not because they are addressed to the Imagination, which is Spiritual Sensation, & but mediately to the Understanding of Reason? Such is True Painting, and such was alone valued by the Greeks & the best modern Artists. Consider what Lord Bacon says: "Sense sends over to Imagination before Reason have judged, & Reason sends over to Imagination before the Decree can be acted". See Advancemt. of Learning, Part 2 P.47 of first Edition.[3]

But I am happy to find a Great Majority of Fellow Mortals who can Elucidate My Visions, & Particularly they have been Elucidated by Children, who have taken a greater delight in contemplating my Pictures than I even hoped. Neither Youth nor Childhood is Folly or Incapacity. Some Children are Fools & so are some Old Men. But There is a vast Majority on the side of Imagination or Spiritual Sensation.

[2] *Nature all Ridicule & Deformity:* alluding probably to Sir Joshua Reynolds' *Discourses on Art*, and especially to Discourse III on ideal beauty, in which Reynolds remarks that all objects in nature "have their blemishes and defects".

[3] *Advancement of Learning*, Book 2, XII. 1.

To Engrave after another Painter is infinitely more laborious than to Engrave one's own Inventions. And of the size you require my price has been Thirty Guineas, & I cannot afford to do it for less. I had Twelve for the Head I sent you as a specimen; but after my own designs I could do at least Six times the quantity of labour in the same time, which will account for the difference of price as also that Chalk Engraving⁴ is at least six times as laborious as Aqua tinta.⁵ I have no objection to Engraving after another Artist. Engraving is the profession I was apprenticed to, & should never have attempted to live by anything else, If orders had not come in for my Designs & Paintings, which I have the pleasure to tell you are increasing Every Day. Thus If I am a Painter it is not to be attributed to seeking after. But I am contented whether I live by Painting or Engraving.

I am, Revd. Sir, your very obedient servant,

William Blake.

FROM A LETTER TO THOMAS BUTTS⁶

April 25, 1803

But none can know the Spiritual Acts of my three years' Slumber on the banks of the Ocean, unless he has seen them in the Spirit, or unless he should read My long Poem descriptive of those Acts; for I have in these three years composed an immense number of verses on One Grand Theme, Similar to Homer's Iliad or Milton's Paradise Lost, the Persons & Machinery intirely new to the Inhabitants of Earth (some of the Persons Excepted). I have written this Poem from immediate Dictation, twelve or sometimes twenty or thirty lines at a time without Premeditation & even against my Will; the Time it has taken in writing was thus render'd Non Existent, & an immense Poem⁷ Exists which seems to be the Labour of a long Life, all produc'd without Labour or Study. I mention

---

⁴ *Chalk Engraving:* a method of etching in which the artist attempts with his tools to imitate the broken lines of crayon or chalk drawings.

⁵ *Aqua tinta:* aquatint, a method of etching on copper to produce an effect resembling water-colour drawing.

⁶ *Butts:* Thomas Butts (died 1845), friend and patron of Blake.

⁷ *Poem: Vala,* or *The Four Zoas.*

this to shew you what I think the Grand Reason of my being brought down here.

Annotations to SIR JOSHUA REYNOLDS—DISCOURSE VIII (written about 1808)[8]

BURKE'S Treatise on the Sublime & Beautiful[9] is founded on the Opinions of Newton & Locke; on this Treatise Reynolds has grounded many of his assertions in all his Discourses. I read Burke's Treatise when very Young; at the same time I read Locke on Human Understanding & Bacon's Advancement of Learning; on Every one of these Books I wrote my Opinions, & on looking them over find that my Notes on Reynolds in this Book are exactly Similar. I felt the Same Contempt & Abhorrence then that I do now. They mock Inspiration & Vision. Inspiration & Vision was then, & now is, & I hope will always Remain, my Element, my Eternal Dwelling place; how can I then hear it Contemned without returning Scorn for Scorn?

Notes for Blake's picture, VISION OF THE LAST JUDGMENT (written in 1810)

THIS world of Imagination is the world of Eternity; it is the divine bosom into which we shall all go after the death of the Vegetated body. This World of Imagination is Infinite & Eternal, whereas the world of Generation, or Vegetation, is Finite & Temporal. There Exist in that Eternal World the Permanent Realities of Every Thing which we see reflected in this Vegetable Glass of Nature. All Things are comprehended in their Eternal Forms in the divine body of the Saviour, the True Vine of Eternity, The Human Imagination, who appear'd to Me as Coming to Judgment among his Saints & throwing off the Temporal that the Eternal might be Establish'd; around him were seen the Images of Existences according to a certain order Suited to my Imaginative Eye as follows.

[8] *The Discourses on Art* were delivered at the Royal Academy between 1769 and 1790, and first published as a whole in 1797. Discourse VIII is concerned with the value and place of rules in the work of an artist.

[9] Edmund Burke's essay was first published in 1756.

Annotations to POEMS BY WILLIAM WORDSWORTH,
VOL. I, LONDON, MDCCCXV (*written in 1826*)[10]

*The powers requisite for the production of poetry are, first, those of
observation and description . . . 2dly, Sensibility.*

One Power alone makes a Poet; Imagination, The Divine Vision.

(Sub-title): *Poems Referring to the Period of Childhood.*

I see in Wordsworth the Natural Man rising up against the
Spiritual Man Continually, & then he is No Poet but a Heathen
Philosopher at Enmity against all true Poetry or Inspiration.

> *Influence of Natural Objects
> In calling forth and strengthening the Imagination
> in Boyhood and early Youth.*

Natural Objects always did & now do weaken, deaden & obliter-
ate Imagination in Me. Wordsworth must know that what he
Writes Valuable is Not to be found in Nature.

[10] See below, p. 61.

William Wordsworth

1770–1850

PREFACE TO *LYRICAL BALLADS* 1800; REVISED 1802

THE first edition of *Lyrical Ballads* (1798), experimental poems by Wordsworth and Coleridge written with a new simplicity of manner and emphasis on feeling as giving "importance to the action and situation" (see below, p. 29) was prefaced by an advertisement only. For the second edition, issued in London in 1800, Wordsworth provided a preface by way of a defence of his poems; this was altered in many details, and substantially expanded at one or two points when *Lyrical Ballads* was issued again in 1802. The following reprint is based on the text of 1800, but the most important additions made in 1802 are included, and printed within square brackets. Wordsworth also added an appendix in 1802, to explain what he meant by the phrase "poetic diction", as a mode of language "differing materially from the real language of men in *any situations*"; I have not reprinted this, for it comments on what is already sufficiently clear in the Preface itself (see p. 33).

The central importance of the Preface resides in Wordsworth's setting forth of the proposition that poetry "takes its origin from emotion" (p. 43), is valuable because of its expression of feeling, and that "whatever passions" the poet "communicates to his Reader, those passions, if his Reader's mind be sound and vigorous, should always be accompanied with an overbalance of pleasure" (p. 43). Along with this emphasis on feeling as central in poetic creation and in the reader's response goes a conception of the poet as distinguished from other men by his possession primarily of a "more lively sensibility, more enthusiasm and tenderness"; he is like other men, but superior in his "more comprehensive soul", his sensitivity and sympathy (p. 34); the idea of poetry as an overflow of feeling tends to thrust aside any notion of art, of the poet's craft and skill. There follows, however, from the central theory, a necessary attention to diction, since the language of the poetry of feeling must be a "selection of the language really spoken by men" (p. 33) if it is to convey feelings directly and honestly. The true poet will never "break in upon the sanctity and truth of his pictures by transitory and accidental ornaments" (p. 39), or use an artificial poetic diction.

This essay was written as an apology for the poems presented in *Lyrical Ballads*, but it proved in many ways seminal, as a kind of Romantic manifesto, as a memorable statement of an expressive theory of poetry, and as a starting-point for much later criticism; see, for example, the selections from Coleridge, Keble and Mill in this volume.

THE First Volume of these Poems has already been submitted to general perusal. It was published, as an experiment which, I hoped, might be of some use to ascertain, how far, by fitting to metrical arrangement a selection of the real language of men in a state of vivid sensation, that sort of pleasure and that quantity of pleasure may be imparted, which a Poet may rationally endeavour to impart.

I had formed no very inaccurate estimate of the probable effect of those Poems: I flattered myself that they who should be pleased with them would read them with more than common pleasure: and on the other hand I was well aware that by those who should dislike them they would be read with more than common dislike. The result has differed from my expectation in this only, that I have pleased a greater number, than I ventured to hope I should please.

For the sake of variety and from a consciousness of my own weakness I was induced to request the assistance of a Friend,[1] who furnished me with the Poems of the ANCIENT MARINER, the FOSTER-MOTHER'S TALE, the NIGHTINGALE, the DUNGEON, and the Poem entitled LOVE. I should not, however, have requested this assistance, had I not believed that the poems of my Friend would in a great measure have the same tendency as my own, and that, though there would be found a difference, there would be found no discordance in the colours of our style; as our opinions on the subject of poetry do almost entirely coincide.

Several of my Friends are anxious for the success of these Poems from a belief, that if the views, with which they were composed, were indeed realized, a class of Poetry would be produced, well adapted to interest mankind permanently, and not unimportant in the multiplicity and in the quality of its moral relations: and on this account they have advised me to prefix a systematic defence of the theory, upon which the poems were written. But I was unwilling to undertake the task, because I knew that on this occasion the Reader would look coldly upon my arguments, since I might be suspected

[1] *Friend:* Samuel Taylor Coleridge.

of having been principally influenced by the selfish and foolish hope of *reasoning* him into an approbation of these particular Poems: and I was still more unwilling to undertake the task, because adequately to display my opinions and fully to enforce my arguments would require a space wholly disproportionate to the nature of a preface. For to treat the subject with the clearness and coherence, of which I believe it susceptible, it would be necessary to give a full account of the present state of the public taste in this country, and to determine how far this taste is healthy or depraved; which again could not be determined, without pointing out, in what manner language and the human mind act and react on each other, and without retracing the revolutions not of literature alone but likewise of society itself. I have therefore altogether declined to enter regularly upon this defence; yet I am sensible, that there would be some impropriety in abruptly obtruding upon the Public, without a few words of introduction, Poems so materially different from those, upon which general approbation is at present bestowed.

It is supposed, that by the act of writing in verse an Author makes a formal engagement that he will gratify certain known habits of association, that he not only thus apprizes the Reader that certain classes of ideas and expressions will be found in his book, but that others will be carefully excluded. This exponent or symbol held forth by metrical language must in different aeras of literature have excited very different expectations: for example, in the age of Catullus, Terence and Lucretius, and that of Statius or Claudian,[2] and in our own country, in the age of Shakespeare and Beaumont and Fletcher, and that of Donne and Cowley, or Dryden, or Pope. I will not take upon me to determine the exact import of the promise which by the act of writing in verse an Author in the present day makes to his Reader; but I am certain it will appear to many persons that I have not fulfilled the terms of an engagement thus voluntarily contracted. [*1802:* They who have been accustomed to the gaudiness and inane phraseology of many modern writers, if they persist in reading this book to its conclusion, will, no doubt, frequently have to struggle with feelings of strangeness and awkwardness: they will

[2] Of these Roman writers, Catullus, Terence and Lucretius lived in the first and second centuries B.C., Statius in the first century A.D., and Claudian in the fourth century A.D.

look round for poetry, and will be induced to inquire by what species of courtesy these attempts can be permitted to assume that title.] I hope therefore the Reader will not censure me, if I attempt to state what I have proposed to myself to perform, and also (as far as the limits of a preface will permit), to explain some of the chief reasons which have determined me in the choice of my purpose: that at least he may be spared any unpleasant feeling of disappointment, and that I myself may be protected from the most dishonorable accusation which can be brought against an Author, namely, that of an indolence which prevents him from endeavouring to ascertain what is his duty, or, when his duty is ascertained, prevents him from performing it.

The principal object then which I proposed to myself in these Poems was [*1802*: to chuse incidents and situations from common life, and to relate or describe them, throughout, as far as was possible, in a selection of language really used by men; and, at the same time, to throw over them a certain colouring of imagination, whereby ordinary things should be presented to the mind in an unusual way; and further, and above all,] to make the[se] incidents of common life[3] [and situations] interesting by tracing in them, truly though not ostentatiously, the primary laws of our nature: chiefly as far as regards the manner in which we associate ideas in a state of excitement. Low and rustic life was generally chosen because in that situation the essential passions of the heart find a better soil in which they can attain their maturity, are less under restraint, and speak a plainer and more emphatic language; because in that situation our elementary feelings exist in a state of greater simplicity and consequently may be more accurately contemplated and more forcibly communicated; because the manners of rural life germinate from those elementary feelings; and from the necessary character of rural occupations are more easily comprehended; and are more durable; and lastly, because in that situation the passions of men are incorporated with the beautiful and permanent forms of nature. The language too of these men is adopted (purified indeed from what appear to be its real defects, from all lasting and rational causes of dislike or disgust) because such men hourly communicate with the best objects from which the

[3] "of common life" omitted 1802.

best part of language is originally derived; and because, from their rank in society and the sameness and narrow circle of their intercourse, being less under the action of social vanity they convey their feelings and notions in simple and unelaborated expressions. Accordingly such a language arising out of repeated experience and regular feelings is a more permanent and a far more philosophical language than that which is frequently substituted for it by Poets, who think that they are conferring honour upon themselves and their art in proportion as they separate themselves from the sympathies of men, and indulge in arbitrary and capricious habits of expression in order to furnish food for fickle taste and fickle appetites of their own creation.*

I cannot be insensible of the present outcry against the triviality and meanness both of thought and language, which some of my contemporaries have occasionally introduced into their metrical compositions; and I acknowledge that this defect, where it exists, is more dishonorable to the Writer's own character than false refinement or arbitrary innovation, though I should contend at the same time that it is far less pernicious in the sum of its consequences. From such verses the Poems in these volumes will be found distinguished at least by one mark of difference, that each of them has a worthy *purpose*. Not that I mean to say, that I always began to write with a distinct purpose formally conceived; but I believe that my habits of meditation have so formed my feelings, as that my descriptions of such objects as strongly excite those feelings, will be found to carry along with them a *purpose*. If in this opinion I am mistaken I can have little right to the name of a Poet. For all good poetry is the spontaneous overflow of powerful feelings; but though this be true, Poems to which any value can be attached, were never produced on any variety of subjects but by a man who being possessed of more than usual organic sensibility had also thought long and deeply. For our continued influxes of feeling are modified and directed by our thoughts, which are indeed the representatives of all our past feelings; and as by contemplating the relation of these general representatives to each other, we discover

* It is worth while here to observe that the affecting parts of Chaucer are almost always expressed in language pure and universally intelligible even to this day.

what is really important to men, so by the repetition and continuance of this act feelings connected with important subjects will be
nourished, till at length, if we be originally possessed of much
organic sensibility, such habits of mind will be produced that by
obeying blindly and mechanically the impulses of those habits we
shall describe objects and utter sentiments of such a nature and in
such connection with each other, that the understanding of the
being to whom we address ourselves, if he be in a healthful state of
association, must necessarily be in some degree enlightened, his
taste exalted, and his affections ameliorated.

I have said that each of these poems has a purpose. I have also
informed my Reader what this purpose will be found principally
to be: namely to illustrate the manner in which our feelings and
ideas are associated in a state of excitement. But speaking in less
general language, it is to follow the fluxes and refluxes of the mind
when agitated by the great and simple affections of our nature.
This object I have endeavoured in these short essays to attain by
various means; by tracing the maternal passion through many of
its more subtle windings, as in the poems of the IDIOT BOY and the
MAD MOTHER; by accompanying the last struggles of a human being
at the approach of death, cleaving in solitude to life and society, as
in the Poem of the FORSAKEN INDIAN; by shewing, as in the Stanzas
entitled WE ARE SEVEN, the perplexity and obscurity which in childhood attend our notion of death, or rather our utter inability to
admit that notion; or by displaying the strength of fraternal, or to
speak more philosophically, of moral attachment when early
associated with the great and beautiful objects of nature, as in THE
BROTHERS; or, as in the Incident of SIMON LEE, by placing my Reader
in the way of receiving from ordinary moral sensations another
and more salutary impression than we are accustomed to receive
from them. It has also been part of my general purpose to attempt to
sketch characters under the influence of less impassioned feelings,
as in the OLD MAN TRAVELLING, THE TWO THIEVES, &c., characters of
which the elements are simple, belonging rather to nature than to
manners, such as exist now and will probably always exist, and
which from their constitution may be distinctly and profitably
contemplated. I will not abuse the indulgence of my Reader by
dwelling longer upon this subject; but it is proper that I should

mention one other circumstance which distinguishes these Poems from the popular Poetry of the day; it is this, that the feeling therein developed gives importance to the action and situation and not the action and situation to the feeling. My meaning will be rendered perfectly intelligible by referring my Reader to the Poems entitled POOR SUSAN and the CHILDLESS FATHER, particularly to the last Stanza of the latter Poem.

I will not suffer a sense of false modesty to prevent me from asserting, that I point my Reader's attention to this mark of distinction far less for the sake of these particular Poems than from the general importance of the subject. The subject is indeed important! For the human mind is capable of excitement without the application of gross and violent stimulants; and he must have a very faint perception of its beauty and dignity who does not know this, and who does not further know that one being is elevated above another in proportion as he possesses this capability. It has therefore appeared to me that to endeavour to produce or enlarge this capability is one of the best services in which, at any period, a Writer can be engaged; but this service, excellent at all times, is especially so at the present day. For a multitude of causes unknown to former times are now acting with a combined force to blunt the discriminating powers of the mind, and unfitting it for all voluntary exertion to reduce it to a state of almost savage torpor. The most effective of these causes are the great national events which are daily taking place, and the increasing accumulation of men in cities, where the uniformity of their occupations produces a craving for extraordinary incident which the rapid communication of intelligence hourly gratifies. To this tendency of life and manners the literature and theatrical exhibitions of the country have conformed themselves. The invaluable works of our elder writers, I had almost said the works of Shakespeare and Milton, are driven into neglect by frantic novels, sickly and stupid German Tragedies, and deluges of idle and extravagant stories in verse.[4]—When I think upon this degrading

4 *novels . . . Tragedies . . . stories in verse:* Wordsworth is thinking probably of novels like the sensational *The Monk* (1796) by M. G. Lewis, and of the spate of German-influenced drama and translations of plays by Kotzebue and Schiller that were popular in the 1790s. The "stories in verse" are less easy to identify.

thirst after outrageous stimulation I am almost ashamed to have spoken of the feeble effort with which I have endeavoured to counteract it; and reflecting upon the magnitude of the general evil, I should be oppressed with no dishonorable melancholy, had I not a deep impression of certain inherent and indestructible qualities of the human mind, and likewise of certain powers in the great and permanent objects that act upon it which are equally inherent and indestructible; and did I not further add to this impression a belief that the time is approaching when the evil will be systematically opposed by men of greater powers and with far more distinguished success.

Having dwelt thus long on the subjects and aim of these Poems, I shall request the Reader's permission to apprize him of a few circumstances relating to their *style*, in order, among other reasons, that I may not be censured for not having performed what I never attempted. Except in a very few instances the Reader will find no personifications of abstract ideas in these volumes, not that I mean to censure such personifications: they may be well fitted for certain sorts of composition, but in these Poems I propose to myself to imitate, and, as far as possible, to adopt the very language of men, and I do not find that such personifications make any regular or natural part of that language. I wish to keep my Reader in the company of flesh and blood, persuaded that by so doing, I shall interest him. Not but that I believe that others who pursue a different track may interest him likewise: I do not interfere with their claim, I only wish to prefer a different claim of my own. There will also be found in these volumes little of what is usually called poetic diction; I have taken as much pains to avoid it as others ordinarily take to produce it; this I have done for the reason already alleged, to bring my language near to the language of men, and further, because the pleasure which I have proposed to myself to impart is of a kind very different from that which is supposed by many persons to be the proper object of poetry. I do not know how without being culpably particular I can give my Reader a more exact notion of the style in which I wished these poems to be written than by informing him that I have at all times endeavoured to look steadily at my subject, consequently I hope it will be found that there is in these Poems little falsehood of description, and that my ideas are expressed in language fitted to their respective importance. Something I must have gained by this practice, as it is friendly to one property of all good poetry, namely good sense; but it has necessarily cut me off from a large portion of phrases and figures of speech which from father to son have long been regarded as the common inheritance of Poets. I have also thought it expedient to restrict myself still further, having abstained from the use of many expressions, in themselves proper and beautiful, but which have been foolishly repeated by bad Poets till such feelings of disgust are connected with them as it is scarcely possible by any art of association to overpower.

If in a Poem there should be found a series of lines, or even a single line, in which the language, though naturally arranged and according to the strict laws of metre, does not differ from that of prose, there is a numerous class of critics who, when they stumble upon these prosaisms as they call them, imagine that they have made a notable discovery, and exult over the Poet as over a man ignorant of his own profession. Now these men would establish a canon of criticism which the Reader will conclude he must utterly reject if he wishes to be pleased with these volumes. And it would be a most easy task to prove to him that not only the language of a large portion of every good poem, even of the most elevated character, must necessarily, except with reference to the metre, in no respect differ from that of good prose, but likewise that some of the most interesting parts of the best poems will be found to be strictly the language of prose when prose is well written. The truth of this assertion might be demonstrated by innumerable passages from almost all the poetical writings, even of Milton himself. I have not space for much quotation; but, to illustrate the subject in a general manner, I will here adduce a short composition of Gray,[5] who was at the head of those who by their reasonings have attempted to widen the space of separation betwixt Prose and Metrical composition, and was more than any other man curiously elaborate in the structure of his own poetic diction.

[5] *Gray:* Thomas Gray (1716–71); the sonnet cited here was written in 1742 on the death of Gray's friend Richard West.

In vain to me the smiling mornings shine,
And reddening Phoebus lifts his golden fire:
The birds in vain their amorous descant join,
Or chearful fields resume their green attire:
These ears alas! for other notes repine;
A different object do these eyes require;
My lonely anguish melts no heart but mine;
And in my breast the imperfect joys expire;
Yet Morning smiles the busy race to cheer,
And new-born pleasure brings to happier men;
The fields to all their wonted tribute bear;
To warm their little loves the birds complain.
I fruitless mourn to him that cannot hear
And weep the more because I weep in vain.

It will easily be perceived that the only part of this Sonnet which is of any value is the lines printed in Italics: it is equally obvious that except in the rhyme, and in the use of the single word "fruitless" for fruitlessly, which is so far a defect, the language of these lines does in no respect differ from that of prose.

Is there, then, it will be asked, no essential difference between the language of prose and metrical composition? I answer that there neither is nor can be any essential difference.[6] We are fond of tracing the resemblance between Poetry and Painting, and, accordingly, we call them Sisters: but where shall we find bonds of connection sufficiently strict to typify the affinity betwixt metrical and prose composition? They both speak by and to the same organs; the bodies in which both of them are clothed may be said to be of the same substance, their affections are kindred and almost identical, not

[6] "Is there then . . . any essential difference" becomes, *1802:* "By the foregoing quotation I have shewn that the language of Prose may yet be well adapted to Poetry; and I have previously asserted that a large portion of the language of every good poem can in no respect differ from that of good Prose. I will go further. I do not doubt that it may be safely affirmed that there neither is, nor can be, any essential difference between the language of prose and metrical composition."

necessarily differing even in degree; Poetry* sheds no tears "such as Angels weep,"[7] but natural and human tears; she can boast of no celestial Ichor[8] that distinguishes her vital juices from those of prose; the same human blood circulates through the veins of them both.

If it be affirmed that rhyme and metrical arrangement of themselves constitute a distinction which overturns what I have been saying on the strict affinity of metrical language with that of prose, and paves the way for other distinctions which the mind voluntarily admits, I answer that [1802:[9] the language of such Poetry as I am recommending is, as far as is possible, a selection of the language really spoken by men; that this selection, wherever it is made with true taste and feeling, will of itself form a distinction far greater than would at first be imagined, and will entirely separate the composition from the vulgarity and meanness of ordinary life; and, if metre be super-added thereto, I believe that a dissimilitude will be produced altogether sufficient for the gratification of a rational mind. What other distinction would we have? Whence is it to come? And where is it to exist? Not, surely, where the Poet speaks through the mouths of his characters: it cannot be necessary here, either for elevation of style, or any of its supposed ornaments: for, if the Poet's subject be judiciously chosen, it will naturally, and upon fit occasion, lead him to passions the language of which, if selected truly and judiciously, must necessarily be dignified and variegated, and alive with metaphors and figures. I forbear to speak of an incongruity which would shock the intelligent Reader, should the Poet interweave any foreign splendour of his own with that which

* I here use the word "Poetry" (though against my own judgment) as opposed to the word Prose, and synonymous with metrical composition. But much confusion has been introduced into criticism by this contradistinction of Poetry and Prose, instead of the more philosophical one of Poetry and Science. The only strict antithesis to Prose is Metre [1802: nor is this, in truth a strict antithesis; because lines and passages of metre so naturally occur in writing prose, that it would be scarcely possible to avoid them, even were it desirable].

[7] Cited from Milton, *Paradise Lost*, I. 620.

[8] *Ichor*: the fluid that was supposed to circulate, instead of blood, in the veins of the Greek Gods.

[9] The 1800 text is continued on page 40.

B

the passion naturally suggests: it is sufficient to say that such addition is unnecessary. And, surely, it is more probable that those passages, which with propriety abound with metaphors and figures, will have their due effect, if, upon other occasions where the passions are of a milder character, the style also be subdued and temperate.

But, as the pleasure which I hope to give by the Poems I now present to the Reader must depend entirely on just notions upon this subject, and, as it is in itself of the highest importance to our taste and moral feelings, I cannot content myself with these detached remarks. And if, in what I am about to say, it shall appear to some that my labour is unnecessary, and that I am like a man fighting a battle without enemies, I would remind such persons, that, whatever may be the language outwardly holden by men, a practical faith in the opinions which I am wishing to establish is almost unknown. If my conclusions are admitted, and carried as far as they must be carried if admitted at all, our judgments concerning the works of the greatest Poets both ancient and modern will be far different from what they are at present, both when we praise, and when we censure: and our moral feelings influencing, and influenced by these judgments will, I believe, be corrected and purified.

Taking up the subject, then, upon general grounds, I ask what is meant by the word Poet? What is a Poet? To whom does he address himself? And what language is to be expected from him? He is a man speaking to men: a man, it is true, endued with more lively sensibility, more enthusiasm and tenderness, who has a greater knowledge of human nature, and a more comprehensive soul, than are supposed to be common among mankind; a man pleased with his own passions and volitions, and who rejoices more than other men in the spirit of life that is in him; delighting to contemplate similar volitions and passions as manifested in goings-on of the Universe, and habitually impelled to create them where he does not find them. To these qualities he has added a disposition to be affected more than other men by absent things as if they were present; an ability of conjuring up in himself passions, which are indeed far from being the same as those produced by real events, yet (especially in those parts of the general sympathy which are pleasing and delightful) do more nearly resemble the passions produced by real events, than anything which, from the motions of their own minds merely, other men are accustomed to feel in themselves; whence, and from practice, he has acquired a greater readiness and power in expressing what he thinks and feels, and especially those thoughts and feelings which, by his own choice, or from the structure of his own mind, arise in him without immediate external excitement.

But, whatever portion of this faculty we may suppose even the greatest Poet to possess, there cannot be a doubt but that the language which it will suggest to him, must, in liveliness and truth, fall far short of that which is uttered by men in real life, under the actual pressure of those passions, certain shadows of which the Poet thus produces, or feels to be produced, in himself. However exalted a notion we would wish to cherish of the character of a Poet, it is obvious, that, while he describes and imitates passions, his situation is altogether slavish and mechanical, compared with the freedom and power of real and substantial action and suffering. So that it will be the wish of the Poet to bring his feelings near to those of the persons whose feelings he describes, nay, for short spaces of time perhaps, to let himself slip into an entire delusion, and even confound and identify his own feelings with theirs; modifying only the language which is thus suggested to him, by a consideration that he describes for a particular purpose, that of giving pleasure. Here, then, he will apply the principle on which I have so much insisted, namely, that of selection; on this he will depend for removing what would otherwise be painful or disgusting in the passion; he will feel that there is no necessity to trick out or to elevate nature: and, the more industriously he applies this principle, the deeper will be his faith that no words, which his fancy or imagination can suggest, will be to be compared with those which are the emanations of reality and truth.

But it may be said by those who do not object to the general spirit of these remarks, that, as it is impossible for the Poet to produce upon all occasions language as exquisitely fitted for the passion as that which the real passion itself suggests, it is proper that he should consider himself as in the situation of a translator, who deems himself justified when he substitutes excellences of another kind for those which are unattainable by him; and endeavours occasionally to surpass his original, in order to make some amends for the general inferiority to which he feels that he must submit. But this would be to encourage idleness and unmanly despair. Further, it is the language of men who speak of what they do not understand; who talk of Poetry as of a matter of amusement and idle pleasure; who will converse with us as gravely about a *taste* for Poetry, as they express it, as if it were a thing as indifferent as a taste for Rope-dancing, or Frontiniac[10] or Sherry. Aristotle,[11] I have been told, hath said, that Poetry is the most philosophic of all writing: it is so: its object is truth, not individual and local, but general, and operative; not standing upon external testimony, but carried alive into the heart by passion; truth which is its own testimony, which gives strength and divinity to the tribunal to which it appeals, and receives them from the same tribunal. Poetry is the image of man and nature. The obstacles which stand in the way of the fidelity of the Biographer and Historian, and of their consequent utility, are incalculably greater than those which are to be encountered by the Poet who has an adequate notion of the dignity of his art. The Poet writes under one restriction only, namely, that of the necessity of giving immediate pleasure to a human Being possessed of that information which may be expected from him, not as a lawyer, a physician, a mariner, an astronomer or a natural philosopher, but as a Man. Except this one restriction, there is no object standing between the Poet and the image of things; between this, and the Biographer and Historian there are a thousand.

Nor let this necessity of producing immediate pleasure be considered as a degradation of the Poet's art. It is far otherwise. It is an acknowledgment of the beauty of the universe, an acknowledgment the more sincere, because it is not formal, but indirect; it is a task light and easy to him who looks at the world in the spirit of love: further, it is a homage paid to the native and naked dignity of man, to the grand elementary principle of pleasure, by which he knows, and feels, and lives, and moves. We have no sympathy but what is

[10] *Frontiniac:* a wine made at Frontignan, near Montpellier in the department of Hérault, in Southern France.

[11] Aristotle in fact says, in Chapter IX of the *Poetics*, "poetry is more philosophical and more serious than history".

propagated by pleasure: I would not be misunderstood; but wherever we sympathize with pain it will be found that the sympathy is produced and carried on by subtle combinations with pleasure. We have no knowledge, that is, no general principles drawn from the contemplation of particular facts, but what has been built up by pleasure, and exists in us by pleasure alone. The Man of Science, the Chemist and Mathematician, whatever difficulties and disgusts they may have had to struggle with, know and feel this. However painful may be the objects with which the Anatomist's knowledge is connected, he feels that his knowledge is pleasure; and where he has no pleasure he has no knowledge. What then does the Poet? He considers man and the objects that surround him as acting and re-acting upon each other, so as to produce an infinite complexity of pain and pleasure; he considers man in his own nature and in his ordinary life as contemplating this with a certain quantity of immediate knowledge, with certain convictions, intuitions, and deductions which by habit become of the nature of intuitions; he considers him as looking upon this complex scene of ideas and sensations, and finding everywhere objects that immediately excite in him sympathies which, from the necessities of his nature, are accompanied by an overbalance of enjoyment.

To this knowledge which all men carry about with them, and to these sympathies in which without any other discipline than that of our daily life we are fitted to take delight, the Poet principally directs his attention. He considers man and nature as essentially adapted to each other, and the mind of man as naturally the mirror of the fairest and most interesting qualities of nature. And thus the Poet, prompted by this feeling of pleasure which accompanies him through the whole course of his studies, converses with general nature with affections akin to those, which, through labour and length of time, the Man of Science has raised up in himself, by conversing with those particular parts of nature which are the objects of his studies. The knowledge both of the Poet and the Man of Science is pleasure; but the knowledge of the one cleaves to us as a necessary part of our existence, our natural and unalienable inheritance; the other is a personal and individual acquisition, slow to come to us, and by no habitual and direct sympathy connecting us with our fellow-beings. The Man of Science seeks truth as a remote and unknown benefactor; he cherishes and loves it in his solitude: the Poet, singing a song in which all human beings join with him, rejoices in the presence of truth as our visible friend and hourly companion. Poetry is the breath and finer spirit of all knowledge: it is the impassioned expression which is in the countenance of all Science. Emphatically may it be said of the Poet, as Shakespeare hath said of man, "that he looks before and after."[12] He is the rock of defence of human nature; an upholder and preserver, carrying every where with him relationship and love. In spite of difference of soil and climate, of language and manners, of laws and customs, in spite of things silently gone out of mind and things violently destroyed, the Poet binds together by passion and knowledge the vast empire of human society, as it is spread over the whole earth, and over all time. The objects of the Poet's thoughts are every where; though the eyes and senses of man are, it is true, his favorite guides, yet he will follow wheresoever he can find an atmosphere of sensation in which to move his wings. Poetry is the first and last of all knowledge—it is as immortal as the heart of man. If the labours of men of Science should ever create any material revolution, direct or indirect, in our condition, and in the impressions which we habitually receive, the Poet will sleep then no more than at present, but he will be ready to follow the steps of the Man of Science, not only in those general indirect effects, but he will be at his side, carrying sensation into the midst of the objects of the Science itself. The remotest discoveries of the Chemist, the Botanist, or Mineralogist, will be as proper objects of the Poet's art as any upon which it can be employed, if the time should ever come when these things shall be familiar to us, and the relations under which they are contemplated by the followers of these respective Sciences shall be manifestly and palpably material to us as enjoying and suffering beings. If the time should ever come when what is now called Science, thus familiarized to men, shall be ready to put on, as it were, a form of flesh and blood, the Poet will lend his divine spirit to aid the transfiguration, and will welcome the Being thus produced, as a dear and genuine inmate of the household of man.— It is not, then, to be supposed that any one, who holds that sublime

[12] Alluding to *Hamlet*, V. iv. 37.

notion of Poetry which I have attempted to convey, will break in upon the sanctity and truth of his pictures by transitory and accidental ornaments, and endeavour to excite admiration of himself by arts, the necessity of which must manifestly depend upon the assumed meanness of his subject.

What I have thus far said applies to Poetry in general; but especially to those parts of composition where the Poet speaks through the mouths of his characters; and upon this point it appears to have such weight that I will conclude, there are few persons of good sense who would not allow that the dramatic parts of composition are defective, in proportion as they deviate from the real language of nature, and are coloured by a diction of the Poet's own, either peculiar to him as an individual Poet, or belonging simply to Poets in general, to a body of men who, from the circumstance of their compositions being in metre, it is expected will employ a particular language.

It is not, then, in the dramatic parts of composition that we look for this distinction of language; but still it may be proper and necessary where the Poet speaks to us in his own person and character. To this I answer by referring my Reader to the description which I have before given of a Poet. Among the qualities which I have enumerated as principally conducing to form a Poet, is implied nothing differing in kind from other men, but only in degree. The sum of what I have there said is, that the Poet is chiefly distinguished from other men by a greater promptness to think and feel without immediate external excitement, and a greater power in expressing such thoughts and feelings as are produced in him in that manner. But these passions and thoughts and feelings are the general passions and thoughts and feelings of men. And with what are they connected? Undoubtedly with our moral sentiments and animal sensations, and with the causes which excite these; with the operations of the elements and the appearances of the visible universe; with storm and sun-shine, with the revolutions of the seasons, with cold and heat, with loss of friends and kindred, with injuries and resentments, gratitude and hope, with fear and sorrow. These, and the like, are the sensations and objects which the Poet describes, as they are the sensations of other men, and the objects which interest them. The Poet thinks and feels in the spirit of the passions of men. How, then, can his language differ in any material degree from that of all other men who feel vividly and see clearly? It might be *proved* that it is impossible. But supposing that this were not the case, the Poet might then be allowed to use a peculiar language when expressing his feelings for his own gratification, or that of men like himself. But Poets do not write for Poets alone, but for men. Unless therefore we are advocates for that admiration which depends upon ignorance, and that pleasure which arises from hearing what we do not understand, the Poet must descend from this supposed height, and, in order to excite rational sympathy, he must express himself as other men express themselves. To this it may be added, that while he is only selecting from the real language of men, or, which amounts to the same thing, composing accurately in the spirit of such selection, he is treading upon safe ground, and we know what we are to expect from him. Our feelings are the same with respect to metre; for, as it may be proper to inform the Reader,] the distinction of rhyme and metre is regular and uniform, and not, like that which is produced by what is usually called poetic diction, arbitrary and subject to infinite caprices upon which no calculation whatever can be made. In the one case the Reader is utterly at the mercy of the Poet respecting what imagery or diction he may choose to connect with the passion, whereas in the other the metre obeys certain laws, to which the Poet and Reader both willingly submit because they are certain, and because no interference is made by them with the passion but such as the concurring testimony of ages has shewn to heighten and improve the pleasure which co-exists with it.

It will now be proper to answer an obvious question, namely, why, professing these opinions have I written in verse? To this in the first place I reply, because, however I may have restricted myself, there is still left open to me what confessedly constitutes the most valuable object of all writing whether in prose or verse, the great and universal passions of men, the most general and interesting of their occupations, and the entire world of nature, from which I am at liberty to supply myself with endless combinations of forms and imagery. Now, granting for a moment that whatever is interesting in these objects may be as vividly described in prose, why am I to be condemned if to such description I have endeavoured to superadd the charm which by the consent of all nations is acknowledged to exist in metrical language? To this it will be answered, that a very small part of the pleasure given by Poetry depends upon the metre, and that it is injudicious to write in metre unless it be accompanied with the other artificial distinctions of style with which metre is usually accompanied, and that by such deviation more will be lost from the shock which will be thereby given to the Reader's associations than will be counterbalanced by any pleasure which he can derive from the general power of numbers. In answer to those who thus contend for the necessity of accompanying metre with certain appropriate colours of style in order to the accomplishment of its appropriate end, and who also, in my opinion, greatly under-rate the power of metre in itself, it might perhaps be almost sufficient to observe that poems are extant, written upon more humble subjects, and in a more naked and simple style than what I have aimed at, which poems have continued to give pleasure from generation to generation. Now, if nakedness and simplicity be a defect, the fact here mentioned affords a strong presumption that poems somewhat less naked and simple are capable of affording pleasure at the present day; and all that I am now attempting is to justify myself for having written under the impression of this belief.

But I might point out various causes why, when the style is manly, and the subject of some importance, words metrically arranged will long continue to impart such a pleasure to mankind as he who is sensible of the extent of that pleasure will be desirous to impart. The end of Poetry is to produce excitement in coexistence with an overbalance of pleasure. Now, by the supposition, excitement is an unusual and irregular state of the mind; ideas and feelings do not in that state succeed each other in accustomed order. But if the words by which this excitement is produced are in themselves powerful, or the images and feelings have an undue proportion of pain connected with them, there is some danger that the excitement may be carried beyond its proper bounds. Now the co-presence of something regular, something to which the mind has been accustomed when in an unexcited or a less excited state, cannot but have great efficacy in tempering and restraining the passion by an intertexture of ordinary feeling [*1802:* and of feeling not strictly and necessarily connected with the passion. This is unquestionably

true, and hence, though the opinion will at first appear paradoxical, from the tendency of metre to divest language in a certain
degree of its reality, and thus to throw a sort of half-conciousness
of unsubstantial existence over the whole composition, there can
be little doubt but that more pathetic situations and sentiments, that
is, those which have a greater proportion of pain connected with
them, may be endured in metrical composition, especially in
rhyme, than in prose. The metre of the old ballads is very artless;
yet they contain many passages which would illustrate this opinion,
and, I hope, if the following Poems be attentively perused, similar
instances will be found in them]. This [opinion] may be [further]
illustrated by appealing to the Reader's own experience of the
reluctance with which he comes to the re-perusal of the distressful
parts of Clarissa Harlowe,[13] or the Gamester.[14] While Shakespeare's
writings, in the most pathetic scenes, never act upon us as pathetic
beyond the bounds of pleasure—an effect which is in a great degree
to be ascribed to small, but continual and regular impulses of
pleasurable surprise from the metrical arrangement.—On the other
hand (what it must be allowed will much more frequently happen)
if the Poet's words should be incommensurate with the passion, and
inadequate to raise the Reader to a height of desirable excitement,
then (unless the Poet's choice of his metre has been grossly injudicious), in the feelings of pleasure which the Reader has been accustomed to connect with metre in general, and in the feeling, whether
chearful or melancholy, which he has been accustomed to connect
with that particular movement of metre, there will be found
something which will greatly contribute to impart passion to the
words, and to effect the complex end which the Poet proposes to
himself.

If I had undertaken a systematic defence of the theory upon which
these poems are written, it would have been my duty to develop
the various causes upon which the pleasure received from metrical
language depends. Among the chief of these causes is to be reckoned
a principle which must be well known to those who have made any
of the Arts the object of accurate reflection; I mean the pleasure

[13] *Clarissa Harlowe:* a novel issued in 1747–8 by Samuel Richardson
(1689–1761).

[14] *The Gamester:* a tragedy written in 1753 by Edward Moore (1712–57).

which the mind derives from the perception of similitude in dissimilitude. This principle is the great spring of the activity of our minds and their chief feeder. From this principle the direction of the sexual appetite, and all the passions connected with it take their origin: It is the life of our ordinary conversation; and upon the accuracy with which similitude in dissimilitude, and dissimilitude in similitude are perceived, depend our taste and our moral feelings. It would not have been a useless employment to have applied this principle to the consideration of metre, and to have shown that metre is hence enabled to afford much pleasure, and to have pointed out in what manner that pleasure is produced. But my limits will not permit me to enter upon this subject, and I must content myself with a general summary.

I have said that Poetry is the spontaneous overflow of powerful feelings: it takes its origin from emotion recollected in tranquillity: the emotion is contemplated till by a species of reaction the tranquillity gradually disappears, and an emotion, similar to that which was before the subject of contemplation, is gradually produced, and does itself actually exist in the mind. In this mood successful composition generally begins, and in a mood similar to this it is carried on; but the emotion, of whatever kind and in whatever degree, from various causes is qualified by various pleasures, so that in describing any passions whatsoever, which are voluntarily described, the mind will upon the whole be in a state of enjoyment. Now if Nature be thus cautious in preserving in a state of enjoyment a being thus employed, the Poet ought to profit by the lesson thus held forth to him, and ought especially to take care, that whatever passions he communicates to his Reader, those passions, if his Reader's mind be sound and vigorous, should always be accompanied with an overbalance of pleasure. Now the music of harmonious metrical language, the sense of difficulty overcome, and the blind association of pleasure which has been previously received from works of rhyme or metre of the same or similar construction, [*1802:* an indistinct perception perpetually renewed of language closely resembling that of real life, and yet, in the circumstance of metre, differing from it so widely,] all these imperceptibly make up a complex feeling of delight, which is of the most important use in tempering the painful feeling which will always be found intermingled with powerful descriptions of the deeper passions. This effect is always produced in pathetic and impassioned poetry; while in lighter compositions the ease and gracefulness with which the Poet manages his numbers are themselves confessedly, a principal source of the gratification of the Reader. I might perhaps include all which it is *necessary* to say upon this subject by affirming what few persons will deny, that of two descriptions either of passions, manners, or characters, each of them equally well executed, the one in prose and the other in verse, the verse will be read a hundred times where the prose is read once. We see that Pope by the power of verse alone, has contrived to render the plainest common sense interesting, and even frequently to invest it with the appearance of passion. In consequence of these convictions I related in metre the Tale of GOODY BLAKE and HARRY GILL, which is one of the rudest of this collection. I wished to draw attention to the truth that the power of the human imagination is sufficient to produce such changes even in our physical nature as might almost appear miraculous. The truth is an important one; the fact (for it is a *fact*) is a valuable illustration of it. And I have the satisfaction of knowing that it has been communicated to many hundreds of people who would never have heard of it, had it not been narrated as a Ballad, and in a more impressive metre than is usual in Ballads.

Having thus adverted to a few of the reasons why I have written in verse, and why I have chosen subjects from common life, and endeavoured to bring my language near to the real language of men, if I have been too minute in pleading my own cause, I have at the same time been treating a subject of general interest; and it is for this reason that I request the Reader's permission to add a few words with reference solely to these particular poems, and to some defects which will probably be found in them. I am sensible that my associations must have sometimes been particular instead of general, and that, consequently, giving to things a false importance, sometimes from diseased impulses I may have written upon unworthy subjects; but I am less apprehensive on this account, than that my language may frequently have suffered from those arbitrary connections of feelings and ideas with particular words, from which no man can altogether protect himself. Hence I have no doubt that in some instances feelings even of the ludicrous may be given to my Readers by expressions which appeared to me tender and pathetic. Such faulty expressions, were I convinced they were faulty at present, and that they must necessarily continue to be so, I would willingly take all reasonable pains to correct. But it is dangerous to make these alterations on the simple authority of a few individuals, or even of certain classes of men; for where the under-standing of an Author is not convinced, or his feelings altered, this cannot be done without great injury to himself: for his own feelings are his stay and support, and if he sets them aside in one instance, he may be induced to repeat this act till his mind loses all confidence in itself and becomes utterly debilitated. To this it may be added, that the Reader ought never to forget that he is himself exposed to the same errors as the Poet, and perhaps in a much greater degree: for there can be no presumption in saying that it is not probable he will be so well acquainted with the various stages of meaning through which words have passed, or with the fickleness or stability of the relations of particular ideas to each other; and above all, since he is so much less interested in the subject, he may decide lightly and carelessly.

Long as I have detained my Reader, I hope he will permit me to caution him against a mode of false criticism which has been applied to Poetry in which the language closely resembles that of life and nature. Such verses have been triumphed over in parodies of which Dr. Johnson's Stanza is a fair specimen.[15]

> "I put my hat upon my head,
>   And walk'd into the Strand,
>   And there I met another man
>   Whose hat was in his hand."

Immediately under these lines I will place one of the most justly admired stanzas of the "*Babes* in the Wood".[16]

[15] Dr. Johnson's lines were published in 1785, and are to be found in his *Poems*, edited D. Nichol Smith and E. L. McAdam (1941), pp. 157-8.

[16] "*Babes in the Wood*": The lines are quoted from the version of this popular ballad printed as "The Children in the Wood" in Bishop Thomas Percy's *Reliques of Ancient English Poetry* (1765), 3rd Series, Book II, Number 18, lines 113-16.

"These pretty Babes with hand in hand
Went wandering up and down;
But never more they saw the Man
Approaching from the Town."

In both of these stanzas the words, and the order of the words, in no respect differ from the most unimpassioned conversation. There are words in both, for example, "the Strand," and "the Town," connected with none but the most familiar ideas; yet the one stanza we admit as admirable, and the other as a fair example of the superlatively contemptible. Whence arises this difference? Not from the metre, not from the language, not from the order of the words; but the *matter* expressed in Dr. Johnson's stanza is contemptible. The proper method of treating trivial and simple verses to which Dr. Johnson's stanza would be a fair parallelism is not to say this is a bad kind of poetry, or this is not poetry, but this wants sense; it is neither interesting in itself, nor can *lead* to anything interesting; the images neither originate in that sane state of feeling which arises out of thought, nor can excite thought or feeling in the Reader. This is the only sensible manner of dealing with such verses: Why trouble yourself about the species till you have previously decided upon the genus? Why take pains to prove that an Ape is not a Newton when it is self-evident that he is not a man?

I have one request to make of my Reader, which is, that in judging these Poems he would decide by his own feelings genuinely, and not by reflection upon what will probably be the judgment of others. How common is it to hear a person say, "I myself do not object to this style of composition or this or that expression, but to such and such classes of people it will appear mean or ludicrous." This mode of criticism so destructive of all sound unadulterated judgment is almost universal: I have therefore to request that the Reader would abide independently by his own feelings, and that if he finds himself affected he would not suffer such conjectures to interfere with his pleasure.

If an Author by any single composition has impressed us with respect for his talents, it is useful to consider this as affording a presumption, that, on other occasions where we have been displeased, he nevertheless may not have written ill or absurdly; and, further, to give him so much credit for this one composition as may induce us to review what has displeased us with more care than we should otherwise have bestowed upon it. This is not only an act of justice, but in our decisions upon poetry especially, may conduce in a high degree to the improvement of our own taste: for an *accurate* taste in Poetry and in all the other arts, as Sir Joshua Reynolds[17] has observed, is an *acquired* talent, which can only be produced by thought and a long continued intercourse with the best models of composition. This is mentioned not with so ridiculous a purpose as to prevent the most inexperienced Reader from judging for himself, (I have already said that I wish him to judge for himself;) but merely to temper the rashness of decision, and to suggest that if Poetry be a subject on which much time has not been bestowed, the judgment may be erroneous, and that in many cases it necessarily will be so.

I know nothing would have so effectually contributed to further the end which I have in view as to have shewn of what kind the pleasure is, and how the pleasure is produced which is confessedly produced by metrical composition essentially different from what I have here endeavoured to recommend; for the Reader will say that he has been pleased by such composition and what can I do more for him? The power of any art is limited; and he will suspect that if I propose to furnish him with new friends it is only upon condition of his abandoning his old friends. Besides, as I have said, the Reader is himself conscious of the pleasure which he has received from such composition, composition to which he has peculiarly attached the endearing name of Poetry; and all men feel an habitual gratitude, and something of an honorable bigotry for the objects which have long continued to please them: we not only wish to be pleased, but to be pleased in that particular way in which we have been accustomed to be pleased. There is a host of arguments in these feelings; and I should be the less able to combat them successfully, as I am willing to allow, that, in order entirely to enjoy the Poetry which I am recommending, it would be necessary to give up much of what is ordinarily enjoyed. But would my limits have permitted

[17] *Reynolds:* The reference is to Discourse VII (delivered December 1776), on the theme of taste, published in his *Discourses on Art* (printed 1797). See p. 21.

me to point out how this pleasure is produced, I might have removed many obstacles, and assisted my Reader in perceiving that the powers of language are not so limited as he may suppose; and that it is possible that poetry may give other enjoyments, of a purer, more lasting, and more exquisite nature. But this part of my subject I have been obliged altogether to omit: as it has been less my present aim to prove that the interest excited by some other kinds of poetry is less vivid, and less worthy of the nobler powers of the mind, than to offer reasons for presuming, that, if the object which I have proposed to myself were adequately attained, a species of poetry would be produced, which is genuine poetry; in its nature well adapted to interest mankind permanently, and likewise important in the multiplicity and quality of its moral relations.

From what has been said, and from a perusal of the Poems, the Reader will be able clearly to perceive the object which I have proposed to myself: he will determine how far I have attained this object; and, what is a much more important question, whether it be worth attaining; and upon the decision of these two questions will rest my claim to the approbation of the public.

August Wilhelm von Schlegel

1767–1845

FROM ON DRAMATIC ART AND LITERATURE
1808; TRANSLATED INTO ENGLISH 1815

SCHLEGEL (1767–1845) had already earned a reputation as a critic, and translator of Shakespeare into German, when he delivered his lectures on dramatic art and literature in Vienna in 1808. These were published in 1809–11 and, unlike other critical writings of Schlegel, were quickly translated into English by John Black (1815). Schlegel had studied the development of critical ideas in German through the eighteenth century, and, with his talent for lucid and orderly exposition, he provided, especially in the introductory lecture to the series, a brilliant summary of some central ideas in German Romantic critical theory. The early publication of a translation of these lectures gave them a special importance, for it was in these that many Englishmen were able to acquaint themselves with the latest in German thought. They became so well known that Henry Bohn reprinted them in his "Standard Library" in 1846, still in Black's translation, and the extracts below are taken from this edition (pp. 19–27, 340, and 342–3).

In his opening lecture, Schlegel attempts to define "modern" or romantic art, in contrast to ancient, or classical art. He links romantic art especially with the picturesque and with melancholy, and further associates it with the development of Christianity; perhaps his sharpest insight here is into the harmony of the "Grecian ideal", as contrasted with the sense of "internal discord" in modern poets, whose "endeavour is to reconcile these two worlds between which we find ourselves divided, and to blend them indissolubly together" (pp. 57–8). The finite and the infinite worlds relate to the objective and subjective reconciled in Coleridge's theory of the imagination. More important, perhaps, is Schlegel's distinction between mechanical and organic form, which was developed also by Coleridge, who came to know Schlegel's essays after 1811, but always asserted that he arrived at his ideas independently (see, for example, his note in *Biographia Literaria*, Chapter II, edited J. Shawcross, I. 22 *n.*, and his letter of December 1811, in *Letters*, edited E. L. Griggs, Volume III, 1959, p. 359). Schlegel also influenced

Carlyle directly, especially in his emphasis on poetic creation as a largely unconscious or spontaneous activity, and on the originality of Romantic art, "striving after new and marvellous births" (p. 59).

FROM LECTURE 1

LET us now apply the idea which we have been developing, of the universality of true criticism, to the history of poetry and the fine arts. This, like the so-called universal history, we generally limit (even though beyond this range there may be much that is both remarkable and worth knowing) to whatever has had a nearer or more remote influence on the present civilisation of Europe: consequently, to the works of the Greeks and Romans, and of those of the modern European nations, who first and chiefly distinguished themselves in art and literature. It is well known that, three centuries and a-half ago, the study of ancient literature received a new life by the diffusion of the Grecian language (for the Latin never became extinct); the classical authors were brought to light, and rendered universally accessible by means of the press; and the monuments of ancient art were diligently disinterred and preserved. All this powerfully excited the human mind, and formed a decided epoch in the history of human civilisation; its manifold effects have extended to our times, and will yet extend to an incalculable series of ages. But the study of the ancients was forthwith most fatally perverted. The learned, who were chiefly in the possession of this knowledge, and who were incapable of distinguishing themselves by works of their own, claimed for the ancients an unlimited authority, and with great appearance of reason, since they are models in their kind. Maintaining that nothing could be hoped for the human mind but from an imitation of antiquity, in the works of the moderns they only valued what resembled, or seemed to bear a resemblance to, those of the ancients. Everything else they rejected as barbarous and unnatural. With the great poets and artists it was quite otherwise. However strong their enthusiasm for the ancients, and however determined their purpose of entering into competition with them, they were compelled by their independence and originality of mind to strike out a path of their own, and to impress upon their productions the stamp of their own genius. Such was the case with Dante among the Italians, the father of modern poetry;

acknowledging Virgil for his master, he has produced a work which, of all others, most differs from the Æneid, and in our opinion far excels its pretended model in power, truth, compass, and profundity. It was the same afterwards with Ariosto, who has most unaccountably been compared to Homer, for nothing can be more unlike. So in art with Michael Angelo and Raphael, who had no doubt deeply studied the antique. When we ground our judgment of modern painters merely on their greater or less resemblance to the ancients, we must necessarily be unjust towards them, as Winkelmann[1] undoubtedly has [been] in the case of Raphael. As the poets for the most part had their share of scholarship, it gave rise to a curious struggle between their natural inclination and their imaginary duty. When they sacrificed to the latter, they were praised by the learned; but by yielding to the former, they became the favourites of the people. What preserves the heroic poems of a Tasso and a Camoëns to this day alive in the hearts and on the lips of their countrymen, is by no means their imperfect resemblance to Virgil, or even to Homer, but in Tasso the tender feeling of chivalrous love and honour, and in Camoëns the glowing inspiration of heroic patriotism.

Those very ages, nations, and ranks, who felt least the want of a poetry of their own, were the most assiduous in their imitation of the ancients; accordingly, its results are but dull school exercises, which at best excite a frigid admiration. But in the fine arts, mere imitation is always fruitless; even what we borrow from others, to assume a true poetical shape, must, as it were, be born again within us. Of what avail is all foreign imitation? Art cannot exist without nature, and man can give nothing to his fellow-men but himself.

Genuine successors and true rivals of the ancients, who, by virtue of congenial talents and cultivation have walked in their path and worked in their spirit, have ever been as rare as their mechanical spiritless copyists are common. Seduced by the form, the great body of critics have been but too indulgent to these servile imitators. These were held up as correct modern classics, while the great truly living and popular poets, whose reputation was a part of their nations' glory, and to whose sublimity it was impossible to be

[1] *Winkelmann:* Johann Joachim Winckelmann (1717–68), a great German classical scholar.

altogether blind, were at best but tolerated as rude and wild natural geniuses. But the unqualified separation of genius and taste on which such a judgment proceeds, is altogether untenable. Genius is the almost unconscious choice of the highest degree of excellence, and, consequently, it is taste in its highest activity.

In this state, nearly, matters continued till a period not far back, when several inquiring minds, chiefly Germans, endeavoured to clear up the misconception, and to give the ancients their due, without being insensible to the merits of the moderns, although of a totally different kind. The apparent contradiction did not intimidate them. The groundwork of human nature is no doubt everywhere the same; but in all our investigations, we may observe that, throughout the whole range of nature, there is no elementary power so simple, but that it is capable of dividing and diverging into opposite directions. The whole play of vital motion hinges on harmony and contrast. Why, then, should not this phenomenon recur on a grander scale in the history of man? In this idea we have perhaps discovered the true key to the ancient and modern history of poetry and the fine arts. Those who adopted it, gave to the peculiar spirit of *modern* art, as contrasted with the *antique* or *classical*, the name of *romantic*. The term is certainly not inappropriate; the word is derived from *romance*—the name originally given to the languages which were formed from the mixture of the Latin and the old Teutonic dialects, in the same manner as modern civilisation is the fruit of the heterogeneous union of the peculiarities of the northern nations and the fragments of antiquity; whereas the civilisation of the ancients was much more of a piece.

The distinction which we have just stated can hardly fail to appear well founded, if it can be shown, so far as our knowledge of an-tiquity extends, that the same contrast in the labours of the ancients and moderns runs symmetrically, I might almost say systematically, throughout every branch of art—that it is as evident in music and the plastic arts as in poetry. This is a problem which, in its full extent, still remains to be demonstrated, though, on particular portions of it, many excellent observations have been advanced already.

Among the foreign authors who wrote before this school can be said to have been formed in Germany, we may mention Rousseau, who acknowledged the contrast in music, and showed that rhythm and melody were the prevailing principles of ancient, as harmony is that of modern music. In his prejudices against harmony, however, we cannot at all concur. On the subject of the arts of design an ingenious observation was made by Hemsterhuys,[2] that the ancient painters were perhaps too much of sculptors, and the modern sculptors too much of painters. This is the exact point of difference; for, as I shall distinctly show in the sequel, the spirit of ancient art and poetry is *plastic*, but that of the moderns *picturesque*.

By an example taken from another art, that of architecture, I shall endeavour to illustrate what I mean by this contrast. Throughout the Middle Ages there prevailed, and in the latter centuries of that area was carried to perfection, a style of architecture, which has been called Gothic, but ought really to have been termed old German. When, on the general revival of classical antiquity, the imitation of Grecian architecture became prevalent, and but too frequently without a due regard to the difference of climate and manners or the purpose of the building, the zealots of this new taste, passing a sweeping sentence of condemnation on the Gothic, reprobated it as tasteless, gloomy, and barbarous. This was in some degree pardonable in the Italians, among whom a love for ancient architecture, cherished by hereditary remains of classical edifices, and the similarity of their climate to that of the Greeks and Romans, might, in some sort, be said to be innate. But we Northerns are not so easily to be talked out of the powerful, solemn impressions which seize upon the mind at entering a Gothic cathedral. We feel, on the contrary, a strong desire to investigate and to justify the source of this impression. A very slight attention will convince us, that the Gothic architecture displays not only an extraordinary degree of mechanical skill, but also a marvellous power of invention; and, on a closer examination, we recognise its profound significance, and perceive that as well as the Grecian it constitutes in itself a complete and finished system.

To the application!—The Pantheon is not more different from

[2] *Hemsterhuys:* François Hemsterhuis (1721–90), a Dutch aesthetician and philosopher who wrote in French; the reference is to his *Letter on Sculpture* (1769).

Westminster Abbey or the church of St. Stephen at Vienna,[3] than the structure of a tragedy of Sophocles from a drama of Shakespeare. The comparison between these wonderful productions of poetry and architecture might be carried still farther. But does our admiration of the one compel us to depreciate the other? May we not admit that each is great and admirable in its kind, although the one is, and is meant to be, different from the other? The experiment is worth attempting. We will quarrel with no man for his predilection either for the Grecian or the Gothic. The world is wide, and affords room for a great diversity of objects. Narrow and blindly adopted prepossessions will never constitute a genuine critic or connoisseur, who ought, on the contrary, to possess the power of dwelling with liberal impartiality on the most discrepant views, renouncing the while all personal inclinations.

For our present object, the justification, namely, of the grand division which we lay down in the history of art, and according to which we conceive ourselves equally warranted in establishing the same division in dramatic literature, it might be sufficient merely to have stated this contrast between the ancient, or classical, and the romantic. But as there are exclusive admirers of the ancients, who never cease asserting that all deviation from them is merely the whim of a new school of critics, who, expressing themselves in language full of mystery, cautiously avoid conveying their sentiments in a tangible shape, I shall endeavour to explain the origin and spirit of the *romantic*, and then leave the world to judge if the use of the word, and of the idea which it is intended to convey, be thereby justified.

The mental culture of the Greeks was a finished education in the school of Nature. Of a beautiful and noble race, endowed with susceptible senses and a cheerful spirit under a mild sky, they lived and bloomed in the full health of existence; and, favoured by a rare combination of circumstances, accomplished all that the finite nature of man is capable of. The whole of their art and poetry is the expression of a consciousness of this harmony of all their faculties. They invented the poetry of joy.

[3] *The Pantheon . . . Vienna:* The Pantheon in Rome was built as a classical temple to all the gods; Westminster Abbey and St. Stephen's are examples of the Gothic style in architecture.

Their religion was the deification of the powers of nature and of the earthly life: but this worship, which, among other nations, clouded the imagination with hideous shapes, and hardened the heart to cruelty, assumed, among the Greeks, a mild, a grand, and a dignified form. Superstition, too often the tyrant of the human faculties, seemed to have here contributed to their freest development. It cherished the arts by which it was adorned, and its idols became the models of ideal beauty.

But however highly the Greeks may have succeeded in the Beautiful, and even in the Moral, we cannot concede any higher character to their civilisation than that of a refined and ennobled sensuality. Of course this must be understood generally. The conjectures of a few philosophers, and the irradiations of poetical inspiration, constitute an occasional exception. Man can never altogether turn aside his thoughts from infinity, and some obscure recollections will always remind him of the home he has lost; but we are now speaking of the predominant tendency of his endeavours.

Religion is the root of human existence. Were it possible for man to renounce all religion, including that which is unconscious, independent of the will, he would become a mere surface without any internal substance. When this centre is disturbed, the whole system of the mental faculties and feelings takes a new shape.

And this is what has actually taken place in modern Europe through the introduction of Christianity. This sublime and beneficent religion has regenerated the ancient world from its state of exhaustion and debasement; it is the guiding principle in the history of modern nations, and even at this day, when many suppose they have shaken off its authority, they still find themselves much more influenced by it in their views of human affairs than they themselves are aware.

After Christianity, the character of Europe has, since the commencement of the Middle Ages, been chiefly influenced by the Germanic race of northern conquerors, who infused new life and vigour into a degenerated people. The stern nature of the North drives man back within himself; and what is lost in the free sportive development of the senses, must, in noble dispositions, be compensated by earnestness of mind. Hence the honest cordiality with which Christianity was welcomed by all the Teutonic tribes, so that among no other race of men has it penetrated more deeply into the inner man, displayed more powerful effects, or become more interwoven with all human feelings and sensibilities.

The rough, but honest heroism of the northern conquerors, by its admixture with the sentiments of Christianity, gave rise to chivalry, of which the object was, by vows which should be looked upon as sacred, to guard the practice of arms from every rude and ungenerous abuse of force into which it was so likely to sink.

With the virtues of chivalry was associated a new and purer spirit of love, an inspired homage for genuine female worth, which was now revered as the acme of human excellence, and, maintained by religion itself under the image of a virgin mother, infused into all hearts a mysterious sense of the purity of love.

As Christianity did not, like the heathen worship, rest satisfied with certain external acts, but claimed an authority over the whole inward man and the most hidden movements of the heart; the feeling of moral independence took refuge in the domain of honour, a worldly morality, as it were, which subsisting alongside of, was often at variance with that of religion, but yet in so far resembling it that it never calculated consequences, but consecrated unconditionally certain principles of action, which, like the articles of faith, were elevated far beyond the investigation of a casuistical reasoning.

Chivalry, love, and honour, together with religion itself, are the subjects of that poetry of nature which poured itself out in the Middle Ages with incredible fulness, and preceded the more artistic cultivation of the romantic spirit. This age had also its mythology, consisting of chivalrous tales and legends; but its wonders and its heroism were the very reverse of those of the ancient mythology.

Several inquirers who, in other respects, entertain the same conception of the peculiarities of the moderns, and trace them to the same source that we do, have placed the essence of the northern poetry in melancholy; and to this, when properly understood, we have nothing to object.

Among the Greeks human nature was in itself all-sufficient; it was conscious of no defects, and aspired to no higher perfection than that which it could actually attain by the exercise of its own energies. We, however, are taught by superior wisdom that man, through a grievous transgression, forfeited the place for which he was originally destined; and that the sole destination of his earthly existence is to struggle to regain his lost position, which, if left to his own strength, he can never accomplish. The old religion of the senses sought no higher possession than outward and perishable blessings; and immortality, so far as it was believed, stood shadow-like in the obscure distance, a faint dream of this sunny waking life. The very reverse of all this is the case with the Christian view: everything finite and mortal is lost in the contemplation of infinity; life has become shadow and darkness, and the first day of our real existence dawns in the world beyond the grave. Such a religion must waken the vague foreboding, which slumbers in every feeling heart, into a distinct consciousness that the happiness after which we are here striving is unattainable; that no external object can ever entirely fill our souls; and that all earthly enjoyment is but a fleeting and momentary illusion. When the soul, resting as it were under the willows of exile,* breathes out its longing for its distant home, what else but melancholy can be the key-note of its songs? Hence the poetry of the ancients was the poetry of enjoyment, and ours is that of desire: the former has its foundation in the scene which is present, while the latter hovers betwixt recollection and hope. Let me not be understood as affirming that everything flows in one unvarying strain of wailing and complaint, and that the voice of melancholy is always loudly heard. As the austerity of tragedy was not incompatible with the joyous views of the Greeks, so that romantic poetry whose origin I have been describing, can assume every tone, even that of the liveliest joy; but still it will always, in some indescribable way, bear traces of the source from which it originated. The feeling of the moderns is, upon the whole, more in-ward, their fancy more incorporeal, and their thoughts more contemplative. In nature, it is true, the boundaries of objects run more into one another, and things are not so distinctly separated as we must exhibit them in order to convey distinct notions of them.

The Grecian ideal of human nature was perfect unison and proportion between all the powers,—a natural harmony. The moderns, on the contrary, have arrived at the consciousness of an internal discord which renders such an ideal impossible; and hence the endeavour of their poetry is to reconcile these two worlds between

* *willows of exile:* an allusion to Psalm 137 [translator's note].

which we find ourselves divided, and to blend them indissolubly together. The impressions of the senses are to be hallowed, as it were, by a mysterious connexion with higher feelings; and the soul, on the other hand, embodies its forebodings, or indescribable intuitions of infinity, in types and symbols borrowed from the visible world.

In Grecian art and poetry we find an original and unconscious unity of form and matter; in the modern, so far as it has remained true to its own spirit, we observe a keen struggle to unite the two, as being naturally in opposition to each other. The Grecian executed what it proposed in the utmost perfection; but the modern can only do justice to its endeavours after what is infinite by approximation; and, from a certain appearance of imperfection, is in greater danger of not being duly appreciated.

FROM LECTURE 22

THE poetic spirit requires to be limited, that it may move with a becoming liberty, within its proper precincts, as has been felt by all nations on the first invention of metre; it must act according to laws derivable from its own essence, otherwise its strength will evaporate in boundless vacuity.

The works of genius cannot therefore be permitted to be without form; but of this there is no danger. However, that we may answer this objection of want of form, we must understand the exact meaning of the term form, since most critics, and more especially those who insist on a stiff regularity, interpret it merely in a mechanical, and not in an organical sense. Form is mechanical when, through external force, it is imparted to any material merely as an accidental addition without reference to its quality; as, for example, when we give a particular shape to a soft mass that it may retain the same after its induration. Organical form, again, is innate; it unfolds itself from within, and acquires its determination contemporaneously with the perfect development of the germ. We everywhere discover such forms in nature throughout the whole range of living powers, from the crystallization of salts and minerals to plants and flowers, and from these again to the human body. In the fine arts, as well as in the domain of nature—the supreme artist, all genuine forms are organical, that is determined by the quality of the work.

In a word, the form is nothing but a significant exterior, the speaking physiognomy of each thing, which, as long as it is not disfigured by any destructive accident, gives a true evidence of its hidden essence.

Hence it is evident that the spirit of poetry, which, though imperishable, migrates, as it were, through different bodies, must, so often as it is newly born in the human race, mould to itself, out of the nutrimental substance of an altered age, a body of a different conformation. The forms vary with the direction taken by the poetical sense; and when we give to the new kinds of poetry the old names, and judge of them according to the ideas conveyed by these names, the application which we make of the authority of classical antiquity is altogether unjustifiable. No one should be tried before a tribunal to which he is not amenable. . . .

Of the origin and essence of the romantic I treated in my first Lecture, and I shall here, therefore, merely briefly mention the subject. The ancient art and poetry rigorously separate things which are dissimilar; the romantic delights in indissoluble mixtures; all contrarieties: nature and art, poetry and prose, seriousness and mirth, recollection and anticipation, spirituality and sensuality, terrestrial and celestial, life and death, are by it blended together in the most intimate combination. As the oldest lawgivers delivered their mandatory instructions and prescriptions in measured melodies; as this is fabulously ascribed to Orpheus, the first softener of the yet untamed race of mortals; in like manner the whole of the ancient poetry and art is, as it were, a *rhythmical nomos* (law), an harmonious promulgation of the permanently established legislation of a world submitted to a beautiful order, and reflecting in itself the eternal images of things. Romantic poetry, on the other hand, is the expression of the secret attraction to a chaos which lies concealed in the very bosom of the ordered universe, and is perpetually striving after new and marvellous births; the life-giving spirit of primeval love broods here anew on the face of the waters. The former is more simple, clear, and like to nature in the self-existent perfection of her separate works; the latter, notwithstanding its fragmentary appearance, approaches more to the secret of the universe. For Conception can only comprise each object separately, but nothing in truth can ever exist separately and by itself; Feeling perceives all in all at one and the same time.

William Wordsworth

FROM THE PREFACE TO *POEMS* 1815

THE famous distinction drawn between imagination and fancy in S. T. Coleridge's *Biographia Literaria* (see below, p. 89) emerged out of a continuing dialogue with Wordsworth, and has its roots in theories of the association of ideas developed much earlier in the eighteenth century. Coleridge announced his disagreement with the argument Wordsworth presented in the preface to the 1815 edition of his poems (see below, p. 77), and Wordsworth in turn was taking issue with a definition of imagination and fancy offered by Coleridge in 1812 (see below, p. 68). Their concern with these terms has its origin in earlier attempts to identify that power of the mind by which images are associated and brought together. Already the superiority of the imagination, as linked with the coherence of a whole, over the fancy as concerned with a mechanical association of images, was so far indicated as to ensure that it would remain the dominant term. Wordsworth reacted strongly to the definition of these terms he cites from William Taylor's *British Synonyms Discriminated* (1813), as leaving them too much alike, and merely names for functions of memory. For him, the imagination takes on a loftier sense, as associated with the shaping art of the poet, and as creative in "consolidating numbers into unity, and dissolving and separating unity into number" (p. 66). However, fancy has much the same powers, and differs it seems, in dealing with the definite and limited, while imagination "recoils from everything but the plastic, the pliant, and the indefinite" (p. 68). Both are creative faculties, but the fancy relates to the "temporal part of our nature", the imagination is given to "support the eternal" (p. 69).

The distinction Wordsworth seems about to establish in sharp clarity slips away from him, and, richly as he contributes here to the argument about the terms, he remains finally content with a formulation which distinguishes imagination from fancy mainly in terms of the areas of experience with which they deal, and the difference is one of degree not of kind. It was left to Coleridge to define the difference more radically in terms of their nature and function, and clarify the distinction between organic, or unifying functions, and purely mechanical operations of the mind, a distinction which remains blurred in this Preface. Some sections are omitted from the text as reprinted here, namely, a short opening paragraph, referring to the Preface to *Lyrical*

Ballads, a few pages describing the "kinds" of poetry, a concluding account of Charles Cotton's poem "Ode upon Winter" as exemplifying the work of the fancy, and a footnote on the selection of poems for the volume.

THE powers requisite for the production of poetry are: first, those of Observation and Description,—i.e. the ability to observe with accuracy things as they are in themselves, and with fidelity to describe them, unmodified by any passion or feeling existing in the mind of the describer; whether the things depicted be actually present to the senses, or have a place only in the memory. This power, though indispensable to a Poet, is one which he employs only in submission to necessity, and never for a continuance of time: as its exercise supposes all the higher qualities of the mind to be passive, and in a state of subjection to external objects, much in the same way as a translator or engraver ought to be to his original. 2ndly, Sensibility,—which, the more exquisite it is, the wider will be the range of a poet's perceptions; and the more will he be incited to observe objects, both as they exist in themselves and as re-acted upon by his own mind. (The distinction between poetic and human sensibility has been marked in the character of the Poet delineated in the original preface).[1] 3rdly, Reflection,—which makes the Poet acquainted with the value of actions, images, thoughts, and feelings; and assists the sensibility in perceiving their connection with each other. 4thly, Imagination and Fancy,—to modify, to create and to associate. 5thly, Invention,—by which characters are composed out of materials supplied by observation; whether of the Poet's own heart and mind, or of external life and nature; and such incidents and situations produced as are most impressive to the imagination, and most fitted to do justice to the characters, sentiments, and passions, which the Poet undertakes to illustrate. And, lastly, Judgment,—to decide how and where, and in what degree, each of these faculties ought to be exerted; so that the less shall not be sacrificed to the greater; nor the greater, slighting the less, arrogate, to its own injury, more than its due. By judgment, also, is determined what are the laws and appropriate graces of every species of composition. . . .

Let us come now to the consideration of the words Fancy and

[1] *Preface:* the Preface to *Lyrical Ballads;* see above, p. 34.

Imagination, as employed in the classification of the following
Poems. "A man," says an intelligent author, "has imagination in
proportion as he can distinctly copy in idea the impression of sense:
it is the faculty which images within the mind the phenomena of
sensation. A man has fancy in proportion as he can call up, connect
or associate, at pleasure, those internal images ($\phi\alpha\nu\tau\acute{\alpha}\zeta\epsilon\iota\nu$ is to
cause to appear) so as to complete ideal representations of absent
objects. Imagination is the power of depicting, and fancy of revok-
ing and combining. The imagination is formed by patient observation; the fancy by a voluntary activity in shifting the scenery of the
mind. The more accurate the imagination, the more safely may a
painter, or a poet, undertake a delineation, or a description, without
the presence of the objects to be characterised. The more versatile
the fancy, the more original and striking will be the decorations
produced".—*British Synonyms discriminated, by W. Taylor.*[2]

Is not this as if a man should undertake to supply an account of a
building, and be so intent upon what he had discovered of the
foundations, as to conclude his task without once looking up at the
superstructure? Here, as in other instances throughout the volume,
the judicious Author's mind is enthralled by Etymology; he takes
up the original word as his guide and escort, and too often does not
perceive how soon he becomes its prisoner, without liberty to
tread in any path but that to which it confines him. It is not easy to
find out how imagination, thus explained, differs from distinct
remembrance of images; or fancy from quick and vivid recollection
of them: each is nothing more than a mode of memory. If the two
words bear the above meaning, and no other, what term is left to
designate that faculty of which the Poet is "all compact";[3] he
whose eye glances from earth to heaven, whose spiritual attributes
body forth what his pen is prompt in turning to shape; or what
is left to characterise Fancy, as insinuating herself into the heart of
objects with creative activity?—Imagination, in the sense of the
word as giving title to a class of the following Poems, has no
reference to images that are merely a faithful copy, existing in the
mind, of absent external objects; but is a word of higher import,
denoting operations of the mind upon those objects, and processes

[2] *Taylor:* Published in 1813; see above, p. 60.

[3] *all compact:* recalling Shakespeare, *A Midsummer Night's Dream* V i. 8.

of creation or of composition, governed by certain fixed laws. I proceed to illustrate my meaning by instances. A parrot *hangs* from the wires of his cage by his beak or by his claws; or a monkey from the bough of a tree by his paws or his tail. Each creature does so literally and actually. In the first Eclogue of Virgil, the shepherd, thinking of the time when he is to take leave of his farm, thus addressed his goats:

> "Non ego vos posthac viridi projectus in antro
> Dumosa *pendere* procul de rupe videbo".[4]

> "Half way down
> *Hangs* one who gathers samphire",[5]

is the well-known expression of Shakespeare, delineating an ordinary image upon the cliffs of Dover. In these two instances is a slight exertion of the faculty which I denominate imagination, in the use of one word: neither the goats nor the samphire-gatherer do literally hang, as does the parrot or the monkey; but, presenting to the senses something of such an appearance, the mind in its activity, for its own gratification, contemplates them as hanging.

> "As when far off at sea a fleet descried
> *Hangs* in the clouds, by equinoctial winds
> Close sailing from Bengala, or the isles
> Of Ternate or Tidore, whence merchants bring
> Their spicy drugs; they on the trading flood
> Through the wide Ethiopian to the Cape
> Ply, stemming nightly toward the Pole: so seemed
> Far off the flying Fiend".[6]

Here is the full strength of the imagination involved in the word *hangs*, and exerted upon the whole image: First, the fleet, an aggregate of many ships, is represented as one mighty person, whose track we know and feel is upon the waters; but taking advantage of its appearance to the senses, the Poet dares to represent it as *hanging in the clouds*, both for the gratification of the mind in

[4] Virgil, *Eclogue* I, 75–6: "Never again shall I, reclining in some green dell, watch you [my goats] hang far above from the bushy cliffs".

[5] Shakespeare, *King Lear*, II. vi. 14–15.

[6] Milton, *Paradise Lost*, II. 636–43.

contemplating the image itself, and in reference to the motion and appearance of the sublime objects to which it is compared.

From images of sight we will pass to those of sound; which, as they must necessarily be of a less definite character, shall be selected from these volumes:

"Over his own sweet voice the Stock-dove *broods*;"[7]

of the same bird,

"His voice was *buried* among trees,
    Yet to be come at by the breeze;"[8]

"O, Cuckoo! shall I call thee *Bird*,
    Or but a wandering *Voice?*"[9]

The stock-dove is said to *coo*, a sound well imitating the note of the bird; but, by the intervention of the metaphor *broods*, the affections are called in by the imagination to assist in marking the manner in which the bird reiterates and prolongs her soft note, as if herself delighting to listen to it, and participating of a still and quiet satisfaction, like that which may be supposed inseparable from the continuous process of incubation. "His voice was buried among trees", a metaphor expressing the love of *seclusion* by which this Bird is marked; and characterising its note in not partaking of the shrill and the piercing, and therefore more easily deadened by the intervening shade; yet a note so peculiar and withal so pleasing, that the breeze, gifted with that love of the sound which the Poet feels, penetrates the shades in which it is entombed, and conveys it to the ear of the listener.

"Shall I call thee Bird,
    Or but a wandering Voice?"

This concise interrogation characterises the seeming ubiquity of the voice of the cuckoo, and dispossesses the creature almost of a corporeal existence; the Imagination being tempted to this exertion of her power by a consciousness in the memory that the cuckoo is

7 Wordsworth, "Resolution and Independence," line 5.
8 Wordsworth, "O Nightingale! thou surely art", lines 13–14.
9 Wordsworth, "To the Cuckoo," lines 3–4.

almost perpetually heard throughout the season of spring, but seldom becomes an object of sight.

Thus far of images independent of each other, and immediately endowed by the mind with properties that do not inhere in them, upon an incitement from properties and qualities the existence of which is inherent and obvious. These processes of imagination are carried on either by conferring additional properties upon an object, or abstracting from it some of those which it actually possesses, and thus enabling it to re-act upon the mind which hath performed the process, like a new existence.

I pass from the Imagination acting upon an individual image to a consideration of the same faculty employed upon images in a conjunction by which they modify each other. The Reader has already had a fine instance before him in the passage quoted from Virgil, where the apparently perilous situation of the goat, hanging upon the shaggy precipice, is contrasted with that of the shepherd contemplating it from the seclusion of the cavern in which he lies stretched at ease and in security. Take these images separately, and how unaffecting the picture compared with that produced by their being thus connected with, and opposed to, each other!

> "As a huge stone is sometimes seen to lie
> Couched on the bald top of an eminence,
> Wonder to all who do the same espy
> By what means it could thither come, and whence,
> So that it seems a thing endued with sense,
> Like a sea-beast crawled forth, which on a shelf
> Of rock or sand reposeth, there to sun himself.
>
> Such seemed this Man; not all alive or dead
> Nor all asleep, in his extreme old age.
>
> . . . .
>
> Motionless as a cloud the old Man stood,
> That heareth not the loud winds when they call,
> And moveth altogether if it move at all".[10]

In these images, the conferring, the abstracting, and the modifying powers of the Imagination, immediately and mediately acting, are

[10] Wordsworth, "Resolution and Independence," lines 57-65, 75-7.

C

all brought into conjunction. The stone is endowed with something of the power of life to approximate it to the sea-beast; and the sea-beast stripped of some of its vital qualities to assimilate it to the stone; which intermediate image is thus treated for the purpose of bringing the original image, that of the stone, to a nearer resemblance to the figure and condition of the aged Man; who is divested of so much of the indications of life and motion as to bring him to the point where the two objects unite and coalesce in just comparison. After what has been said, the image of the cloud need not be commented upon.

Thus far of an endowing or modifying power: but the Imagination also shapes and *creates*; and how? By innumerable processes; and in none does it more delight than in that of consolidating numbers into unity, and dissolving and separating unity into number,—alternations proceeding from, and governed by, a sublime consciousness of the soul in her own mighty and almost divine powers. Recur to the passage already cited from Milton. When the compact Fleet, as one Person, has been introduced "sailing from Bengala," "They," i.e. the "merchants," representing the fleet resolved into a multitude of ships, "ply" their voyage towards the extremities of the earth: "So," (referring to the word "As" in the commencement) "seemed the flying Fiend;" the image of his Person acting to recombine the multitude of ships, into one body,—the point from which the comparison set out. "So seemed," and to whom seemed? To the heavenly Muse who dictates the poem, to the eye of the Poet's mind, and to that of the Reader, present at one moment in the wide Ethiopian, and the next in the solitudes, then first broken in upon, of the infernal regions!

"Modo me Thebis, modo ponit Athenis."[11]

Hear again this mighty Poet,—speaking of the Messiah going forth to expel from heaven the rebellious angels,

"Attended by ten thousand thousand Saints
He onward came: far off his coming shone,"[12]

[11] Horace, *Epistles* II. 1. 213: "Let me down now at Thebes, now at Athens".

[12] Milton, *Paradise Lost*, VI. 767-8.

the retinue of Saints, and the Person of the Messiah himself, lost almost and merged in the splendour of that indefinite abstraction "His coming!"

As I do not mean here to treat this subject further than to throw some light upon the present Volumes, and especially upon one division of them, I shall spare myself and the Reader the trouble of considering the Imagination as it deals with thoughts and sentiments, as it regulates the composition of characters, and determines the course of actions: I will not consider it (more than I have already done by implication) as that power which, in the language of one of my most esteemed Friends, "draws all things to one; which makes things animate or inanimate, beings with their attributes, subjects with their accessories, take one colour and serve to one effect."[13] The grand store-houses of enthusiastic and meditative Imagination, of poetical, as contra-distinguished from human and dramatic Imagination, are the prophetic and lyrical parts of the Holy Scriptures, and the works of Milton; to which I cannot forbear to add those of Spenser. I select these writers in preference to those of ancient Greece and Rome, because the anthropomorphitism of the Pagan religion subjected the minds of the greatest poets in those countries too much to the bondage of definite form; from which the Hebrews were preserved by their abhorrence of idolatry. This abhorrence was almost as strong in our great epic Poet, both from circumstances of his life, and from the constitution of his mind. However imbued the surface might be with classical literature, he was a Hebrew in soul; and all things tended in him towards the sublime. Spenser, of a gentler nature, maintained his freedom by aid of his allegorical spirit, at one time inciting him to create persons out of abstractions; and, at another, by a superior effort of genius, to give the universality and permanence of abstractions to his human beings, by means of attributes and emblems that belong to the highest moral truths and the purest sensations,—of which his character of Una is a glorious example. Of the human and dramatic Imagination the works of Shakespeare are an inexhaustible source.

[13] The quotation is from Charles Lamb's essay "On the Genius and Character of Hogarth" (*Collected Essays*, 1929, II. 244).

"I tax not you, ye Elements, with unkindness,
I never gave you kingdoms, call'd you Daughters!"[14]

And if, bearing in mind the many Poets distinguished by this prime quality, whose names I omit to mention; yet justified by recollection of the insults which the ignorant, the incapable, and the presumptuous, have heaped upon these and my other writings, I may be permitted to anticipate the judgment of posterity upon myself, I shall declare (censurable, I grant, if the notoriety of the fact above stated does not justify me) that I have given in these unfavourable times, evidence of exertions of this faculty upon its worthiest objects, the external universe, the moral and religious sentiments of Man, his natural affections, and his acquired passions; which have the same ennobling tendency as the productions of men, in this kind, worthy to be holden in undying remembrance.

To the mode in which Fancy has already been characterised as the power of evoking and combining, or, as my friend Mr. Coleridge has styled it, "the aggregative and associative power,"[15] my objection is only that the definition is too general. To aggregate and to associate, to evoke and to combine, belong as well to the Imagination as to the Fancy; but either the materials evoked and combined are different; or they are brought together under a different law, and for a different purpose. Fancy does not require that the materials which she makes use of should be susceptible of change in their constitution, from her touch; and, where they admit of modification, it is enough for her purpose if it be slight, limited, and evanescent. Directly the reverse of these, are the desires and demands of the Imagination. She recoils from everything but the plastic, the pliant, and the indefinite. She leaves it to Fancy to describe Queen Mab as coming,

"In shape no bigger than an agate-stone
On the fore-finger of an alderman."[16]

---

[14] *King Lear*, III. ii. 16–17.
[15] Wordsworth refers to an essay contributed by Coleridge to Southey's *Omniana*, No. 174. See *Biographia Literaria*, ed. J. Shawcross, 1907, I. 193, 270.
[16] Shakespeare, *Romeo and Juliet*, I. iv. 55–6.

Having to speak of stature, she does not tell you that her gigantic Angel was as tall as Pompey's Pillar;[17] much less that he was twelve cubits, or twelve hundred cubits high; or that his dimensions equalled those of Teneriffe or Atlas;—because these, and if they were a million times as high it would be the same, are bounded: The expression is, "His stature reached the sky!" the illimitable firmament!—When the Imagination frames a comparison, if it does not strike on the first presentation, a sense of the truth of the likeness, from the moment that it is perceived, grows—and continues to grow—upon the mind; the resemblance depending less upon outline of form and feature, than upon expression and effect; less upon casual and outstanding, than upon inherent and internal, properties: moreover, the images invariably modify each other.—The law under which the processes of Fancy are carried on is as capricious as the accidents of things, and the effects are surprising, playful, ludicrous, amusing, tender, or pathetic, as the objects happen to be appositely produced or fortunately combined. Fancy depends upon the rapidity and profusion with which she scatters her thoughts and images; trusting that their number, and the felicity with which they are linked together, will make amends for the want of individual value: or she prides herself upon the curious subtilty and the successful elaboration with which she can detect their lurking affinities. If she can win you over to her purpose, and impart to you her feelings, she cares not how unstable or transitory may be her influence, knowing that it will not be out of her power to resume it upon an apt occasion. But the Imagination is conscious of an indestructible dominion;—the Soul may fall away from it, not being able to sustain its grandeur; but, if once felt and acknowledged, by no act of any other faculty of the mind can it be relaxed, impaired, or diminished.—Fancy is given to quicken and to beguile the temporal part of our nature, Imagination to incite and to support the eternal.—Yet is it not the less true that Fancy, as she is an active, is also, under her own laws and in her own spirit, a creative faculty. In what manner Fancy ambitiously aims at a rivalship with Imagination, and Imagination stoops to work with the materials of

[17] *Pompey's Pillar:* This was erected in Alexandria to record the Roman conquest of the city in the reign of Diocletian, A.D. 296; it has no connection with Pompey.

Fancy, might be illustrated from the compositions of all eloquent writers, whether in prose or verse; and chiefly from those of our own Country. Scarcely a page of the impassioned parts of Bishop Taylor's Works[18] can be opened that shall not afford examples.— Referring the Reader to those inestimable volumes, I will content myself with placing a conceit (ascribed to Lord Chesterfield) in contrast with a passage from the Paradise Lost:

> "The dews of the evening most carefully shun,
>   They are the tears of the sky for the loss of the sun."[19]

After the transgression of Adam, Milton, with other appearances of sympathising Nature, thus marks the immediate consequence,

> "Sky lowered, and, muttering thunder, some sad drops
>   Wept at completion of the mortal sin."[20]

The associating link is the same in each instance: Dew and rain, not distinguishable from the liquid substance of tears, are employed as indications of sorrow. A flash of surprise is the effect in the former case; a flash of surprise, and nothing more; for the nature of things does not sustain the combination. In the latter, the effects from the act, of which there is this immediate consequence and visible sign, are so momentous, that the mind acknowledges the justice and reasonableness of the sympathy in nature so manifested; and the sky weeps drops of water as if with human eyes, as "Earth had before trembled from her entrails, and Nature given a second groan."[21]

[18] *Bishop Taylor's Works;* Jeremy Taylor (1613–67)

[19] Cited from "Advice to a lady in Autumn" by Philip Stanhope, Earl of Chesterfield (1693–1773); the second line should read "Those tears of the sky ..."

[20] *Paradise Lost*, IX. 1002–3; line 2 should read "completing" for "completion".

[21] *Paradise Lost*, IX. 1000–1; the lines are altered from Milton's text, which reads:

> Earth trembl'd from her entrails, as again
>   In pangs, and Nature gave a second groan.

Samuel Taylor Coleridge

1772–1834

FROM *BIOGRAPHIA LITERARIA* 1817

COLERIDGE had for some years envisaged writing a major philosophical treatise, when in 1815 he composed the major part of his *Biographia Literaria; or Biographical Sketches of My Literary Life and Opinions*. This was at first conceived as a preface to the *magnum opus* for which outline schemes and plans are drawn up in his letters and notebooks. The great work was never completed, and the *Biographia Literaria*, published in 1817, has itself become his best-known critical work. It is diffuse and unsystematic, but richly sums up the insights resulting from years of study and thought. In the excerpts that follow, Coleridge attempts to identify the nature and function of imagination, and of poetry itself. His ideas on the imagination spring perhaps in origin from Kant's concept of the "productive imagination" as aiming at "unity in the synthesis of what is manifold in appearance" (see p. 215). The theses of Chapter XII, here reprinted without Coleridge's annotations of them, are in part borrowed from the writings of the German philosopher Friedrich W. J. von Schelling (1775–1854), whose system of "transcendental idealism", and emphasis on intuition as the centre of the self-consciousness, proved useful in affording material for the groundwork of a definition of imagination. The theses show how Coleridge's idea of the imagination was bound up with his attempt to find a unifying principle which would resolve the Cartesian duality of spirit and matter; in other words, Coleridge's critical theories were rooted in an attempt to solve a philosophical problem, and find a way of mediating between the Knowing subject and the object Known. The self-consciousness is identified as bringing about "the most original union of both"; and the imagination, as the "prime agent of all human perception", is the servant of the self-consciousness in achieving this unity of subject and object, repeating the "eternal act of creation in the infinite I AM" (p. 89).

This philosophical idea of the imagination, as mediating in the act of Knowledge, and as the means of apprehending God, lent a special colouring and elevation to the idea of the poetic or secondary imagination, which functions to resolve a critical rather than a philosophical problem. Coleridge departs from Wordsworth here (see p. 90) in appropriating to the idea of imagination exclusively the power to "idealise and unify". He makes a more radical contrast between the imagination as "essentially *vital*" (p. 90), and the fancy as tied to the mechanical memory. The fancy proceeds by steps, whereas the imagination seizes wholes, "blends and harmonizes", by the "sacred power of self-intuition", into an organic unity (p. 79). The poet thus comes to have a special status, as bringing "the whole soul of men into activity" (p. 92) and a kind of religious grandeur attaches to him; at the same time, Coleridge found a powerful and convincing way of elucidating the process of poetic creation, and the nature of a poem, in conceiving of the imagination as magically fusing the discordant and irreconcilable in an instantaneous grasp of a new harmony, and working organically to effect a change, not a mere assembling of images, just as "we our food into our nature change" (Coleridge citing Sir John Davies, p. 93). In this explanation, Coleridge seems to have perceived something central in poetic activity, and his *Biographia Literaria* has formed the starting-point for much independent discussion. It should perhaps be noted that Coleridge's theory emphasises intuition somewhat at the expense of art, and that it takes little account of the poet as "maker" or craftsman.

FROM CHAPTER IV

I w A s in my twenty-fourth year when I had the happiness of knowing Mr. Wordsworth personally,[1] and, while memory lasts, I shall hardly forget the sudden effect produced on my mind by his recitation of a manuscript poem, which still remains unpublished, but of which the stanza and tone of style were the same as those of "The Female Vagrant", as originally printed in the first volume of the *Lyrical Ballads*.[2] There was here no mark of strained thought or forced diction, no crowd or turbulence of imagery; and, as the poet hath himself well described in his lines[3] "on re-visiting the Wye", manly reflection and human associations had given both variety and an additional interest to natural objects, which in the

[1] Coleridge met Wordsworth in Bristol in 1795.

[2] "The Female Vagrant", printed in the first issue of *Lyrical Ballads* (1798), was incorporated into a much larger poem published as "Guilt and Sorrow" in 1842.

[3] *lines*: alluding to "Lines written above Tintern Abbey" (1798), especially lines 89–112.

passion and appetite of the first love they had seemed to him neither to need or permit. The occasional obscurities, which had risen from an imperfect controul over the resources of his native language, had almost wholly disappeared, together with that worse defect of arbitrary and illogical phrases, at once hackneyed and fantastic, which hold so distinguished a place in the *technique* of ordinary poetry, and will, more or less, alloy the earlier poems of the truest genius, unless the attention has been specifically directed to their worthlessness and incongruity. I did not perceive anything particular in the mere style of the poem alluded to during its recitation, except indeed such difference as was not separable from the thought and manner; and the Spenserian stanza, which always, more or less, recalls to the reader's mind Spenser's own style, would doubtless have authorized, in my then opinion, a more frequent descent to the phrases of ordinary life than could, without an ill effect, have been hazarded in the heroic couplet. It was not however the freedom from false taste, whether as to common defects or to those more properly his own, which made so unusual an impression on my feelings immediately, and subsequently on my judgment. It was the union of deep feeling with profound thought; the fine balance of truth in observing, with the imaginative faculty in modifying the objects observed; and above all the original gift of spreading the tone, the *atmosphere*, and with it the depth and height of the ideal world, around forms, incidents, and situations of which, for the common view, custom had bedimmed all the lustre, had dried up the sparkle and the dew-drops. "To find no contradiction in the union of old and new; to contemplate the Ancient of Days and all his works with feelings as fresh as if all had then sprang forth at the first creative fiat, characterizes the mind that feels the riddle of the world and may help to unravel it. To carry on the feelings of childhood into the powers of manhood; to combine the child's sense of wonder and novelty with the appearances which every day for perhaps forty years had rendered familiar:

> With sun and moon and stars throughout the year
> And man and woman;[4]

[4] Cited inaccurately from John Milton, "To Mr. Cyriack Skinner upon his Blindness", lines 5–6.

this is the character and privilege of genius, and one of the marks which distinguish genius from talents. And therefore it is the prime merit of genius, and its most unequivocal mode of manifestation, so to represent familiar objects as to awaken in the minds of others a kindred feeling concerning them, and that freshness of sensation which is the constant accompaniment of mental no less than of bodily convalescence. Who has not a thousand times seen snow fall on water? Who has not watched it with a new feeling from the time that he has read Burns' comparison of sensual pleasure:

> To snow that falls upon a river
> A moment white—then gone for ever![5]

In poems, equally as in philosophic disquisitions, genius produces the strongest impressions of novelty while it rescues the most admitted truths from the impotence caused by the very circumstance of their universal admission. Truths of all others the most awful and mysterious, yet being at the same time of universal interest, are too often considered as *so* true, that they lose all the life and efficiency of truth, and lie bed-ridden in the dormitory of the soul side by side with the most despised and exploded errors." *The Friend*, p. 76, No. 5.[6]

This excellence, which in all Mr Wordsworth's writings is more or less predominant, and which constitutes the character of his mind, I no sooner felt than I sought to understand. Repeated meditations led me first to suspect (and a more intimate analysis of the human faculties, their appropriate marks, functions and effects, matured my conjecture into full conviction), that fancy and imagination were two distinct and widely different faculties, instead of being, according to the general belief, either two names with one meaning, or, at furthest, the lower and higher degree of one and the same power. It is not, I own, easy to conceive a more apposite translation of the Greek *Phantasia* than the Latin Imaginatio; but it is equally true that in all societies there exists an instinct of growth, a certain collective, unconscious good sense working progressively

---

[5] Cited inaccurately from "Tam O'Shanter", lines 61–2.

[6] Coleridge wrote and issued *The Friend* as a weekly paper in 1809–10; the whole series was published as three volumes of essays in 1818.

to desynonymize* those words originally of the same meaning, which the conflux of dialects had supplied to the more homogeneous languages, as the Greek and German; and which the same cause, joined with accidents of translation from original works of different countries, occasion in mixt languages like our own. The first and most important point to be proved is, that two conceptions perfectly distinct are confused under one and the same word, and (this done) to appropriate that word exclusively to one meaning, and the synonym (should there be one) to the other. But if (as will be often the case in the arts and sciences) no synonym exists, we must either invent or borrow a word. In the present instance the appropriation had already begun, and been legitimated in the derivative adjective: Milton had a highly *imaginative*, Cowley a very *fanciful* mind. If therefore I should succeed in establishing the actual existences of two faculties generally different, the nomenclature would be at once determined. To the faculty by which I had characterized

* This is effected either by giving to the one word a general and to the other an exclusive use; as "to put on the back" and "to indorse"; or by an actual distinction of meanings as "naturalist", and "physician"; or by difference of relation as "I", and "Me"; (each of which the rustics of our different provinces still use in all the cases singular of the first personal pronoun). Even the mere difference or corruption in the *pronunciation* of the same word, if it have become general, will produce a new word with a distinct signification; thus "property" and "propriety", the latter of which even to the time of Charles II was the *written* word for all the senses of both. Thus too "mister" and "master", both hasty pronunciations of the same word "magister", "mistress", and "miss", "if", and "give", etc. etc. There is a sort of *minim immortal* among the *animalcula infusoria* [that is, protozoa (Ed.)] which has not naturally either birth, or death, absolute beginning or absolute end: for at a certain period a small point appears on its back, which deepens and lengthens till the creature divides in two and the same process recommences in each of the halves now become integral. This may be a fanciful but it is by no means a bad emblem of the formation of words, and may facilitate the conception how immense a nomenclature may be organised from a few simple sounds by rational beings in a social state. For each new application or excitement of the same sound will call forth a different sensation, which cannot but affect the pronunciation. The after recollection of the sound without the same vivid sensation will modify it still further; till at length all trace of the original likeness is worn away.

Milton, we should confine the term *imagination*; while the other would be contra-distinguished as *fancy*. Now were it once fully ascertained that this division is no less grounded in nature than that of delirium from mania, or Otway's

Lutes, laurels, seas of milk and ships of amber,[7]

from Shakespeare's

What! have his daughters brought him to this pass?[8]

or from the preceding apostrophe to the elements, the theory of the fine arts, and of poetry in particular, could not, I thought, but derive some additional and important light. It would in its immediate effects furnish a torch of guidance to the philosophical critic, and ultimately to the poet himself. In energetic minds truth soon changes by domestication into power; and from directing the discrimination and appraisal of the product, becomes influencive in the production. To admire on principle is the only way to imitate without loss of originality.

It has been already hinted that metaphysics and psychology have long been my hobby-horse. But to have a hobby-horse, and to be vain of it, are so commonly found together that they pass almost for the same. I trust therefore that there will be more good humour than contempt in the smile with which the reader chastises my self-complacency, if I confess myself uncertain whether the satisfaction from the perception of a truth new to myself may not have been rendered more poignant by the conceit that it would be equally so to the public. There was a time, certainly, in which I took some little credit to myself in the belief that I had been the first of my countrymen who had pointed out the diverse meaning of which the two terms were capable, and analysed the faculties to which they should be appropriated. Mr W. Taylor's recent volume of synonyms I have not yet seen; but his specification of the terms in question has been clearly shown to be both insufficient and erroneous by Mr Wordsworth in the Preface added to the late collection of his

[7] *Venice Preserved* (1682), V. ii; the first edition of *Biographia Literaria* has "lobsters" for "laurels".

[8] *King Lear*, III. iv. 62.

Lyrical Ballads and other poems.[9] The explanation which Mr Wordsworth has himself given will be found to differ from mine, chiefly perhaps, as our objects are different. It could scarcely indeed happen otherwise, from the advantage I have enjoyed of frequent conversation with him on a subject to which a poem of his own first directed my attention, and my conclusions concerning which he had made more lucid to myself by many happy instances drawn from the operation of natural objects on the mind. But it was Mr Wordsworth's purpose to consider the influences of fancy and imagination as they are manifested in poetry, and from the different effects to conclude their diversity in kind; while it is my object to investigate the seminal principle, and then from the kind to deduce the degree. My friend has drawn a masterly sketch of the branches with their *poetic* fruitage. I wish to add the trunk, and even the roots, as far as they lift themselves above ground and are visible to the naked eye of our common consciousness.

. . . .

FROM CHAPTER VII

Most of my readers will have observed a small water-insect on the surface of rivulets, which throws a cinque-spotted shadow fringed with prismatic colours on the sunny bottom of the brook; and will have noticed how the little animal *wins* its way up against the stream, by alternate pulses of active and passive motion, now resisting the current, and now yielding to it in order to gather strength and a momentary *fulcrum* for a further propulsion. This is no unapt emblem of the mind's self-experience in the act of thinking. There are evidently two powers at work, which relatively to each other are active and passive; and this is not possible without an intermediate faculty, which is at once both active and passive. (In philosophical language we must denominate this intermediate faculty in all its degrees and determinations the IMAGINATION. But, in common language, and especially on the subject of poetry, we appropriate the name to a superior degree of the faculty, joined to a superior voluntary control over it.)

. . . .

[9] See above, pp. 60 and 62.

FROM CHAPTER XII

But it is time to tell the truth; though it requires some courage to
avow it in an age and country in which disquisitions on all subjects,
not privileged to adopt technical terms or scientific symbols, must be
addressed to the public. I say then, that it is neither possible or
necessary for all men, or for many, to be PHILOSOPHERS. There is a
philosophic (and inasmuch as it is actualized by an effort of freedom,
an *artificial*) *consciousness*, which lies beneath or (as it were) *behind*
the spontaneous consciousness natural to all reflecting beings. As
the elder Romans distinguished their northern provinces into Cis-
Alpine and Trans-Alpine, so may we divide all the objects of human
knowledge into those on this side, and those on the other side of the
spontaneous consciousness: citra et trans conscientiam communem.
The latter is exclusively the domain of PURE philosophy, which is
therefore properly entitled *transcendental*, in order to discriminate it
at once, both from mere reflection and *re*-presentation on the one
hand, and on the other from those flights of lawless speculation
which, abandoned by *all* distinct consciousness, because trans-
gressing the bounds and purposes of our intellectual faculties, are
justly condemned as *transcendent*. The first range of hills that
encircles the scanty vale of human life is the horizon for the majority
of its inhabitants. On *its* ridges the common sun is born and departs.
From *them* the stars rise, and touching *them* they vanish. By the
many even this range, the natural limit and bulwark of the vale,
is but imperfectly known. Its higher ascents are too often hidden by
mists and clouds from uncultivated swamps, which few have
courage or curiosity to penetrate. To the multitude below these
vapours appear, now as the dark haunts of terrific agents, on which
none may intrude with impunity; and now all *a-glow* with colours
not their own, they are gazed at as the splendid palaces of happiness
and power. But in all ages there have been a few who, measuring
and sounding the rivers of the vale at the feet of their furthest in-
accessible falls, have learnt that the sources must be far higher and
far inward; a few who even in the level streams have detected
elements which neither the vale itself nor the surrounding mountains
contained or could supply. How and whence to these thoughts,

these strong probabilities, the ascertaining vision, the intuitive knowledge, may finally supervene, can be learnt only by the fact. I might oppose to the question the words with which Plotinus supposes NATURE to answer a similar difficulty: "Should any one interrogate her, how she works, if graciously she vouchsafe to listen and speak, she will reply, it behoves thee not to disquiet me with interrogatories, but to understand in silence even as I am silent, and work without words."[10]

Likewise in the fifth book of the fifth Ennead,[11] speaking of the highest and intuitive knowledge as distinguished from the discursive, or in the language of Wordsworth,

The vision and the faculty divine;[12]

he says: "it is not lawful to inquire from whence it sprang, as if it were a thing subject to place and motion, for it neither approached hither, nor again departs from hence to some other place; but it either appears to us or it does not appear. So that we ought not to pursue it with a view of detecting its secret source, but to watch in quiet till it suddenly shines upon us; preparing ourselves for the blessed spectacle as the eye waits patiently for the rising sun." They and they only can acquire the philosophic imagination, the sacred power of self-intuition, who within themselves can interpret and understand the symbol, that the wings of the air-sylph are forming within the skin of the caterpillar; those only who feel in their own spirits the same instinct which impels the chrysalis of the horned fly to leave room in its involucrum for antennae yet to come. They know and feel that the *potential* works *in* them, even as the *actual* works on them! In short, all the organs of sense are framed for a corresponding world of sense; and we have it. All the organs of spirit are framed for a correspondent world of spirit:

[10] The works of the neo-platonist Plotinus (A.D. 204–70) were published by his follower Porphyry in 301, arranged as six *Enneads*. These religious and philosphical speculations were translated in part by Thomas Taylor (1767–1835), beginning with *Concerning the Beautiful* (1787), and had a powerful influence on Blake, Coleridge and Shelley in particular. The reference here is to *Ennead* III. 8 .3.

[11] *Ennead* V. 5. 8.

[12] Wordsworth, *The Excursion* (1814), I. 79.

though the latter organs are not developed in all alike. But they exist in all, and their first appearance discloses itself in the *moral* being. How else could it be that even worldlings, not wholly debased, will contemplate the man of simple and disinterested goodness with contradictory feelings of pity and respect? "Poor man! he is not made for *this* world." Oh! herein they utter a prophecy of universal fulfilment; for man *must* either rise or sink.

FROM CHAPTER XII

All knowledge rests on the coincidence of an object with a subject. (My readers have been warned in a former chapter that, for their convenience as well as the writer's, the term *subject* is used by me in its scholastic sense as equivalent to mind or sentient being, and as the necessary correlative of object or *quicquid objicitur menti*.) [13] For we can *know* that only which is true; and the truth is universally placed in the coincidence of the thought with the thing, of the representation with the object represented.

Now the sum of all that is merely OBJECTIVE we will henceforth call NATURE, confining the term to its passive and material sense, as comprising all the phaenomena by which its existence is made known to us. On the other hand, the sum of all that is SUBJECTIVE we may comprehend in the name of the SELF or INTELLIGENCE. Both conceptions are in necessary antithesis. Intelligence is conceived of as exclusively representative, nature as exclusively represented; the one as conscious, the other as without consciousness. Now in all acts of positive knowledge there is required a reciprocal concurrence of both, namely of the conscious being and of that which is in itself unconscious. Our problem is to explain this concurrence, its possibility and its necessity.

During the act of knowledge itself, the objective and subjective are so instantly united that we cannot determine to which of the two the priority belongs. There is here no first and no second; both are coinstantaneous and one. While I am attempting to explain this intimate coalition, I must suppose it dissolved. I must necessarily set out from the one, to which therefore I give hypothetical antecedence, in order to arrive at the other. But as there are but two

[13] *quicquid objicitur menti:* "whatever offers itself to the mind".

factors or elements in the problem, subject and object, and as it is left indeterminate from which of them I should commence, there are two cases equally possible.

1. EITHER THE OBJECTIVE IS TAKEN AS THE FIRST, AND THEN WE HAVE TO ACCOUNT FOR THE SUPERVENTION OF THE SUBJECTIVE WHICH COALESCES WITH IT.

The notion of the subjective is not contained in the notion of the objective. On the contrary, they mutually exclude each other. The subjective therefore must supervene to the objective. The conception of nature does not apparently involve the co-presence of an intelligence making an ideal duplicate of it, i.e. representing it. This desk for instance would (according to our natural notions) be, though there should exist no sentient being to look at it. This then is the problem of natural philosophy. It assumes the objective or unconscious nature as the first, and has therefore to explain how intelligence can supervene to it, or how itself can grow into intelligence. If it should appear that all enlightened naturalists, without having distinctly proposed the problem to themselves, have yet constantly moved in the line of its solution, it must afford a strong presumption that the problem itself is founded in nature. For if all knowledge has as it were two poles reciprocally required and pre-supposed, all sciences must proceed from the one or the other, and must tend toward the opposite as far as the equatorial point in which both are reconciled and become identical. The necessary tendence therefore of all natural philosophy is from nature to intelligence; and this, and no other, is the true ground and occasion of the instinctive striving to introduce theory into our views of natural phaenomena. The highest perfection of natural philosophy would consist in the perfect spiritualization of all the laws of nature into laws of intuition and intellect. The phaenomena (*the material*) must wholly disappear, and the laws alone (*the formal*) must remain. Thence it comes, that in nature itself the more the principle of law breaks forth, the more does the *husk* drop off, the phaenomena themselves become more spiritual and at length cease altogether in our consciousness. The optical phaenomena are but a geometry, the lines of which are drawn by light, and the materiality of this light itself has already become matter of doubt. In the appearances of magnetism all trace of matter is lost, and of the phaenomena of gravitation, which not a few among the most illustrious Newtonians have declared no otherwise comprehensible than as an immediate spiritual influence, there remains nothing but its law, the execution of which on a vast scale is the mechanism of the heavenly motions. The theory of natural philosophy would then be completed, when all nature was demonstrated to be identical in essence with that which in its highest known power exists in man as intelligence and self-consciousness; when the heavens and the earth shall declare not only the power of their maker, but the glory and the presence of their God, even as he appeared to the great prophet during the vision of the mount in the skirts of his divinity.[14]

This may suffice to show that even natural science, which commences with the material phaenomenon as the reality and substance of things existing, does yet, by the necessity of theorizing unconsciously, and as it were instinctively, end in nature as an intelligence; and by this tendency the science of nature becomes finally natural philosophy, the one of the two poles of fundamental science.

2. OR THE SUBJECTIVE IS TAKEN AS THE FIRST, AND THE PROBLEM THEN IS, HOW THERE SUPERVENES TO IT A COINCIDENT OBJECTIVE.

In the pursuit of these sciences, our success in each depends on an austere and faithful adherence to its own principles with a careful separation and exclusion of those which appertain to the opposite science. As the natural philosopher, who directs his views to the objective, avoids above all things the intermixture of the subjective in his knowledge, as for instance arbitrary suppositions or rather suffictions,[15] occult qualities, spiritual agents and the substitution of final for efficient causes; so on the other hand, the transcendental or intelligential philosopher is equally anxious to preclude all interpolation of the objective into the subjective principles of his science, as for instance the assumption of impresses or configurations in the brain, correspondent to miniature pictures on the retina painted by rays of light from supposed originals, which are not the immediate and real objects of vision, but deductions from it for the purpose of explanation. This purification of the mind is effected by an absolute

[14] Alluding to the vision of Moses, *Exodus*, xxiv. 9–10.

[15] *suffictions:* Coleridge coined this word to mean a fiction taken as a hypothesis.

and scientific scepticism, to which the mind voluntarily determines itself for the specific purpose of future certainty. Des Cartes who (in his meditations) himself first, at least of the moderns, gave a beautiful example of this voluntary doubt, this self-determined indetermination, happily expresses its utter difference from the scepticism of vanity or irreligion: "Nec tamen in eo scepticos imitabar, qui dubitant tantum ut dubitent, et praeter incertitudinem ipsam nihil quaerunt. Nam contra totus in eo eram ut aliquid certi reperirem." Des Cartes, de Methodo.[16] Nor is it less distinct in its motives and final aim than in its proper objects, which are not as in ordinary scepticism the prejudices of education and circumstance, but those original and innate prejudices which nature herself has planted in all men, and which to all but the philosopher are the first principles of knowledge and the final test of truth.

Now these essential prejudices are all reducible to the one fundamental presumption, THAT THERE EXIST THINGS WITHOUT US. As this on the one hand originates neither in grounds or arguments, and yet on the other hand remains proof against all attempts to remove it by grounds or arguments (*naturam furca expellas tamen usque recurret*);[17] on the one hand lays claim to IMMEDIATE certainty as a position at once indemonstrable and irresistible, and yet on the other hand, inasmuch as it refers to something essentially different from ourselves, nay even in opposition to ourselves, leaves it inconceivable how it could possibly become a part of our immediate consciousness (in other words, how that, which *ex hypothesi* is and continues to be extrinsic and alien to our being, should become a modification of our being); the philosopher therefore compels himself to treat this faith as nothing more than a prejudice, innate indeed and connatural,[18] but still a prejudice.

---

[16] Descartes, *Discourse on Method*. Part 3. See *The Philosophical Works of Descartes*, translated by Elizabeth Haldane and G. R. T. Ross, Vol. I (1911), p. 99, where this passage is rendered as follows: "Not that indeed I imitated the sceptics, who only doubt for the sake of doubting, and pretend to be always uncertain; for, on the contrary, my design was only to provide myself with good ground for assurance."

[17] Horace, *Epistles*, I. x. 24, meaning "You may drive out Nature with a pitchfork, yet she will hurry back".

[18] *connatural:* natural to man, born in us.

The other position, which not only claims but necessitates the admission of its immediate certainty, equally for the scientific reason of the philosopher as for the common sense of mankind at large, namely I AM, cannot so properly be entitled a prejudice. It is groundless indeed; but then in the very idea it precludes all ground, and separated from the immediate consciousness loses its whole sense and import. It is groundless; but only because it is itself the ground of all other certainty. Now the apparent contradiction that the former position, namely the existence of things without us, which from its nature cannot be immediately certain, should be received as blindly and as independently of all grounds as the existence of our own being, the transcendental philosopher can solve only by the supposition that the former is unconsciously involved in the latter; that it is not only coherent but identical, and one and the same thing with our own immediate self-consciousness. To demonstrate this identity is the office and object of his philosophy.

If it be said that this is Idealism, let it be remembered that it is only so far idealism as it is at the same time, and on that very account, the truest and most binding realism. For wherein does the realism of mankind properly consist? In the assertion that there exists a something without them, what, or how, or where they know not, which occasions the objects of their perception? Oh no! This is neither connatural or universal. It is what a few have taught and learnt in the schools, and which the many repeat without asking themselves concerning their own meaning. The realism common to all mankind is far elder and lies infinitely deeper than this hypothetical explanation of the origin of our perceptions, an explanation skimmed from the mere surface of mechanical philosophy. It is the table itself which the man of common sense believes himself to see, not the phantom of a table, from which he may argumentatively deduce the reality of a table which he does not see. If to destroy the reality of all that we actually behold be idealism, what can be more egregiously so than the system of modern metaphysics which banishes us to a land of shadows, surrounds us with apparitions, and distinguishes truth from illusion only by the majority of those who dream the same dream? "*I* asserted that the world was mad," exclaimed poor Lee, "and the world said that I was mad, and confound them, they outvoted me."[19]

It is to the true and original realism that I would direct the attention. This believes and requires neither more nor less than that the object which it beholds or presents to itself is the real and very object. In this sense, however much we may strive against it, we are all collectively born idealists, and therefore and only therefore are we at the same time realists. But of this the philosophers of the schools know nothing, or despise the faith as the prejudice of the ignorant vulgar, because they live and move in a crowd of phrases and notions from which human nature has long ago vanished. Oh, ye that reverence yourselves, and walk humbly with the divinity in your own hearts, ye are worthy of a better philosophy! Let the dead bury the dead, but do you preserve your human nature, the depth of which was never yet fathomed by a philosophy made up of notions and mere logical entities. . . .

THESIS I

Truth is correlative to being. Knowledge without a correspondent reality is no knowledge; if we know, there must be somewhat known by us. To know is in its very essence a verb active.

THESIS II

All truth is either mediate, that is, derived from some other truth or truths; or immediate and original. . . .

THESIS III

We are to seek therefore for some absolute truth capable of communicating to other positions a certainty which it has not itself borrowed; a truth self-grounded, unconditional and known by its own light. In short, we have to find a somewhat which *is*, simply because it *is*. In order to be such, it must be one which is its own predicate, so far at least that all other nominal predicates must be modes and repetitions of itself. Its existence too must be such as to preclude the possibility of requiring a cause or antecedent without an absurdity.

[19] Alluding to Nathaniel Lee, the dramatist, who was confined in Bedlam for five years from 1684, and died in 1692.

THESIS IV

That there can be but one such principle may be proved a priori; for were there two or more, each must refer to some other by which its equality is affirmed; consequently neither would be self-established, as the hypothesis demands. And a posteriori, it will be proved by the principle itself when it is discovered, as involving universal antecedents in its very conception. . . .

THESIS V

Such a principle cannot be any THING or OBJECT. Each thing is what it is in consequence of some other thing. An infinite, independent *thing* is no less a contradiction than an infinite circle or a sideless triangle. Besides a thing is that which is capable of being an object of which itself is not the sole percipient. But an object is inconceivable without a subject as its antithesis. *Omne perceptum percipientem supponit.*[20]

But neither can the principle be found in a subject as a subject, contra-distinguished from an object: for *unicuique percipienti aliquid objicitur perceptum.*[21] It is to be found therefore neither in object nor subject taken separately, and consequently, as no other third is conceivable, it must be found in that which is neither subject nor object exclusively, but which is the identity of both.

THESIS VI

This principle, and so characterized, manifests itself in the SUM or I AM, which I shall hereafter indiscriminately express by the words spirit, self and self-consciousness. In this, and in this alone, object and subject, being and knowing, are identical, each involving and supposing the other. In other words, it is a subject which becomes a subject by the act of constructing itself objectively to itself; but which never is an object except for itself, and only so far as by the very same act it becomes a subject. It may be described therefore as a perpetual self-duplication of one and the same power into

[20] *Omne . . . supponit:* "each thing perceived implies a perceiver".
[21] *unicuique . . . perceptum:* "something to be perceived will offer itself to each perceiver".

object and subject, which presuppose each other, and can exist only as antitheses.

SCHOLIUM.[22] If a man be asked how he *knows* that he is, he can only answer, *sum quia sum*.[23] But if (the absoluteness of this certainty having been admitted) he be again asked how he, the individual person, came to be, then in relation to the ground of his *existence*, not to the ground of his *knowledge* of that existence, he might reply, *sum quia deus est*,[24] or still more philosophically, *sum quia in deo sum*.[25]

But if we elevate our conception to the absolute self, the great eternal I AM, then the principle of being, and of knowledge, of idea, and of reality, the ground of existence, and the ground of the knowledge of existence, are absolutely identical, *Sum quia sum*; I am, because I affirm myself to be; I affirm myself to be, because I am.

THESIS VII

If then I know myself only through myself, it is contradictory to require any other predicate of self but that of self-consciousness. Only in the self-consciousness of a spirit is there the required identity of object and of representation; for herein consists the essence of a spirit, that it is self-representative. If therefore this be the one only immediate truth in the certainty of which the reality of our collective knowledge is grounded, it must follow that the spirit in all the objects which it views, views only itself. If this could be proved, the immediate reality of all intuitive knowledge would be assured. It has been shown that a spirit is that which is its own object, yet not originally an object, but an absolute subject for which all, itself included, may become an object. It must therefore be an act; for every object is, as an *object*, dead, fixed, incapable in itself of any action, and necessarily finite. Again, the spirit (originally the identity of object and subject) must in some sense dissolve this identity, in order to be conscious of it: *fit alter et idem*.[26] But this implies an act, and it follows therefore that intelligence or

[22] *Scholium:* explanatory comment.
[23] *sum quia sum:* "I exist because I exist".
[24] *sum quia deus est:* "I exist because God exists".
[25] *sum quia in deo sum:* "I exist because I exist in God".
[26] *fit alter et idem:* "it is made different and the same".

self-consciousness is impossible, except by and in a will. The self-conscious spirit therefore is a will; and freedom must be assumed as a *ground* of philosophy, and can never be deduced from it.

THESIS VIII

Whatever in its origin is objective is likewise as such necessarily finite. Therefore, since the spirit is not originally an object, and as the subject exists in antithesis to an object, the spirit cannot originally be finite. But neither can it be a subject without becoming an object, and as it is originally the identity of both, it can be conceived neither as infinite nor finite exclusively, but as the most original union of both. In the existence, in the reconciling and the recurrence of this contradiction consists the process and mystery of production and life.

THESIS IX

This *principium commune essendi et cognoscendi*,[27] as subsisting in a WILL or primary ACT of self-duplication, is the mediate or indirect principle of every science; but it is the immediate and direct principle of the ultimate science alone, i.e. of transcendental philosophy alone. For it must be remembered, that all these Theses refer solely to one of the two Polar Sciences, namely, to that which commences with and rigidly confines itself within the subjective, leaving the objective (as far as it is exclusively objective) to natural philosophy, which is its opposite pole. In its very idea therefore as a systematic knowledge of our collective KNOWING (*scientia scientiae*), it involves the necessity of some one highest principle of knowing, as at once the source and accompanying form in all particular acts of intellect and perception. This, it has been shown, can be found only in the act and evolution of self-consciousness. We are not investigating an absolute *principium essendi*; for then, I admit, many valid objections might be started against our theory; but an absolute *principium cognoscendi*. The result of both the sciences, or their equatorial point, would be the principle of a total and undivided philosophy, as for prudential reasons I have chosen to anticipate in the Scholium to Thesis VI and the note subjoined. In other words, philosophy would

[27] *principium . . . cognoscendi:* "common principle of being and of knowing".

pass into religion, and religion become inclusive of philosophy. We begin with the I KNOW MYSELF, in order to end with the absolute I AM. We proceed from the SELF, in order to lose and find all self in GOD.

THESIS X

The transcendental philosopher does not inquire what ultimate ground of our knowledge there may lie out of our knowing, but what is the last in our knowing itself, beyond which *we* cannot pass. The principle of our knowing is sought within the sphere of our knowing. It must be something therefore which can itself be known. It is asserted only that the act of self-consciousness is for *us* the source and principle of all *our* possible knowledge. Whether abstracted from us there exists anything higher and beyond this primary self-knowing, which is for us the form of all our knowing, must be decided by the result.

That the self-consciousness is the fixt point to which for *us* all is morticed and annexed, needs no further proof. But that the self-consciousness may be the modification of a higher form of being, perhaps of a higher consciousness, and this again of a yet higher, and so on in an infinite regressus; in short, that self-consciousness may be itself something explicable into something which must lie beyond the possibility of our knowledge, because the whole synthesis of our intelligence is first formed in and through the self-consciousness, does not at all concern us as transcendental philosophers. For to us, self-consciousness is not a kind of *being*, but a kind of *knowing*, and that too the highest and farthest that exists for *us*. . . .

FROM CHAPTER XIII

The IMAGINATION then I consider either as primary, or secondary. The primary IMAGINATION I hold to be the living Power and prime Agent of all human Perception, and as a repetition in the finite mind of the eternal act of creation in the infinite I AM. The secondary Imagination I consider as an echo of the former, co-existing with the conscious will, yet still as identical with the primary in the *kind* of its agency, and differing only in *degree*, and in the *mode* of its operation. It dissolves, diffuses, dissipates, in order to re-create; or where this process is rendered impossible, yet still at all events it struggles to idealize and to unify. It is essentially *vital*, even as all objects (*as* objects) are essentially fixed and dead.

FANCY, on the contrary, has no other counters to play with but fixities and definites. The Fancy is indeed no other than a mode of memory emancipated from the order of time and space; while it is blended with, and modified by that empirical phaenomenon of the will which we express by the word CHOICE. But equally with the ordinary memory the Fancy must receive all its materials ready made from the law of association. . . .

FROM CHAPTER XIV

But the communication of pleasure may be the immediate object of a work not metrically composed; and that object may have been in a high degree attained, as in novels and romances. Would then the mere superaddition of metre, with or without rhyme, entitle *these* to the name of poems? The answer is that nothing can permanently please which does not contain in itself the reason why it is so, and not otherwise. If metre be superadded, all other parts must be made consonant with it. They must be such as to justify the perpetual and distinct attention to each part which an exact correspondent recurrence of accent and sound are calculated to excite. The final definition then, so deduced, may be thus worded. A poem is that species of composition which is opposed to works of science by proposing for its *immediate* object pleasure, not truth; and from all other species (having *this* object in common with it) it is discriminated by proposing to itself such delight from the *whole* as is compatible with a distinct gratification from each component *part*.

Controversy is not seldom excited in consequence of the disputants attaching each a different meaning to the same word; and in few instances has this been more striking than in disputes concerning the present subject. If a man chooses to call every composition a poem which is rhyme, or measure, or both, I must leave his opinion uncontroverted. The distinction is at least competent to characterize the writer's intention. If it were subjoined that the whole is likewise

entertaining or affecting as a tale or as a series of interesting reflec-
tions, I of course admit this as another fit ingredient of a poem and
an additional merit. But if the definition sought for be that of a
legitimate poem, I answer, it must be one, the parts of which
mutually support and explain each other; all in their proportion
harmonizing with, and supporting the purpose and known influences of metrical arrangement. The philosophic critics of all ages
coincide with the ultimate judgment of all countries in equally
denying the praises of a just poem on the one hand to a series of
striking lines or distiches, each of which absorbing the whole
attention of the reader to itself disjoins it from its context and
makes it a separate whole, instead of a harmonizing part; and on the
other hand, to an unsustained composition, from which the reader
collects rapidly the general result, unattracted by the component
parts. The reader should be carried forward, not merely or chiefly
by the mechanical impulse of curiosity, or by a restless desire to
arrive at the final solution; but by the pleasurable activity of mind
excited by the attractions of the journey itself. Like the motion of a
serpent, which the Egyptians made the emblem of intellectual
power; or like the path of sound through the air; at every step he
pauses and half recedes, and from the retrogressive movement
collects the force which again carries him onward. "Praecipitandus
est *liber* spiritus," says Petronius Arbiter most happily.[28] The
epithet *liber* here balances the preceding verb; and it is not easy to
conceive more meaning condensed in fewer words.

But if this should be admitted as a satisfactory character of a
poem, we have still to seek for a definition of poetry. The writings
of PLATO, and Bishop TAYLOR[29] and the *Theoria Sacra* of BURNET,[30]
furnish undeniable proofs that poetry of the highest kind may exist
without metre, and even without the contradistinguishing objects
of a poem. The first chapter of Isaiah (indeed a very large proportion of the whole book) is poetry in the most emphatic sense; yet it

[28] *Satyricon*, 118, "The free spirit must plunge headlong." (The quotation
comes from a speech by Eumolpus on the qualities that make a good poet.)

[29] Jeremy Taylor (1613–67), best known for his *Holy Living* and *Holy
Dying*.

[30] Thomas Burnet (died 1715), whose *Sacred Theory of the Earth* appeared
in 1684–9.

would be not less irrational than strange to assert that pleasure, and not truth, was the immediate object of the prophet. In short, whatever *specific* import we attach to the word poetry, there will be found involved in it, as a necessary consequence, that a poem of any length neither can be, nor ought to be, all poetry. Yet if a harmonious whole is to be produced, the remaining parts must be preserved *in keeping* with the poetry; and this can be no otherwise effected than by such a studied selection and artificial arrangement as will partake of *one*, though not a *peculiar*, property of poetry. And this again can be no other than the property of exciting a more continuous and equal attention than the language of prose aims at, whether colloquial or written.

My own conclusions on the nature of poetry, in the strictest use of the word, have been in part anticipated in the preceding disquisition on the fancy and imagination. What is poetry? is so nearly the same question with, what is a poet? that the answer to the one is involved in the solution of the other. For it is a distinction resulting from the poetic genius itself, which sustains and modifies the images, thoughts and emotions of the poet's own mind.

The poet, described in *ideal* perfection, brings the whole soul of man into activity, with the subordination of its faculties to each other, according to their relative worth and dignity. He diffuses a tone and spirit of unity that blends and (as it were) *fuses*, each into each, by that synthetic and magical power to which we have exclusively appropriated the name of imagination. This power, first put in action by the will and understanding and retained under their irremissive, though gentle and unnoticed, controul (*laxis effertur habenis*)[31] reveals itself in the balance or reconciliation of opposite or discordant qualities: of sameness, with difference; of the general, with the concrete; the idea, with the image; the individual, with the representative; the sense of novelty and freshness, with old and familiar objects; a more than usual state of emotion, with more than usual order; judgement ever awake and steady self-possession, with enthusiasm and feeling profound or vehement; and while it blends and harmonizes the natural and the artificial, still subordinates art to nature; the manner to the matter;

[31] Virgil, *Georgics*, II. 364 ("laxis . . . inmissus habenis"), "given its head on loose reins".

and our admiration of the poet to our sympathy with the poetry. "Doubtless," as Sir John Davies observes of the soul (and his words may with slight alteration be applied, and even more appropriately, to the poetic IMAGINATION):

> Doubtless this could not be, but that she turns
> Bodies to spirit by sublimation strange,
> As fire converts to fire the things it burns,
> As we our food into our nature change.
>
> From their gross matter she abstracts their forms,
> And draws a kind of quintessence from things;
> Which to her proper nature she transforms
> To bear them light on her celestial wings.
>
> Thus does she, when from individual states
> She doth abstract the universal kinds;
> Which then re-clothed in divers names and fates
> Steal access through our senses to our minds.[32]

Finally, GOOD SENSE, is the BODY of poetic genius, FANCY its DRAPERY, MOTION its LIFE, and IMAGINATION the SOUL that is every where, and in each; and forms all into one graceful and intelligent whole.

[32] Sir John Davies (1569–1626), whose *Nosce Teipsum* ("Know Thyself") was written in 1599. Coleridge quotes lines 537–48, but the last stanza should read:

> This doth she when from things particular
> She doth abstract the universal kinds,
> Which bodiless and immaterial are
> And can be lodg'd but only in our minds.

John Keats

1795–1821

PASSAGES FROM THE LETTERS 1817-1819

KEATS was no theorist, but in the letters he wrote to his family and friends he threw off comments, sometimes extended, more frequently asides in a sentence or two, about his own art, or more generally about poetry and the imagination. The letters reveal a remarkable development in his thinking in a very short period, and the excerpts printed here show well enough how rash it would be to take any of the poet's famous phrases as typifying his views. It is well known that Keats continually refreshed his mind by studying Shakespeare, and that Milton influenced him strongly when he was writing *Hyperion*. His ideas, however, were formed more importantly through his reactions to his contemporaries, especially Wordsworth and Coleridge. In speaking out his private thoughts with a young man's ardour, Keats seems to exemplify something central in romanticism, a passionate utterance unlike the more subdued and cautious public statements of Wordsworth's prefaces. He belongs, in any case, to the next generation of poets, and can take for granted positions which Wordsworth and Coleridge had laboriously to work towards. So his sense of the "holiness of the heart's affections" (p. 95), his use of the term "imagination" (p. 96, for example), his tendency to elevate passion and intuition above intellect and "consequitive reasoning" (p. 95), and his inability "to feel certain of any truth but from a clear perception of its Beauty" (p. 106), all reflect elements in the thinking of Wordsworth and Coleridge. It is true that Keats moves beyond them in some respects, as in his rejection of the "egotistical sublime" in favour of "negative capability" (p. 104), but much of what he says may be seen as adapting, making personal, and proving on the pulses of a gifted and passionate individual, what remains abstract and general in the Preface to the *Lyrical Ballads*, or in *Biographia Literaria*.

FROM A LETTER TO BENJAMIN BAILEY [1]

Saturday, November 22, 1817

O I wish I was as certain of the end of all your troubles as that of your momentary start about the authenticity of the Imagination. I am certain of nothing but of the holiness of the Heart's affections and the truth of Imagination—What the imagination seizes as Beauty must be truth—whether it existed before or not—for I have the same Idea of all our Passions as of Love they are all in their sublime, creative of essential Beauty—In a Word, you may know my favorite Speculation by my first Book [2] and the little song [3] I sent in my last—which is a representation from the fancy of the probable mode of operating in these Matters—The Imagination may be compared to Adam's dream [4]—he awoke and found it truth. I am the more zealous in this affair, because I have never yet been able to perceive how any thing can be known for truth by consequitive reasoning—and yet it must be—Can it be that even the greatest Philosopher ever arrived at his goal without putting aside numerous objections—However it may be, O for a Life of Sensations [5] rather than of Thoughts! It is "a Vision in the form of Youth" a Shadow of reality to come—and this consideration has further convinced me for it has come as auxiliary to another favorite Speculation of mine, that we shall enjoy ourselves here after by having what we called happiness on Earth repeated in a finer tone and so repeated—And yet such a fate can only befall those who delight in Sensation rather than hunger as you do after Truth— Adam's dream will do here and seems to be a conviction that Imagination and its empyreal reflection is the same as human Life and its spiritual repetition. But as I was saying—the simple imaginative Mind may have its rewards in the repeti[ti]on of its own silent Working coming continually on the Spirit with a fine

[1] At first Benjamin Bailey (1791–1853) was valued as a friend by Keats, but their friendship came to an end in 1819.

[2] first Book: Book I of *Endymion* (published 1818).

[3] little song: "O Sorrow, why dost borrow . . ."

[4] Adam's dream: in Milton's *Paradise Lost*, VIII. 460–90.

[5] Sensations: Dr. Johnson defined "sensation" as "perception by means of the senses", which indicates what Keats meant here.

Suddenness—to compare great things with small[6]—have you never by being Surprised with an old Melody—in a delicious place—by a delicious voice, fe[ll]t over again your very speculations and surmises at the time it first operated on your Soul—do you not remember forming to yourself the singer's face more beautiful that [*for* than] it was possible and yet with the elevation of the Moment you did not think so—even then you were mounted on the Wings of Imagination so high—that the Prototype must be here after—that delicious face you will see. What a time! I am continually running away from the subject—sure this cannot be exactly the case with a complex Mind—one that is imaginative and at the same time careful of its fruits—who would exist partly on Sensation partly on thought —to whom it is necessary that years should bring the philosophic Mind[7]—such an one I consider your's and therefore it is necessary to your eternal Happiness that you not only drink this old Wine of Heaven, which I shall call the redigestion of our most ethereal Musings on Earth; but also increase in knowledge and know all things.

FROM A LETTER TO GEORGE AND THOMAS KEATS[8]
Sunday, December 21, 1817

THE excellence of every Art is its intensity, capable of making all disagreeables evaporate, from their being in close relationship with Beauty and Truth—Examine King Lear, and you will find this exemplified throughout . . .

I had not a dispute but a disquisition with Dilke[9] on various subjects; several things dove-tailed in my mind, and at once it struck me, what quality went to form a Man of Achievement, especially in Literature and which Shakespeare possessed so enormously—I mean *Negative Capability*, that is, when a man is capable of being in uncertainties, Mysteries, doubts, without any irritable reaching after

[6] *to compare . . . small:* recalling *Paradise Lost*, II. 921–2.

[7] *years . . . Mind:* recalling Wordsworth, *Ode on Intimations of Immortality*, line 190.   [8] Younger brothers of John Keats.

[9] *Dilke:* Charles Wentworth Dilke (1789–1864), friend of Keats and later editor of *The Athenaeum*.

fact and reason—Coleridge, for instance, would let go by a fine isolated verisimilitude caught from the Penetralium of mystery, from being incapable of remaining content with half knowledge. This pursued through volumes would perhaps take us no further than this, that with a great poet the sense of Beauty overcomes every other consideration, or rather obliterates all consideration.

FROM A LETTER TO JOHN TAYLOR[10]
Friday, February, 27, 1818

IT is a sorry thing for me that any one should have to overcome Prejudices in reading my Verses—that affects me more than any hypercriticism on any particular Passage. In *Endymion* I have most likely but moved into the Go-cart from the leading strings. In Poetry I have a few Axioms, and you will see how far I am from their Centre. 1st I think Poetry should surprise by a fine excess and not by Singularity—it should strike the Reader as a wording of his own highest thoughts, and appear almost a Remembrance—2nd Its touches of Beauty should never be half way therby making the reader breathless instead of content: the rise, the progress, the setting of imagery should like the Sun come natural to him—shine over him and set soberly although in magnificence leaving him in the Luxury of twilight—but it is easier to think what Poetry should be than to write it—and this leads me on to another axiom. That if Poetry comes not as naturally as the Leaves to a tree it had better not come at all. However it may be with me I cannot help looking into new countries with "O for a Muse of fire to ascend!"[11] If Endymion serves me as a Pioneer perhaps I ought to be content. I have great reason to be content for thank God I can read and perhaps understand Shakespeare to his depths, and I have I am sure many friends, who, if I fail, will attribute any change in my Life and Temper to Humbleness rather than to Pride—to a cowering under the Wings of great Poets rather than to a Bitterness that I am not appreciated. I am anxious to get *Endymion* printed that I may forget it and proceed.

[10] With James Hessey, John Taylor published all except the first collection of poems Keats issued.

[11] Shakespeare, *Henry V*, Prologue, line 1.

D

FROM A LETTER TO JOHN TAYLOR
Friday, April 24, 1818

I was purposing to travel over the north this Summer—there is but one thing to prevent me—I know nothing I have read nothing and I mean to follow Solomon's directions of "get Wisdom—get understanding"[12]—I find cavalier days are gone by. I find that I can have no enjoyment in the World but continual drinking of Knowledge—I find there is no worthy pursuit but the idea of doing some good for the world—some do it with their society—some with their wit—some with their benevolence—some with a sort of power of conferring pleasure and good humour on all they meet and in a thousand ways all equally dutiful to the command of Great Nature —there is but one way for me—the road lies th[r]ough application study and thought. I will pursue it and to that end purpose retiring for some years. I have been hovering for some time between an exquisite sense of the luxurious and a love for Philosophy—were I calculated for the former I should be glad—but as I am not I shall turn all my soul to the latter.

FROM A LETTER TO
JOHN HAMILTON REYNOLDS[13]
Sunday, May 3, 1818

Were I to study physic or rather Medicine again,—I feel it would not make the least difference in my Poetry; when the Mind is in its infancy a Bias is in reality a Bias, but when we have acquired more strength, a Bias becomes no Bias. Every department of Knowledge we see excellent and calculated towards a great whole. I am so convinced of this, that I am glad at not having given away my medical Books, which I shall again look over to keep alive the little I know thitherwards; and moreover intend through you and Rice[14]

---

[12] *Proverbs*, iv. 5.

[13] Reynolds (1794–1852), a minor poet, was one of the closest friends of Keats.

[14] *Rice:* James Rice (1792–1832), another close friend of Keats.

to become a sort of pip-civilian.[15] An extensive knowledge is needful to thinking people—it takes away the heat and fever; and helps, by widening speculation, to ease the Burden of the Mystery:[16] a thing I begin to understand a little, and which weighed upon you in the most gloomy and true sentence in your Letter. The difference of high Sensations with and without knowledge appears to me this —in the latter case we are falling continually ten thousand fathoms deep and being blown up again without wings and with all [the] horror of a bare shouldered creature—in the former case, our shoulders are fledge[d], and we go thro' the same air and space without fear. This is running one's rigs on the score of abstracted benefit[17]—when we come to human Life and the affections it is impossible [to know] how a parallel of breast and head can be drawn—(you will forgive me for thus privately treading out [of] my depth, and take it for treading as schoolboys tread the water)— it is impossible to know how far Knowledge will console us for the death of a friend and the ill "that flesh is heir to"[18]—With respect to the affections and Poetry you must know by a sympathy my thoughts that way; and I dare say these few lines will be but a ratification: I wrote them on May-day—and intend to finish the ode all in good time.—[19]

> Mother of Hermes! and still youthful Maia!
> May I sing to thee
> As thou wast hymned on the shores of Baiae?
> Or may I woo thee
> In earlier Sicilian? or thy smiles
> Seek as they once were sought, in Grecian isles,
> By Bards who died content in pleasant sward,

[15] *pip-civilian:* a humorous phrase meaning "student of diseases"; "pip" was a half-comic term for any kind of illness, and a "civilian" was a professor or student of civil law.

[16] *Burden of the Mystery:* Wordsworth, "Lines written above Tintern Abbey", line 38.

[17] *running one's rigs . . . abstracted benefit:* i.e. running riot for the sake of an ideal (or abstract) benefit.

[18] Shakespeare, *Hamlet*, III. i. 63.

[19] This Ode to May was never completed.

Leaving great verse unto a little clan?
O give me their old vigour, and unheard,
Save of the quiet Primrose, and the span
    Of Heaven and few ears
Rounded by thee My song should die away
    Content as theirs
Rich in the simple worship of a day.—

You may be anxious to know for fact to what sentence in your letter I allude. You say "I fear there is little chance of any thing else in this life". you seem by that to have been going through with a more painful and acute zest the same labyrinth that I have—I have come to the same conclusion thus far. My Branchings out therefrom have been numerous: one of them is the consideration of Words-worth's genius and as a help, in the manner of gold being the meridian Line of worldly wealth,—how he differs from Milton.— And here I have nothing but surmises, from an uncertainty whether Milton's apparently less anxiety for Humanity proceeds from his seeing further or no than Wordsworth: And whether Wordsworth has in truth epic passion[s], and martyrs himself to the human heart, the main region of his song—In regard to his genius alone—we find what he says true as far as we have experienced and we can judge no further but by larger experience—for axioms in philosophy are not axioms until they are proved upon our pulses: We read fine things but never feel them to the full until we have gone the same steps as the Author.—I know this is not plain; you will know exactly my meaning when I say, that now I shall relish Hamlet more than I ever have done. . . .

This crossing a letter is not without its association—for chequer work leads us naturally to a Milkmaid, a Milkmaid to Hogarth Hogarth to Shakespeare Shakespear to Hazlitt—Hazlitt to Shakes-peare[20] and thus by merely pulling an apron string we set a pretty

---

[20] *Milkmaid to Hogarth . . . Hazlitt to Shakespeare:* a milkmaid is the central figure in Hogarth's "The Enraged Musician", an engraving referred to by William Hazlitt in his essay "On the Works of Hogarth", in *The English Comic Writers* (1818). Hazlitt there mentions Charles Lamb, who, in his essay "On the Genius and Character of Hogarth" (1811), had likened

peal of Chimes at work—Let them chime on while, with your patience,—I will return to Wordsworth—whether or no he has an extended vision or a circumscribed grandeur—whether he is an eagle in his nest, or on the wing—and to be more explicit and to show you how tall I stand by the giant, I will put down a simile of human life as far as I now perceive it; that is, to the point to which I say we both have arrived at—Well—I compare human life to a large Mansion[21] of Many Apartments, two of which I can only describe, the doors of the rest being as yet shut upon me—The first we step into we call the infant or thoughtless Chamber, in which we remain as long as we do not think—We remain there a long while, and notwithstanding the doors of the second Chamber remain wide open, showing a bright appearance, we care not to hasten to it; but are at length imperceptibly impelled by the awakening of the thinking principle within us—we no sooner get into the second Chamber, which I shall call the Chamber of Maiden-Thought, than we become intoxicated with the light and the atmosphere, we see nothing but pleasant wonders, and think of delaying there for ever in delight: However among the effects this breathing is father of is that tremendous one of sharpening one's vision into the heart and nature of Man—of convincing one's nerves that the world is full of Misery[22] and Heartbreak, Pain, Sickness and oppression—whereby This Chamber of Maiden Thought becomes gradually darken'd and at the same time on all sides of it many doors are set open—but all dark—all leading to dark passages—We see not the ballance of good and evil. We are in a Mist—*We* are now in that state—We feel the "burden of the Mystery", To this Point was Wordsworth come, as far as I can conceive when he wrote "Tintern Abbey"[23] and it seems to me that his Genius is explorative of those dark Passages. Now if we live, and go on thinking, we too shall explore them. He is a Genius and superior [to] us, in so far as he can,

Hogarth to Shakespeare; and Hazlitt had also just published his *Characters of Shakespeare's Plays* (1817). The link between chequer work and the milk-maid perhaps lay in the pattern of her traditional dress.

[21] *Mansion:* recalling *John*, xiv. 2.

[22] *Misery:* see the poem by Keats, *The Fall of Hyperion*, lines 147-9.

[23] *Tintern Abbey:* Keats cited the same passage earlier in this letter; see above, p. 99.

more than we, make discoveries, and shed a light in them—Here I must think Wordsworth is deeper than Milton—though I think it has depended more upon the general and gregarious advance of intellect, than individual greatness of Mind—From the Paradise Lost and the other Works of Milton, I hope it is not too presuming, even between ourselves to say, that his Philosophy, human and divine, may be tolerably understood by one not much advanced in years, In his time englishmen were just emancipated from a great superstition—and Men had got hold of certain points and resting places in reasoning which were too newly born to be doubted, and too much opposed by the Mass of Europe not to be thought etherial and authentically divine—who could gainsay his ideas on virtue, vice, and Chastity in Comus, just at the time of the dismissal of Cod-pieces[24] and a hundred other disgraces? who would not rest satisfied with his hintings at good and evil in the Paradise Lost, when just free from the inquisition and burning in Smithfield? The Reformation produced such immediate and great benefits, that Protestantism was considered under the immediate eye of heaven, and its own remaining Dogmas and superstitions, then, as it were, regenerated, constituted those resting places and seeming sure points of Reasoning—from that I have mentioned, Milton, whatever he may have thought in the sequel, appears to have been content with these by his writings—He did not think into the human heart, as Wordsworth has done—Yet Milton as a Philosopher, had sure as great powers as Wordsworth—What is then to be inferr'd? O many things—It proves there is really a grand march of intellect—, It proves that a mighty providence subdues the mightiest Minds to the service of the time being, whether it be in human Knowledge or Religion—I have often pitied a Tutor who has to hear "Nome: Musa"[25]—so often dinn'd into his ears—I hope you may not the same pain in this scribbling—I may have read these things before, but I never had even a thus dim perception of them; and moreover I like to say my lesson to one who will endure my tediousness for

[24] Cod-pieces: pouches attached to the front of tight fitting breeches; the latest use cited in the Oxford English Dictionary is of 1761.

[25] "Nome: Musa": apparently the beginning of the declension of the noun, meaning "nominative: musa"; the student would continue with "accusative: musam", etc.

my own sake—After all there is certainly something real in the
World—Moore's present[26] to Hazlitt is real—I like that Moore, and
am glad I saw him at the Theatre just before I left Town. Tom[27]
has spit a leetle blood this afternoon, and that is rather a damper—
but I know—the truth is there is something real in the World.
Your third Chamber of Life shall be a lucky and a gentle one—
stored with the wine of love—and the Bread of Friendship.

FROM A LETTER TO
JAMES AUGUSTUS HESSEY[28]
Friday, October 8, 1818

YOU are very good in sending me the letter from the Chronicle[29]
—and I am very bad in not acknowledging such a kindness sooner.
—pray forgive me.—It has so chanced that I have had that paper
every day—I have seen today's. I cannot but feel indebted to those
Gentlemen who have taken my part—As for the rest, I begin to get
a little acquainted with my own strength and weakness.—Praise
or blame has but a momentary effect on the man whose love of
beauty in the abstract makes him a severe critic on his own Works.
My own domestic criticism has given me pain without comparison
beyond what Blackwood or the Quarterly could possibly inflict,
and also when I feel I am right, no external praise can give me such
a glow as my own solitary reperception and ratification of what is
fine. J. S. is perfectly right in regard to the slip-shod Endymion.
That it is so is no fault of mine.—No!—though it may sound a little
paradoxical. It is as good as I had power to make it—by myself—

---

[26] *Moore:* Probably a gift of money is meant, by Peter Moore (1753–1828)
a rich man, and a manager of the Drury Lane Theatre.

[27] *Tom:* younger brother of John Keats; he died of consumption in 1818.

[28] Hessey was a partner with John Taylor in the firm which published all
but the first collection of poems by Keats.

[29] *The Morning Chronicle* of October 3 contained a letter by "J. S.", and
another by "R. B." was published in the issue of October 8, both defending
Keats against the attack on *Endymion* by J. W. Croker in the *Quarterly
Review* for September 1818. Keats was also criticised in the August issue of
Blackwood's Edinburgh Magazine.

Had I been nervous about its being a perfect piece, and with that view asked advice, and trembled over every page, it would not have been written; for it is not in my nature to fumble—I will write independently.—I have written independently *without Judgment*.— I may write independently, *and with Judgment* hereafter. The Genius of Poetry must work out its own salvation in a man: It cannot be matured by law and precept, but by sensation and watchfulness in itself. That which is creative must create itself—In Endymion, I leaped headlong into the Sea, and thereby have become better acquainted with the Soundings, the quicksands, and the rocks, than if I had stayed upon the green shore, and piped a silly pipe, and took tea & comfortable advice.—I was never afraid of failure; for I would sooner fail than not be among the greatest.

FROM A LETTER TO RICHARD WOODHOUSE[30]
Tuesday, October 27, 1818

YOUR Letter gave me a great satisfaction; more on account of its friendliness, than any relish of that matter in it which is accounted so acceptable in the "genus irritabile".[31] The best answer I can give you is in a clerklike manner to make some observations on two principle points, which seem to point like indices into the midst of the whole pro and con, about genius, and views and atchievements and ambition and coetera. 1st As to the poetical Character itself (I mean that sort of which, if I am any thing, I am a Member; that sort distinguished from the wordsworthian or egotistical sublime; which is a thing per se and stands alone)[32] it is not itself— it has no self—it is every thing and nothing—It has no character— it enjoys light and shade; it lives in gusto, be it foul or fair, high or low, rich or poor, mean or elevated—It has as much delight in conceiving an Iago as an Imogen. What shocks the virtuous philosopher, delights the camelion Poet. It does no harm from its

---

[30] Richard Woodhouse (1788–1834), friend of Keats, and adviser to his publishers, Taylor and Hessey.

[31] *genus irritabile*: Horace, *Epistles* II. ii. 102, "the moody tribe (of poets)".

[32] *per se, and stands alone*: citing Shakespeare, *Troilus and Cressida*, I. ii. 15–16.

relish of the dark side of things any more than from its taste for the bright one; because they both end in speculation. A Poet is the most unpoetical of any thing in existence; because he has no Identity— he is continually in for—and filling some other Body—The Sun, the Moon, the Sea and Men and Women who are creatures of impulse are poetical and have about them an unchangeable attribute —the poet has none; no identity—he is certainly the most unpoetical of all God's Creatures. If then he has no self, and if I am a Poet, where is the Wonder that I should say I would write no more? Might I not at that very instant have been cogitating on the Characters of Saturn and Ops?[33] It is a wretched thing to confess; but is a very fact that not one word I ever utter can be taken for granted as an opinion growing out of my identical nature—how can it, when I have no nature? When I am in a room with People if I ever am free from speculating on creations of my own brain, then not myself goes home to myself: but the identity of every one in the room begins so to press upon me that I am in a very little time an[ni]hilated —not only among Men; it would be the same in a Nursery of children: I know not whether I make myself wholly understood: I hope enough so to let you see that no dependence is to be placed on what I said that day.

In the second place I will speak of my views, and of the life I purpose to myself. I am ambitious of doing the world some good: if I should be spared that may be the work of maturer years—in the interval I will assay to reach to as high a summit in Poetry as the nerve bestowed upon me will suffer. The faint conceptions I have of Poems to come brings the blood frequently into my forehead— All I hope is that I may not lose all interest in human affairs—that the solitary indifference I feel for applause even from the finest Spirits, will not blunt any acuteness of vision I may have. I do not think it will—I feel assured I should write from the mere yearning and fondness I have for the Beautiful even if my night's labours should be burnt every morning, and no eye ever shine upon them. But even now I am perhaps not speaking from myself: but from some character in whose soul I now live.

[33] *Saturn and Ops:* The theme of Keat's poem *Hyperion* is the overthrow of the Titans, of whom Saturn and his wife Ops were rulers, by the new gods, the Olympians.

FROM A LETTER TO
GEORGE AND GEORGIANA KEATS[34]

Wednesday, December 16, 1818—Monday, January 4, 1819

I HAVE thought so little that I have not one opinion upon any thing except in matters of taste—I never can feel certain of any truth but from a clear perception of its Beauty—and I find myself very young minded even in that perceptive power—which I hope will encrease—

FROM A LETTER TO
JOHN HAMILTON REYNOLDS

Tuesday, August 24, 1819

I HAVE indeed scarcely anything else to say, leading so monotonous a life, except I was to give you a history of sensations, and day-nightmares. You would not find me at all unhappy in it; as all my thoughts and feelings which are of the selfish nature, home speculations every day continue to make me more Iron. I am convinced more and more day by day that fine writing is next to fine doing, the top thing in the world; the Paradise Lost becomes a greater wonder—The more I know what my diligence may in time probably effect; the more does my heart distend with Pride and Obstinacy[35]—I feel it in my power to become a popular Writer —I feel it in my strength to refuse the poisonous suffrage of a public —My own being which I know to be becomes of more consequence to me than the crowds of Shadows in the shape of men and women that inhabit a Kingdom. The Soul is a world of itself, and has enough to do in its own home—Those whom I know already—and who have grown as it were a part of myself, I could not do without: but for the rest of mankind they are as much a dream to me as Milton's Hierarchies.[36] I think if I had a free and healthy and lasting organiza-

[34] George Keats, two years younger than his brother John, emigrated with his wife Georgiana in June 1818 to Louisville, Kentucky, and John wrote several long, chatty letters to them, from one of which this passage comes.

[35] *Pride and Obstinacy:* recalling Milton, *Paradise Lost*, I. 571–2.

[36] *Hierarchies:* of angels; see, for example, *Paradise Lost*, V. 583–601.

tion of heart and lungs—as strong as an ox's—so as to be able [to bear] unhurt the shock of extreme thought and sensation without weariness, I could pass my life very nearly alone though it should last eighty years. But I feel my body too weak to support me to the height; I am obliged continually to check myself and strive to be nothing. It would be vain for me to endeavour after a more reasonable manner of writing to you: I have nothing to speak of but myself —and what can I say but what I feel? If you should have any reason to regret this state of excitement in me, I will turn the tide of your feelings in the right channel by mentioning that it is the only state for the best sort of Poetry—that is all I care for, all I live for.

FROM A LETTER TO
GEORGE AND GEORGIANA KEATS
Friday, September 17—Monday, September 27, 1819

YOU speak of Lord Byron and me—There is this great difference between us. He describes what he sees—I describe what I imagine. Mine is the hardest task. You see the immense difference.

William Hazlitt

1778–1830

FROM "ON POETRY IN GENERAL" 1818

HAZLITT'S inclinations to a sweeping enthusiasm, as when he equates poetry with passion ("Fear is poetry, hope is poetry, love is poetry . . .", p. 110), are tempered by common sense. He is more clear-sighted about some matters than Shelley or Wordsworth; so where Shelley ascribes a decline in the cultivation of poetry to "the accumulation of facts and calculating processes" (pp. 131–2), and Wordsworth relates it to "the great national events which are daily taking place, and the increasing accumulation of men in cities" (p. 29), Hazlitt sees more incisively that the "necessary advances of civilization" (p. 114) are unfavourable to poetry as they make life for most people into a safe and insipid routine. However, Hazlitt lacks their passionate concern as practising poets with the nature of what they are doing. He reflects some of what were becoming commonplaces of Romantic critical thinking, that poetry is the expression of emotion, that it has nevertheless to do with "the moral and intellectual part of our nature" (p. 112), and that poetry is to be more properly related to music than to painting. He has no interest in discriminating accurately, as Coleridge attempts to do, between imagination and fancy, and his use of these terms is muddled and confusing. He casually refers to poetry as the "highest eloquence of passion" (p. 112), but the distinction between eloquence and poetry was to trouble J. S. Mill and Alexander Smith (see below, pp. 158 and 186).

The chief interest of Hazlitt's essay lies less in such matters, where he reflects the mood of the age rather than advances thought, than in his psychological interest in the origins and effects of poetry. He sees all men as living "in a world of their own making" so that "if poetry is a dream, the business of life is much the same" (p. 110). Man "is a poetical animal", because dreams, wishes and aspirations make up his world; poetry by giving perfect expression to "the inmost recesses of thought" (p. 111) or to unrealised passions, relieves "the indistinct and importunate cravings of the will" (p. 113). Poetry thus enables us to know, and so to control the unknown and undefined motions within the mind, "For knowledge is conscious power;

and the mind is no longer, in this case, the dupe, though it may be the victim of vice or folly" (p. 113). In shaping this concept of art as mastering the disorder of the mind (as Coleridge, in *Anima Poetae*, called poets "the true protoplasts who tame the chaos"), Hazlitt helped to give both currency and meaning to the Wordsworthian term "power", which was to be given a new emphasis by De Quincey (see below, p. 141).

The essay appeared as the first of *Lectures on the English Poets* (1818), and is printed from the second issue of 1819.

POETRY is the language of the imagination and the passions. It relates to whatever gives immediate pleasure or pain to the human mind. It comes home to the bosoms and businesses of men;[1] for nothing but what so comes home to them in the most general and intelligible shape, can be a subject for poetry. Poetry is the universal language which the heart holds with nature and itself. He who has a contempt for poetry, cannot have much respect for himself, or for anything else. It is not a mere frivolous accomplishment (as some persons have been led to imagine), the trifling amusement of a few idle readers or leisure hours[2]—it has been the study and delight of mankind in all ages. Many people suppose that poetry is something to be found only in books, contained in lines of ten syllables, with like endings: but wherever there is a sense of beauty, or power, or harmony, as in the motion of a wave of the sea, in the growth of a flower that "spreads its sweet leaves to the air, and dedicates its beauty to the sun,"[3]—*there* is poetry, in its birth. If history is a grave study, poetry may be said to be a graver: its materials lie deeper, and are spread wider. History treats, for the most part, of the cumbrous and unwieldly masses of things, the empty cases in which the affairs of the world are packed, under the heads of intrigue or war, in different states, and from century to century: but there is no thought or feeling that can have entered into the mind of man, which he would be eager to communicate to others, or which they would listen to with delight, that is not a fit subject for poetry. It is not a branch of authorship: it is "the stuff of which our life is made."[4]

[1] A phrase borrowed from the dedication to Lord Bacon's *Essays* (1625).

[2] *frivolous accomplishment . . . leisure hours:* echoing Wordsworth's Preface to *Lyrical Ballads;* see above, p. 36.

[3] Alluding to Shakespeare, *Romeo and Juliet*, I. i. 150-1.

[4] An echo of Shakespeare, *The Tempest*, IV. i. 156-7.

The rest is "mere oblivion,"[5] a dead letter: for all that is worth remembering in life, is the poetry of it. Fear is poetry, hope is poetry, love is poetry, hatred is poetry; contempt, jealousy, remorse, admiration, wonder, pity, despair, or madness, are all poetry. Poetry is that fine particle within us, that expands, rarefies, refines, raises our whole being: without it "man's life is poor as beast's."[6] Man is a poetical animal: and those of us who do not study the principles of poetry, act upon them all our lives, like Molière's *Bourgeois Gentilhomme*, who had always spoken prose without knowing it.[7] The child is a poet in fact, when he first plays at hide-and-seek, or repeats the story of Jack the Giant-killer: the shepherd-boy is a poet, when he first crowns his mistress with a garland of flowers; the countryman, when he stops to look at the rainbow; the city-apprentice, when he gazes after the Lord-Mayor's show; the miser, when he hugs his gold; the courtier, who builds his hopes upon a smile; the savage, who paints his idol with blood; the slave, who worships a tyrant, or the tyrant, who fancies himself a god;— the vain, the ambitious, the proud, the choleric man, the hero and the coward, the beggar and the king, the rich and the poor, the young and the old, all live in a world of their own making; and the poet does no more than describe what all the others think and act. . . .

If poetry is a dream, the business of life is much the same. If it is a fiction, made up of what we wish things to be, and fancy that they are, because we wish them so, there is no other nor better reality.

Poetry then is an imitation of nature, but the imagination and the passions are a part of man's nature. We shape things according to our wishes and fancies, without poetry; but poetry is the most emphatical language that can be found for those creations of the mind "which ecstasy is very cunning in."[8] Neither a mere description of natural objects, nor a mere delineation of natural feelings, however distinct or forcible, constitutes the ultimate end and aim of poetry, without the heightenings of the imagination. The light of

[5] Shakespeare, *As You Like It*, II. vii, 165.

[6] Shakespeare, *King Lear*, II. iv. 266, "Man's life is cheap as beast's".

[7] *Le Bourgeois Gentilhomme* (1670), II. vi.

[8] Shakespeare, *Hamlet*, III. iv. 138–9.

poetry is not only a direct but also a reflected light, that while it shews us the object, throws a sparkling radiance on all around it: the flame of the passions, communicated to the imagination, reveals to us, as with a flash of lightning, the inmost recesses of thought, and penetrates our whole being. Poetry represents forms chiefly as they suggest other forms; feelings, as they suggest forms or other feelings. Poetry puts a spirit of life and motion into the universe. It describes the flowing, not the fixed. It does not define the limits of sense, or analyze the distinctions of the understanding, but signifies the excess of the imagination beyond the actual or ordinary impression of any object or feeling. The poetical impression of any object is that uneasy, exquisite sense of beauty or power that cannot be contained within itself; that is impatient of all limit; that (as flame bends to flame) strives to link itself to some other image of kindred beauty or grandeur; to enshrine itself, as it were, in the highest forms of fancy, and to relieve the aching sense of pleasure by expressing it in the boldest manner, and by the most striking examples of the same quality in other instances. Poetry, according to Lord Bacon,[9] for this reason, 'has something divine in it, because it raises the mind and hurries it into sublimity, by conforming the shows of things to the desires of the soul, instead of subjecting the soul to external things, as reason and history do.' It is strictly the language of the imagination; and the imagination is that faculty which represents objects, not as they are in themselves, but as they are moulded by other thoughts and feelings, into an infinite variety of shapes and combinations of power. This language is not the less true to nature, because it is false in point of fact; but so much the more true and natural, if it conveys the impression which the object under the influence of passion makes on the mind. . . .

Poetry is the high-wrought enthusiasm of fancy and feeling. As in describing natural objects, it impregnates sensible impressions with the forms of fancy, so it describes the feelings of pleasure or pain by blending them with the strongest movements of passion,

[9] *Advancement of Learning*, Book 2, iv. 2, where the passage reads, "it was ever thought to have some participation of divineness, because it doth raise and erect the mind, by submitting the shows of things to the desires of the mind; whereas reason doth buckle and bow the mind unto the nature of things."

and the most striking forms of nature. Tragic poetry, which is the most impassioned species of it, strives to carry on the feeling to the utmost point of sublimity or pathos, by all the force of comparison or contrast; loses the sense of present suffering in the imaginary exaggeration of it; exhausts the terror or pity by an unlimited indulgence of it; grapples with impossibilities in its desperate impatience of restraint; throws us back upon the past, forward into the future; brings every moment of our being or object of nature in startling review before us; and in the rapid whirl of events, lifts us from the depths of woe to the highest contemplations of human life. . . .

Impassioned poetry is an emanation of the moral and intellectual part of our nature, as well as of the sensitive—of the desire to know, the will to act, and the power to feel; and ought to appeal to these different parts of our constitution, in order to be perfect. The domestic or prose tragedy, which is thought to be the most natural, is in this sense the least so, because it appeals almost exclusively to one of these faculties, our sensibility. The tragedies of Moore and Lillo,[10] for this reason, however affecting at the time, oppress and lie like a dead weight upon the mind, a load of misery which it is unable to throw off: the tragedy of Shakespeare which is true poetry, stirs our inmost affections; abstracts evil from itself by combining it with all the forms of imagination, and with the deepest workings of the heart, and rouses the whole man within us. . . .

Poetry is only the highest eloquence of passion, the most vivid form of expression that can be given to our conception of any thing, whether pleasurable or painful, mean or dignified, delightful or distressing. It is the perfect coincidence of the image and the words with the feeling we have, and of which we cannot get rid in any other way, that gives an instant "satisfaction to the thought".[11] This is equally the origin of wit and fancy, of comedy and tragedy, of the sublime and pathetic. When Pope says of the Lord Mayor's shew,—[12]

[10] *Moore and Lillo:* Edward Moore (1712–57), best known for *The Gamester* (1753), and George Lillo (1693–1739), best known for *The London Merchant* (1731).

[11] An echo of *Othello*, III. iii. 97.

[12] Alexander Pope, *The Dunciad*, I. 89–90.

"Now night descending, the proud scene is o'er,
But lives in Settle's numbers one day more!"

—when Collins makes Danger, "with limbs of giant mould",[13]

—"Throw him on the steep
Of some loose hanging rock asleep:"

when Lear calls out in extreme anguish,[14]

"Ingratitude, thou marble-hearted fiend,
How much more hideous shew'st in a child
Than the sea-monster!"

—the passion of contempt in the one case, of terror in the other, and of indignation in the last, is perfectly satisfied. We see the thing ourselves, and shew it to others as we feel it to exist, and as, in spite of ourselves, we are compelled to think of it. The imagination, by thus embodying and turning them to shape, gives an obvious relief to the indistinct and importunate cravings of the will.—We do not wish the thing to be so; but we wish it to appear such as it is. For knowledge is conscious power; and the mind is no longer, in this case, the dupe, though it may be the victim of vice or folly.

Poetry is in all its shapes the language of the imagination and the passions, of fancy and will. Nothing, therefore, can be more absurd than the outcry which has been sometimes raised by frigid and pedantic critics, for reducing the language of poetry to the standard of common sense and reason: for the end and use of poetry, "both at the first and now, was and is to hold the mirror up to nature,"[15] seen through the medium of passion and imagination, not divested of that medium by means of literal truth or abstract reason. The painter of history might as well be required to represent the face of a person who has just trod upon a serpent with the still-life expression of a common portrait, as the poet to describe the most striking and vivid impressions which things can be supposed to make upon the mind, in the language of common conversation. Let who will strip

[13] William Collins (1721–59), "Ode to Fear", lines 10 and 14–15.
[14] *King Lear*, I. iv. 259–61. (The second line should read "More hideous when thou show'st thee in a child".)
[15] *Hamlet*, III. ii. 24.

nature of the colours and the shapes of fancy, the poet is not bound
to do so; the impressions of common sense and strong imagination,
that is, of passion and indifference, cannot be the same, and they
must have a separate language to do justice to either. . . .

The province of the imagination is principally visionary, the
unknown and undefined: the understanding restores things to their
natural boundaries, and strips them of their fanciful pretensions.
Hence the history of religious and poetical enthusiasm is much the
same; and both have received a sensible shock from the progress of
experimental philosophy. It is the undefined and uncommon that
gives birth and scope to the imagination; we can only fancy what we
do not know. As in looking into the mazes of a tangled wood we fill
them with what shapes we please, with ravenous beasts, with
caverns vast, and drear enchantments, so in our ignorance of the
world about us, we make gods or devils of the first object we see,
and set no bounds to the wilful suggestions of our hopes and fears.

> "And visions, as poetic eyes avow,
>   Hang on each leaf and cling to every bough."[16]

There can never be another Jacob's dream. Since that time, the
heavens have gone farther off, and grown astronomical.[17] They have
become averse to the imagination, nor will they return to us on the
squares of the distances, or on Doctor Chalmer's Discourses.[18]
Rembrandt's picture brings the matter nearer to us.—It is not only
the progress of mechanical knowledge, but the necessary advances
of civilization that are unfavourable to the spirit of poetry. We not
only stand in less awe of the preternatural world, but we can calculate more surely, and look with more indifference, upon the regular
routine of this. The heroes of the fabulous ages rid the world of
monsters and giants. At present we are less exposed to the vicissitudes

[16] Misquoting a couplet in a letter of September 1737 from Thomas Gray
to Horace Walpole.

[17] Jacob dreamed of a ladder reaching from earth to heaven; Genesis,
xxviii, 12.

[18] Thomas Chalmers (1780-1847), Professor of Divinity at Edinburgh,
author of A Series of Discourses on the Christian Revelation, viewed in connection
with Modern Astronomy (1817); Hazlitt wrote at some length about him in the
essay on the Rev. Mr. Irving in The Spirit of the Age (1825).

of good or evil, to the incursions of wild beasts or "bandit fierce,"[19] or to the unmitigated fury of the elements. The time has been that "our fell of hair would at a dismal treatise rouse and stir as life were in it."[20] But the police spoils all; and we now hardly so much as dream of a midnight murder. Macbeth is only tolerated in this country for the sake of the music;[21] and in the United States of America, where the philosophical principles of government are carried still farther in theory and practice, we find that the Beggar's Opera is hooted from the stage. Society, by degrees, is constructed into a machine that carries us safely and insipidly from one end of life to the other, in a very comfortable prose style.

> "Obscurity her curtain round them drew,
> And siren Sloth a dull quietus sung."[22]

The remarks which have been here made, would, in some measure, lead to a solution of the question of the comparative merits of painting and poetry. I do not mean to give any preference, but it should seem that the argument which has been sometimes set up, that painting must affect the imagination more strongly, because it represents the image more distinctly, is not well founded. We may assume without much temerity, that poetry is more poetical than painting. When artists or connoisseurs talk on stilts about the poetry of painting, they shew that they know little about poetry, and have little love for the art. Painting gives the object itself; poetry what it implies. Paintings embodies what a thing contains in itself: poetry suggests what exists out of it, in any manner connected with it. But this last is the proper province of the imagination. . . .

Poetry in its matter and form is natural imagery or feeling,

[19] An echo of Milton, *Comus*, line 426.

[20] Shakespeare, *Macbeth*, V. v. 11–13.

[21] *music*: The version of *Macbeth* by Sir William Davenant, "with all the singing and dancing in it . . . being in the nature of an opera", which appealed to London audiences in 1667 after the restoration of Charles II, held the stage for some time, and the music and dances were retained in productions of the play until the 1840s.

[22] Sneyd Davies (1709–69), "To the Honourable and Reverend F. C.", in R. Dodsley's *A Collection of Poems in Six Volumes*, Vol. VI (1763), p. 140.

combined with passion and fancy. In its mode of conveyance, it combines the ordinary use of language with musical expression.

. . . there is nothing either musical or natural in the ordinary construction of language. It is a thing altogether arbitary and conventional. Neither in the sounds themselves, which are the voluntary signs of certain ideas, nor in their grammatical arrangements in common speech, is there any principle of natural imitation, or correspondence to the individual ideas, or to the tone of feeling with which they are conveyed to others. The jerks, the breaks, the inequalities, and harshnesses of prose, are fatal to the flow of a poetical imagination as a jolting road or a stumbling horse disturbs the reverie of an absent man. But poetry makes these odds all even. It is the music of language, answering to the music of the mind, unty'ng as it were "the secret soul of harmony."[23] Wherever any object takes such a hold of the mind as to make us dwell upon it, and brood over it, melting the heart in tenderness, or kindling it to a sentiment of enthusiasm;—wherever a movement of imagination or passion is impressed on the mind, by which it seeks to prolong and repeat the emotion, to bring all other objects into accord with it, and to give the same movement of harmony, sustained and continuous, or gradually varied according to the occasion, to the sounds that express it—this is poetry. The musical in sound is the sustained and continuous; the musical in thought is the sustained and continuous also. There is a near connection between music and deep-rooted passion. Mad people sing. As often as articulation passes naturally into intonation, there poetry begins. Where one idea gives a tone and colour to others, where one feeling melts others into it, there can be no reason why the same principle should not be extended to the sounds by which the voice utters these emotions of the soul, and blends syllables and lines into each other. It is to supply the inherent defect of harmony in the customary mechanism of language, to make the sound an echo to the sense, when the sense becomes a sort of echo to itself—to mingle the tide of verse, "the golden cadences of poetry,"[24] with the tide of feeling, flowing and murmuring as it flows—in short, to take the language of the

[23] Milton, "L'Allegro", line 144, " The hidden soul of harmony"
[24] An echo of Shakespeare, *Love's Labours Lost*, IV. ii. 117.

imagination from off the ground, and enable it to spread its wings
where it may indulge its own impulses—

> "Sailing with supreme dominion
> Through the azure deep of air—"[25]

without being stopped, or fretted, or diverted with the abruptness
and petty obstacles, and discordant flats and sharps of prose, that
poetry was invented. . . .

All is not poetry that passes for such: nor does verse make the
whole difference between poetry and prose. The Iliad does not
cease to be poetry in a literal translation; and Addison's Campaign[26]
has been very properly denominated a Gazette in rhyme. Common
prose differs from poetry, as treating for the most part either of such
trite, familiar, and irksome matters of fact, as convey no extraordinary impulse to the imagination, or else of such difficult and laborious
processes of the understanding, as do not admit of the wayward or
violent movements either of the imagination or the passions.

I will mention three works which come as near to poetry as
possible without absolutely being so, namely, the Pilgrim's Progress,
Robinson Crusoe, and the Tales of Boccaccio. Chaucer and Dryden
have translated some of the last into English rhyme, but the essence
and the power of poetry was there before. That which lifts the
spirit above the earth, which draws the soul out of itself with
indescribable longings, is poetry in kind, and generally fit to become
so in name, by being "married to immortal verse."[27] If it is of the
essence of poetry to strike and fix the imagination, whether we will
or no, to make the eye of childhood glisten with the starting tear,
to be never thought of afterwards with indifference, John Bunyan
and Daniel Defoe may be permitted to pass for poets in their way.

[25] Thomas Gray, "The Progress of Poesy", lines 116–17.

[26] Joseph Addison wrote *The Campaign* in 1705 in heroic couplets to
celebrate Marlborough's victory at Blenheim. It was called a "Gazette in
rhyme" by Joseph Warton in *An Essay on the Genius and Writings of Pope*
(1756), Section 2.

[27] Milton, "L'Allegro", line 137. (The line is cited in Wordsworth's
The Excursion, 1814, VII. 536.)

Percy Bysshe Shelley

1792–1822

FROM "A DEFENCE OF POETRY" 1821;
PUBLISHED 1840

SHELLEY'S famous *Defence of Poetry* was written in response to Thomas Love Peacock's *The Four Ages of Poetry* (1820), a half-serious, half-facetious history of English poetry as beginning from an iron age of rough song, rising to a golden age in the time of Shakespeare, and then declining through a silver age (that of Pope) to the brass age of Wordsworth and Coleridge. In this brass age of his own time, poets are represented as returning to barbarism while professing "to return to nature and revive the age of gold"; and "the highest inspirations of poetry are resolvable into three ingredients: the rant of unregulated passion, the whining of exaggerated feeling, and the cant of factitious sentiment," as found in the writings of that "morbid dreamer, Wordsworth". Shelley's essay takes shape as a rebuttal of Peacock's arguments and begins by claiming that poetry is natural to man, and in its highest forms embraces philosophy and history, in order to proceed to a history of poetry designed to show that the value and social utility of poetry have increased, rather than declined as Peacock had suggested. The last part of the essay, an impassioned plea for poetry as "the centre and circumference of knowledge" (p. 132), presents the articles of Shelley's faith in its power and quasi-divine status, and glows with his excited rhythms and images.

Shelley was much influenced by his study of Plato, whose vision of Essences or eternal Forms hidden by the veil of this life underlies one theme of the essay, that "The story of particular facts is as a mirror which obscures and distorts that which should be beautiful: Poetry is a mirror which makes beautiful that which is distorted" (pp. 125-6). Poetry, then "strips the veil of familiarity from the world, and lays bare the naked and sleeping beauty, which is the spirit of its forms" (p. 135). The poet thus "participates in the eternal, the infinite and the one" (p. 122), and all differences between poems and poets tend to disappear, as they are all doing the same thing, and are subject to one standard of judgment: on this view Shakespeare, Dante, Plato,

Herodotus and Lord Bacon are all poets, and seem to merge into a single grand figure whose business it is to make "immortal all that is best and most beautiful in the world" (p. 134).

Since all values relate to the world of Forms or Essences, poetry is concerned with "the beautiful and the good" (p. 132), and has an autonomous, and non-didactic moral function; by creating "new materials for knowledge and power and pleasure" (p. 132), it raises us above calculating and material considerations, and gives "light and fire" to "Virtue, Love, Patriotism, Friendship" (p. 133). This lofty idea of the moral power of poetry recalls Sir Philip Sidney's *Defence of Poetry* (1595), and reflects a strong neo-platonic line of thought feeding into Romantic criticism. The conviction with which some Romantic critics find a religious function or a healing power in poetry takes strength from this traditional view of its high purpose (see the headnote to the selection from John Keble, p. 192).

Shelley simultaneously offers a more characteristically Romantic theory of poetry as concerned primarily with emotions, and as "the expression of the imagination" (p. 120). Poetry wells up, inspired, from some unconscious region, as "unpremeditated song" (p. 133), and its quality and power reside not in poetic art or poetic form, but in its rendering of eternal truth and beauty. So "the parts of a composition may be poetical, without the composition as a whole being a poem" (p. 126). The idea of the poet as the "wisest, the happiest, and the best" of men (p. 136) looks back to Sir Philip Sidney, but also chimes in with the general tendency of Romantic criticism to regard the poet as a superior being.

ACCORDING to one mode of regarding those two classes of mental action, which are called reason and imagination, the former may be considered as mind contemplating the relations borne by one thought to another, however produced; and the latter, as mind acting upon those thoughts so as to colour them with its own light, and composing from them, as from elements, other thoughts, each containing within itself the principle of its own integrity. The one is the $\tau\grave{o}$ $\pi o\iota\epsilon\hat{\iota}\nu$, or the principle of synthesis, and has for its objects those forms which are common to universal nature and existence itself; the other is the $\tau\grave{o}$ $\lambda o\gamma\acute{\iota}\zeta\epsilon\iota\nu$, or principle of analysis, and its action regards the relations of things, simply as relations; considering thoughts, not in their integral unity, but as the algebraical representations which conduct to certain general results. Reason is the enumeration of quantities already known; imagination is the perception of the value of those quantities, both separately and as a whole. Reason respects the differences, and imagination the similitudes of things. Reason is to imagination as the instrument to the agent, as the body to the spirit, as the shadow to the substance.

Poetry, in a general sense, may be defined to be "the expression of the imagination": and poetry is connate with the origin of man. Man is an instrument over which a series of external and internal impressions are driven, like the alternations of an ever-changing wind over an Æolian lyre, which move it by their motion to ever-changing melody. But there is a principle within the human being, and perhaps within all sentient beings, which acts otherwise than in the lyre, and produces not melody, alone, but harmony, by an internal adjustment of the sounds or motions thus excited to the impressions which excite them. It is as if the lyre could accommodate its chords to the motions of that which strikes them, in a determined proportion of sound; even as the musician can accommodate his voice to the sound of the lyre. A child at play by itself will express its delight by its voice and motions; and every inflexion of tone and every gesture will bear exact relation to a corresponding antitype in the pleasurable impressions which awakened it; it will be the reflected image of that impression; and as the lyre trembles and sounds after the wind has died away, so the child seeks, by prolonging in its voice and motions the duration of the effect, to prolong also a consciousness of the cause. In relation to the objects which delight a child, these expressions are, what poetry is to higher objects. The savage (for the savage is to ages what the child is to years) expresses the emotions produced in him by surrounding objects in a similar manner; and language and gesture, together with plastic or pictorial imitation, become the image of the combined effect of those objects, and of his apprehension of them. Man in society, with all his passions and his pleasures, next becomes the object of the passions and pleasures of man; an additional class of emotions produces an augmented treasure of expressions; and language, gesture, and the imitative arts, become at once the representation and the medium, the pencil and the picture, the chisel and the statue, the chord and the harmony. The social sympathies, or those laws from which, as from its elements, society results, begin to develop themselves from the moment that two human beings coexist; the future is contained within the present, as the plant within the seed; and equality, diversity, unity, contrast, mutual dependence, become the principles alone capable of affording the motives according to which the will of a social being is determined to action, inasmuch as he is social; and constitute pleasure in sensation, virtue in sentiment, beauty in art, truth in reasoning, and love in the intercourse of kind. Hence men, even in the infancy of society, observe a certain order in their words and actions, distinct from that of the objects and the impressions represented by them, all expression being subject to the laws of that from which it proceeds. But let us dismiss those more general considerations which might involve an inquiry into the principles of society itself, and restrict our view to the manner in which the imagination is expressed upon its forms.

In the youth of the world, men dance and sing and imitate natural objects, observing in these actions, as in all others, a certain rhythm or order. And, although all men observe a similar, they observe not the same order, in the motions of the dance, in the melody of the song, in the combinations of language, in the series of their imitations of natural objects. For there is a certain order or rhythm belonging to each of these classes of mimetic representation, from which the hearer and the spectator receive an intenser and purer pleasure than from any other: the sense of an approximation to this order has been called taste by modern writers. Every man in the infancy of art, observes an order which approximates more or less closely to that from which this highest delight results: but the diversity is not sufficiently marked, as that its gradations should be sensible, except in those instances where the predominance of this faculty of approximation to the beautiful (for so we may be permitted to name the relation between this highest pleasure and its cause) is very great. Those in whom it exists in excess are poets, in the most universal sense of the word; and the pleasure resulting from the manner in which they express the influence of society or nature upon their own minds, communicates itself to others, and gathers a sort of reduplication from that community. Their language is vitally metaphorical; that is, it marks the before unapprehended relations of things and perpetuates their apprehension, until the words which represent them, become, through time, signs for portions or classes of thoughts instead of pictures of integral thoughts; and then if no new poets should arise to create afresh the associations which have been thus disorganised, language will be dead to all the nobler purposes of human intercourse. These similitudes or relations are finely said by Lord Bacon to be "the same footsteps of nature impressed upon the various subjects of the world"[1]—and he considers the faculty which perceives them as the storehouse of axioms common to all knowledge. In the infancy of society every author is necessarily a poet, because language itself is poetry; and to be a poet is to apprehend the true and the beautiful, in a word, the good which exists in the relation, subsisting, first between existence and perception, and secondly between perception and expression. Every original language near to its source is in itself the chaos of a cyclic poem: the copiousness of lexicography and the distinctions of grammar are the works of a later age, and are merely the catalogue and the form of the creations of poetry.

But poets, or those who imagine and express this indestructible order, are not only the authors of language and of music, of the dance and architecture, and statuary, and painting; they are the institutors of laws, and the founders of civil society, and the inventors of the arts of life, and the teachers, who draw into a certain propinquity with the beautiful and the true, that partial apprehension of the agencies of the invisible world which is called religion. Hence all original religions are allegorical, or susceptible of allegory, and, like Janus, have a double face of false and true. Poets, according to the circumstances of the age and nation in which they appeared, were called, in the earlier epochs of the world, legislators, or prophets: a poet essentially comprises and unites both these characters. For he not only beholds intensely the present as it is, and discovers those laws according to which present things ought to be ordered, but he beholds the future in the present, and his thoughts are the germs of the flower and the fruit of latest time. Not that I assert poets to be prophets in the gross sense of the word, or that they can foretell the form as surely as they foreknow the spirit of events: such is the pretence of superstition, which would make poetry an attribute of prophecy, rather than prophecy an attribute of poetry. A poet participates in the eternal, the infinite, and the one; as far as relates to his conceptions, time and place and number

[1] *Advancement of Learning*, II. v. 3.

are not. The grammatical forms which express the moods of time, and the difference of persons, and the distinction of place, are convertible with respect to the highest poetry without injuring it as poetry; and the choruses of Æschylus, and the book of Job, and Dante's Paradise, would afford, more than any other writings, examples of this fact, if the limits of this essay did not forbid citation. The creations of sculpture, painting, and music, are illustrations still more decisive.

Language, colour, form, and religious and civil habits of action, are all the instruments and materials of poetry; they may be called poetry by that figure of speech which considers the effect as a synonym of the cause. But poetry in a more restricted sense expresses those arrangements of language, and especially metrical language, which are created by that imperial faculty, whose throne is curtained within the invisible nature of man. And this springs from the nature itself of language, which is a more direct representation of the actions and passions of our internal being, and is susceptible of more various and delicate combinations, than colour, form, or motion, and is more plastic and obedient to the control of that faculty of which it is the creation. For language is arbitrarily produced by the imagination, and has relation to thoughts alone; but all other materials, instruments, and conditions of art, have relations among each other, which limit and interpose between conception and expression. The former is as a mirror which reflects, the latter as a cloud which enfeebles, the light of which both are mediums of communication. Hence the fame of sculptors, painters, and musicians, although the intrinsic powers of the great masters of these arts may yield in no degree to that of those who have employed language as the hieroglyphic of their thoughts, has never equalled that of poets in the restricted sense of the term; as two performers of equal skill will produce unequal effects from a guitar and a harp. The fame of legislators and founders of religions, so long as their institutions last, alone seems to exceed that of poets in the restricted sense; but it can scarcely be a question, whether if we deduct the celebrity which their flattery of the gross opinions of the vulgar usually conciliates, together with that which belonged to them in their higher character of poets, any excess will remain.

We have thus circumscribed the meaning of the word Poetry

within the limits of that art which is the most familiar and the most perfect expression of the faculty itself. It is necessary, however, to make the circle still narrower, and to determine the distinction between measured and unmeasured language; for the popular division into prose and verse is inadmissible in accurate philosophy.

Sounds as well as thoughts have relation both between each other and towards that which they represent, and a perception of the order of those relations has always been found connected with a perception of the order of the relation of thoughts. Hence the language of poets has ever affected a certain uniform and harmonious recurrence of sound, without which it were not poetry, and which is scarcely less indispensable to the communication of its action than the words themselves, without reference to that peculiar order. Hence the vanity of translation; it were as wise to cast a violet into a crucible that you might discover the formal principle of its colour and odour, as seek to transfuse from one language into another the creations of a poet. The plant must spring again from its seed, or it will bear no flower—and this is the burthen of the curse of Babel.[2]

An observation of the regular mode of the recurrence of this harmony in the language of poetical minds, together with its relation to music, produced metre, or a certain system of traditional forms of harmony of language. Yet it is by no means essential that a poet should accommodate his language to this traditional form, so that the harmony, which is its spirit, be observed. The practice is indeed convenient and popular, and to be preferred, especially in such composition as includes much form and action: but every great poet must inevitably innovate upon the example of his predecessors in the exact structure of his peculiar versification. The distinction between poets and prose writers is a vulgar error. The distinction between philosophers and poets has been anticipated. Plato was essentially a poet—the truth and splendour of his imagery, and the melody of his language, is the most intense that it is possible to conceive. He rejected the measure of the epic, dramatic, and lyrical forms, because he sought to kindle a harmony in thoughts divested of shape and action, and he forbore to invent any regular plan of rhythm which should include, under determinate forms, the

[2] Babel: See Genesis, xi. 9, where God brings about a confusion of languages on earth.

varied pauses of his style. Cicero sought to imitate the cadence of his periods, but with little success. Lord Bacon was a poet.* His language has a sweet and majestic rhythm, which satisfies the sense, no less than the almost superhuman wisdom of his philosophy satisfies the intellect; it is a strain which distends, and then bursts the circumference of the hearer's mind, and pours itself forth together with it into the universal element with which it has perpetual sympathy. All the authors of revolutions in opinion are not only necessarily poets as they are inventors, nor even as their words unveil the permanent analogy of things by images which participate in the life of truth; but as their periods are harmonious and rhythmical, and contain in themselves the elements of verse; being the echo of the eternal music. Nor are those supreme poets, who have employed traditional forms of rhythm on account of the form and action of their subjects, less capable of perceiving and teaching the truth of things, than those who have omitted that form. Shakespeare, Dante, and Milton (to confine ourselves to modern writers) are philosophers of the very loftiest power.

A poem is the image of life expressed in its eternal truth. There is this difference between a story and a poem, that a story is a catalogue of detached facts, which have no other bond of connexion than time, place, circumstance, cause and effect; the other is the creation of actions according to the unchangeable forms of human nature, as existing in the mind of the creator, which is itself the image of all other minds. The one is partial, and applies only to a definite period of time, and a certain combination of events which can never again recur; the other is universal, and contains within itself the germ of a relation to whatever motives or actions have place in the possible varieties of human nature. Time, which destroys the beauty and the use of the story of particular facts, stript of the poetry which should invest them, augments that of Poetry, and for ever develops new and wonderful applications of the eternal truth which it contains. Hence epitomes have been called the moths of just history; they eat out the poetry of it.[3] The story of particular facts is as a mirror which obscures and distorts that which should be beautiful:

* *poet:* See the "Filium labyrinthi" and the "Essay on Death" particularly.

[3] *epitomes . . . poetry of it:* See Bacon, *Advancement of Learning*, II. ii. 3.

Poetry is a mirror which makes beautiful that which is distorted.

The parts of a composition may be poetical, without the composition as a whole being a poem. A single sentence may be considered as a whole, though it be found in a series of unassimilated portions; a single word even may be a spark of inextinguishable thought. And thus all the great historians, Herodotus, Plutarch, Livy, were poets; and although the plan of these writers, especially that of Livy, restrained them from developing this faculty in its highest degree, they make copious and ample amends for their subjection, by filling all the interstices of their subjects with living images.

Having determined what is poetry, and who are poets, let us proceed to estimate its effects upon society.

Poetry is ever accompanied with pleasure: all spirits on which it falls open themselves to receive the wisdom which is mingled with its delight. In the infancy of the world, neither poets themselves nor their auditors are fully aware of the excellence of poetry: for it acts in a divine and unapprehended manner, beyond and above consciousness; and it is reserved for future generations to contemplate and measure the mighty cause and effect in all the strength and splendour of their union. Even in modern times, no living poet ever arrived at the fulness of his fame; the jury which sits in judgment upon a poet, belonging as he does to all time, must be composed of his peers: it must be impanneled by Time from the selectest of the wise of many generations. A Poet is a nightingale, who sits in darkness and sings to cheer its own solitude with sweet sounds; his auditors are as men entranced by the melody of an unseen musician, who feel that they are moved and softened, yet know not whence or why. . . .

Few poets of the highest class have chosen to exhibit the beauty of their conceptions in its naked truth and splendour; and it is doubtful whether the alloy of costume, habit, &c., be not necessary to temper this planetary music for mortal ears.

The whole objection, however, of the immorality of poetry rests upon a misconception of the manner in which poetry acts to produce the moral improvement of man. Ethical science arranges the elements which poetry has created, and propounds schemes and proposes examples of civil and domestic life: nor is it for want of admirable doctrines that men hate, and despise, and censure, and deceive, and subjugate one another. But poetry acts in another and diviner manner. It awakens and enlarges the mind itself by rendering it the receptacle of a thousand unapprehended combinations of thought. Poetry lifts the veil from the hidden beauty of the world, and makes familiar objects be as if they were not familiar; it reproduces all that it represents, and the impersonations clothed in its Elysian light stand thenceforward in the minds of those who have once contemplated them, as memorials of that gentle and exalted content which extends itself over all thoughts and actions with which it coexists. The great secret of morals is love; or a going out of our own nature, and an identification of ourselves with the beautiful which exists in thought, action, or person, not our own. A man, to be greatly good, must imagine intensely and comprehensively; he must put himself in the place of another and of many others; the pains and the pleasures of his species must become his own. The great instrument of moral good is the imagination; and poetry administers to the effect by acting upon the cause. Poetry enlarges the circumference of the imagination by replenishing it with thoughts of ever new delight, which have the power of attracting and assimilating to their own nature all other thoughts, and which form new intervals and interstices whose void for ever craves fresh food. Poetry strengthens the faculty which is the organ of the moral nature of man, in the same manner as exercise strengthens a limb. . . .

The poetry of Dante may be considered as the bridge thrown over the stream of time, which unites the modern and ancient World. The distorted notions of invisible things which Dante and his rival Milton have idealised, are merely the mask and the mantle in which these great poets walk through eternity enveloped and disguised. It is a difficult question to determine how far they were conscious of the distinction which must have subsisted in their minds between their own creeds and that of the people. Dante at least appears to wish to mark the full extent of it by placing Riphæus, whom Virgil calls *justissimus unus,* in Paradise,[4] and observing a most heretical caprice in his distribution of rewards and punishments. And Milton's

[4] See the *Paradiso,* Canto XX, 67–9.

poem contains within itself a philosophical refutation of that system, of which, by a strange and natural antithesis, it has been a chief popular support. Nothing can exceed the energy and magnificence of the character of Satan as expressed in "Paradise Lost". It is a mistake to suppose that he could ever have been intended for the popular personification of evil. Implacable hate, patient cunning and a sleepless refinement of device to inflict the extremest anguish on an enemy, these things are evil; and, although venial in a slave, are not to be forgiven in a tyrant; although redeemed by much that ennobles his defeat in one subdued, are marked by all that dishonours his conquest in the victor. Milton's Devil as a moral being is as far superior to his God, as One who perseveres in some purpose which he has conceived to be excellent in spite of adversity and torture, is to One who in the cold security of undoubted triumph inflicts the most horrible revenge upon his enemy, not from any mistaken notion of inducing him to repent of a perserverance in enmity, but with the alleged design of exasperating him to deserve new torments. Milton has so far violated the popular creed (if this shall be judged to be a violation) as to have alleged no superiority of moral virtue to his God over his Devil. And this bold neglect of a direct moral purpose is the most decisive proof of the supremacy of Milton's genius. He mingled as it were the elements of human nature as colours upon a single pallet, and arranged them in the composition of his great picture according to the laws of epic truth; that is, according to the laws of that principle by which a series of actions of the external universe and of intelligent and ethical beings is calculated to excite the sympathy of succeeding generations of mankind. The Divina Commedia and Paradise Lost have conferred upon modern mythology a systematic form; and when change and time shall have added one more superstition to the mass of those which have arisen and decayed upon the earth, commentators will be learnedly employed in elucidating the religion of ancestral Europe, only not utterly forgotten because it will have been stamped with the eternity of genius.

Dante and Milton were both deeply penetrated with the ancient religion of the civilized world; and its spirit exists in their poetry probably in the same proportion as its forms survived in the un-reformed worship of modern Europe. The one preceded and the other followed the Reformation at almost equal intervals. Dante was the first religious reformer, and Luther surpassed him rather in the rudeness and acrimony, than in the boldness of his censures of papal usurpation. Dante was the first awakener of entranced Europe; he created a language, in itself music and persuasion, out of a chaos of inharmonious barbarisms. He was the congregator of those great spirits who presided over the resurrection of learning; the Lucifer of that starry flock which in the thirteenth century shone forth from republican Italy, as from a heaven, into the darkness of the benighted world. His very words are instinct with spirit; each is as a spark, a burning atom of inextinguishable thought; and many yet lie covered in the ashes of their birth, and pregnant with a lightning which has yet found no conductor. All high poetry is infinite; it is as the first acorn, which contained all oaks potentially. Veil after veil may be undrawn, and the inmost naked beauty of the meaning never exposed. A great poem is a fountain for ever overflowing with the waters of wisdom and delight; and after one person and one age has exhausted all its divine effluence which their peculiar relations enable them to share, another and yet another succeeds, and new relations are ever developed, the source of an unforeseen and an unconceived delight.

But poets have been challenged to resign the civic crown to reasoners and mechanists on another plea. It is admitted that the exercise of the imagination is most delightful, but it is alleged, that that of reason is more useful. Let us examine as the grounds of this distinction, what is here meant by utility. Pleasure or good, in a general sense, is that which the consciousness of a sensitive and intelligent being seeks, and in which, when found, it acquiesces. There are two modes or degrees of pleasure, one durable, universal and permanent; the other transitory and particular. Utility may either express the means of producing the former or the latter. In the former sense, whatever strengthens and purifies the affections, enlarges the imagination, and adds spirit to sense, is useful. But the meaning in which the Author[5] of the Four Ages of Poetry seems to have employed the word utility is the narrower one of banishing the importunity of the wants of our animal nature, the surrounding

[5] *Author:* Thomas Love Peacock, to whose essay Shelley's *Defence* is a reply; see above p. 118.

E

men with security of life, the dispersing the grosser delusions of superstition, and the conciliating such a degree of mutual forbearance among men as may consist with the motives of personal advantage.

Undoubtedly the promoters of utility, in this limited sense, have their appointed office in society. They follow the footsteps of poets, and copy the sketches of their creations into the book of common life. They make space, and give time. Their exertions are of the highest value, so long as they confine their administration of the concerns of the inferior powers of our nature within the limits due to the superior ones. But whilst the sceptic destroys gross superstitions, let him spare to deface, as some of the French writers have defaced, the eternal truths charactered upon the imaginations of men. Whilst the mechanist abridges, and the political economist combines, labour, let them beware that their speculations, for want of correspondence with those first principles which belong to the imagination, do not tend, as they have in modern England, to exasperate at once the extremes of luxury and want. They have exemplified the saying, "To him that hath, more shall be given; and from him that hath not, the little that he hath shall be taken away."[6] The rich have become richer, and the poor have become poorer; and the vessel of the state is driven between the Scylla and Charybdis of anarchy and despotism. Such are the effects which must ever flow from an unmitigated exercise of the calculating faculty.

It is difficult to define pleasure in its highest sense; the definition involving a number of apparent paradoxes. For, from an inexplicable defect of harmony in the constitution of human nature, the pain of the inferior is frequently connected with the pleasures of the superior portions of our being. Sorrow, terror, anguish, despair itself, are often the chosen expressions of an approximation to the highest good. Our sympathy in tragic fiction depends on this principle; tragedy delights by affording a shadow of the pleasure which exists in pain. This is the source also of the melancholy which is inseparable from the sweetest melody. The pleasure that is in sorrow is sweeter than the pleasure of pleasure itself. And hence the saying, "It is better to go to the house of mourning, than to the house of

[6] Recalling *Matthew*, xxv. 29.

mirth."[7] Not that this highest species of pleasure is necessarily linked with pain. The delight of love and friendship, the ecstasy of the admiration of nature, the joy of the perception and still more of the creation of poetry is often wholly unalloyed.

The production and assurance of pleasure in this highest sense is true utility. Those who produce and preserve this pleasure are Poets or poetical philosophers.

The exertions of Locke, Hume, Gibbon, Voltaire, Rousseau,* and their disciples, in favour of oppressed and deluded humanity, are entitled to the gratitude of mankind. Yet it is easy to calculate the degree of moral and intellectual improvement which the world would have exhibited, had they never lived. A little more nonsense would have been talked for a century or two; and perhaps a few more men, women, and children, burnt as heretics. We might not at this moment have been congratulating each other on the abolition of the Inquisition in Spain. But it exceeds all imagination to conceive what would have been the moral condition of the world if neither Dante, Petrarch, Boccaccio, Chaucer, Shakespeare, Calderon, Lord Bacon, nor Milton, had ever existed; if Raphael and Michael Angelo had never been born; if the Hebrew poetry had never been translated; if a revival of the study of Greek literature had never taken place; if no monuments of ancient sculpture had been handed down to us; and if the poetry of the religion of the ancient world had been extinguished together with its belief. The human mind could never, except by the intervention of these excitements, have been awakened to the invention of the grosser sciences, and that application of analytical reasoning to the aberrations of society, which it is now attempted to exalt over the direct expression of the inventive and creative faculty itself.

We have more moral, political and historical wisdom, than we know how to reduce into practice; we have more scientific and economical knowledge than can be accommodated to the just distribution of the produce which it multiplies. The poetry in these systems of thought is concealed by the accumulation of facts and

* *Rousseau:* I follow the classification adopted by the Author of the Four Ages of Poetry; but he was essentially a Poet. The others, even Voltaire, were mere reasoners.

[7] Recalling *Ecclesiastes*, vii, 2.

calculating processes. There is no want of knowledge respecting what is wisest and best in morals, government, and political economy, or at least, what is wiser and better than what men now practise and endure. But we let "*I dare not* wait upon *I would*, like the poor cat i' the adage."[8] We want the creative faculty to imagine that which we know; we want the generous impulse to act that which we imagine; we want the poetry of life: our calculations have outrun conception; we have eaten more than we can digest. The cultivation of those sciences which have enlarged the limits of the empire of man over the external world, has, for want of the poetical faculty, proportionally circumscribed those of the internal world; and man, having enslaved the elements, remains himself a slave. To what but a cultivation of the mechanical arts in a degree disproportioned to the presence of the creative faculty, which is the basis of all knowledge, is to be attributed the abuse of all invention for abridging and combining labour, to the exasperation of the inequality of mankind? From what other cause has it arisen that these inventions which should have lightened, have added a weight to the curse imposed on Adam? Thus Poetry, and the principle of Self, of which Money is the visible incarnation, are the God and Mammon of the world.

The functions of the poetical faculty are twofold; by one it creates new materials for knowledge, and power and pleasure; by the other it engenders in the mind a desire to reproduce and arrange them according to a certain rhythm and order which may be called the beautiful and the good. The cultivation of poetry is never more to be desired than at periods when, from an excess of the selfish and calculating principle, the accumulation of the materials of external life exceed the quantity of the power of assimilating them to the internal laws of human nature. The body has then become too unwieldy for that which animates it.

Poetry is indeed something divine. It is at once the centre and circumference of knowledge; it is that which comprehends all science, and that to which all science must be referred. It is at the same time the root and blossom of all other systems of thought; it is that from which all spring, and that which adorns all; and that which, if blighted, denies the fruit and the seed, and withholds from

[8] Shakespeare, *Macbeth*, I. vii. 44–5.

the barren world the nourishment and the succession of the scions of the tree of life. It is the perfect and consummate surface and bloom of things; it is as the odour and the colour of the rose to the texture of the elements which compose it, as the form and the splendour of unfaded beauty to the secrets of anatomy and corruption. What were Virtue, Love, Patriotism, Friendship—what were the scenery of this beautiful Universe which we inhabit; what were our consolations on this side of the grave, and what were our aspirations beyond it, if Poetry did not ascend to bring light and fire from those eternal regions where the owl-winged faculty of calculation dare not ever soar? Poetry is not like reasoning, a power to be exerted according to the determination of the will. A man cannot say, "I will compose poetry." The greatest poet even cannot say it: for the mind in creation is as a fading coal, which some invisible influence, like an inconstant wind, awakens to transitory brightness: this power arises from within, like the colour of a flower which fades and changes as it is developed, and the conscious portions of our natures are unprophetic either of its approach or its departure. Could this influence be durable in its original purity and force, it is impossible to predict the greatness of the results; but when composition begins, inspiration is already on the decline, and the most glorious poetry that has ever been communicated to the world is probably a feeble shadow of the original conception of the Poet. I appeal to the great poets of the present day, whether it be not an error to assert that the finest passages of poetry are produced by labour and study. The toil and the delay recommended by critics, can be justly interpreted to mean no more than a careful observation of the inspired moments, and an artificial connexion of the spaces between their suggestions by the intertexture of conventional expressions; a necessity only imposed by the limitedness of the poetical faculty itself. For Milton conceived the Paradise Lost as a whole before he executed it in portions. We have his own authority also for the Muse having "dictated" to him the "unpremeditated song,"[9] and let this be an answer to those who would allege the fifty-six various readings of the first line of the Orlando Furioso.[10]

[9] Milton, *Paradise Lost*, IX. 24 ("unpremeditated Verse").

[10] *Orlando Furioso:* Ariosto's romantic epic, published in its final form in 1532.

Compositions so produced are to poetry what mosaic is to painting. This instinct and intuition of the poetical faculty is still more observable in the plastic and pictorial arts; a great statue or picture grows under the power of the artist as a child in the mother's womb; and the very mind which directs the hands in formation is incapable of accounting to itself for the origin, the gradations, or the media of the process.

Poetry is the record of the best and happiest moments of the happiest and best minds. We are aware of evanescent visitations of thought and feeling sometimes associated with place or person, sometimes regarding our own mind alone, and always arising unforeseen and departing unbidden, but elevating and delightful beyond all expression: so that even in the desire and the regret they leave, there cannot but be pleasure, participating as it does in the nature of its object. It is as it were the interpenetration of a diviner nature through our own; but its footsteps are like those of a wind over a sea, which the coming calm erases, and whose traces remain only, as on the wrinkled sand which paves it. These and corresponding conditions of being are experienced principally by those of the most delicate sensibility and the most enlarged imagination; and the state of mind produced by them is at war with every base desire. The enthusiasm of virtue, love, patriotism, and friendship, is essentially linked with these emotions; and whilst they last, self appears as what it is, an atom to a Universe. Poets are not only subject to these experiences as spirits of the most refined organisation, but they can colour all that they combine with the evanescent hues of this ethereal world; a word, or a trait in the representation of a scene or a passion, will touch the enchanted chord, and re-animate, in those who have ever experienced these emotions, the sleeping, the cold, the buried image of the past. Poetry thus makes immortal all that is best and most beautiful in the world; it arrests the vanishing apparitions which haunt the interlunations[11] of life, and veiling them, or in language or in form, sends them forth among mankind, bearing sweet news of kindred joy to those with whom their sisters abide—abide, because there is no portal of expression from the caverns of the spirit which they inhabit into

[11] *interlunations:* dark intervals (literally, the periods between the disappearance of the old and the arrival of the new moon).

the universe of things. Poetry redeems from decay the visitations of the divinity in Man.

Poetry turns all things to loveliness; it exalts the beauty of that which is most beautiful, and it adds beauty to that which is most deformed; it marries exultation and horror, grief and pleasure, eternity and change; it subdues to union under its light yoke, all irreconcilable things. It transmutes all that it touches, and every form moving within the radiance of its presence is changed by wondrous sympathy to an incarnation of the spirit which it breathes; its secret alchemy turns to potable gold the poisonous waters which flow from death through life; it strips the veil of familiarity from the world, and lays bare the naked and sleeping beauty, which is the spirit of its forms.

All things exist as they are perceived; at least in relation to the percipient. "The mind is its own place, and of itself can make a Heaven of Hell, a Hell of Heaven."[12] But poetry defeats the curse which binds us to be subjected to the accident of surrounding impressions. And whether it spreads its own figured curtain, or withdraws life's dark veil from before the scene of things, it equally creates for us a being within our being. It makes us the inhabitants of a world to which the familiar world is a chaos. It reproduces the common Universe of which we are portions and percipients, and it purges from our inward sight the film of familiarity[13] which obscures from us the wonder of our being. It compels us to feel that which we perceive, and to imagine that which we know. It creates anew the universe, after it has been annihilated in our minds by the recurrence of impressions blunted by reiteration. It justifies that bold and true word of Tasso: *Non merita nome di creatore, se non Iddio ed il Poeta.*[14]

A poet, as he is the author to others of the highest wisdom, pleasure, virtue and glory, so he ought personally to be the happiest, the best, the wisest, and the most illustrious of men. As to his glory,

---

[12] Milton, *Paradise Lost*, I. 254.

[13] *film of familiarity*: Shelley seems in this passage to be echoing Coleridge's *Biographia Literaria*, Chapter XIV (ed. J. Shawcross, II. 6), where this phrase "film of familiarity" occurs.

[14] I have not traced this phrase from Tasso's voluminous prose writings, which means, "None deserve the name of creator except God and the Poet'.

let Time be challenged to declare whether the fame of any other institutor of human life be comparable to that of a poet. That he is the wisest, the happiest, and the best, inasmuch as he is a poet, is equally incontrovertible: the greatest Poets have been men of the most spotless virtue, of the most consummate prudence, and, if we could look into the interior of their lives, the most fortunate of men: and the exceptions, as they regard those who possessed the imaginative faculty in a high yet inferior degree, will be found on consideration to confirm rather than destroy the rule. Let us for a moment stoop to the arbitration of popular breath, and usurping and uniting in our own persons the incompatible characters of accuser, witness, judge and executioner, let us without trial, testimony, or form, determine that certain motives of those who are "there sitting where we dare not soar,"[15] are reprehensible. Let us assume that Homer was a drunkard, that Virgil was a flatterer, that Horace was a coward, that Tasso was a madman, that Lord Bacon was a peculator, that Raphael was a libertine, that Spenser was a poet laureate. It is inconsistent with this division of our subject to cite living poets, but Posterity has done ample justice to the great names now referred to. Their errors have been weighed and found to have been dust in the balance; if their sins were as scarlet, they are now white as snow: they have been washed in the blood of the mediator and the redeemer, Time. Observe in what a ludicrous chaos the imputations of real or fictitious crime have been confused in the contemporary calumnies against poetry and poets; consider how little is, as it appears—or appears, as it is; look to your own motives, and judge not, lest ye be judged.

Poetry, as has been said, in this respect differs from logic, that it is not subject to the controul of the active powers of the mind, and that its birth and recurrence has no necessary connexion with consciousness or will. It is presumptuous to determine that these are the necessary conditions of all mental causation, when mental effects are experienced insusceptible of being referred to them. The frequent recurrence of the poetical power, it is obvious to suppose, may produce in the mind an habit of order and harmony correlative with its own nature and with its effects upon other minds. But in the intervals of inspiration, and they may be frequent without being

[15] *Paradise Lost*, IV. 829.

durable, a Poet becomes a man, and is abandoned to the sudden reflux of the influences under which others habitually live. But as he is more delicately organized than other men, and sensible to pain and pleasure, both his own and that of others, in a degree unknown to them, he will avoid the one and pursue the other with an ardour proportioned to this difference. And he renders himself obnoxious to calumny, when he neglects to observe the circumstances under which these objects of universal pursuit and flight have disguised themselves in one another's garments.

But there is nothing necessarily evil in this error, and thus cruelty, envy, revenge, avarice, and the passions purely evil, have never formed any portion of the popular imputations on the lives of poets.

I have thought it most favourable to the cause of truth to set down these remarks according to the order in which they were suggested to my mind, by a consideration of the subject itself, instead of following that of the treatise that excited me to make them public. Thus although devoid of the formality of a polemical reply; if the view they contain be just, they will be found to involve a refutation of the doctrines of the Four Ages of Poetry, so far at least as regards the first division of the subject. I can readily conjecture what should have moved the gall of the learned and intelligent author of that paper; I confess myself, like him, unwilling to be stunned by the Theseids of the hoarse Codri of the day. Bavius and Mævius[16] undoubtedly are, as they ever were, insufferable persons. But it belongs to a philosophical critic to distinguish rather than confound.

The first part of these remarks has related to Poetry in its elements and principles; and it has been shewn, as well as the narrow limits assigned them would permit, that what is called poetry, in a restricted sense, has a common source with all other forms of order and of beauty, according to which the materials of human life are susceptible of being arranged, and which is Poetry in an universal sense.

The second part will have for its object an application of these

---

[16] *Theseids . . . Maevius:* Codrus is the name Virgil ascribes to a bad poet in his Eclogue V. 11; Bavius and Maevius are referred to as bad poets in Eclogue III. 90. Juvenal in Satire I. 2 refers to a "Theseid," or poem on Theseus, King of Athens, by Cordus (or Codrus).

principles to the present state of the cultivation of Poetry, and a defence of the attempt to idealize the modern forms of manners and opinions, and compel them into a subordination to the imaginative and creative faculty. For the literature of England, an energetic development of which has ever preceded or accompanied a great and free development of the national will, has arisen as it were from a new birth. In spite of the low-thoughted envy which would undervalue contemporary merit, our own will be a memorable age in intellectual achievements, and we live among such philosophers and poets as surpass beyond comparison any who have appeared since the last national struggle for civil and religious liberty. The most unfailing herald, companion, and follower of the awakening of a great people to work a beneficial change in opinion or institution, is Poetry. At such periods there is an accumulation of the power of communicating and receiving intense and impassioned conceptions respecting man and nature. The persons in whom this power resides, may often as far as regards many portions of their nature, have little apparent correspondence with that spirit of good of which they are the ministers. But even whilst they deny and abjure, they are yet compelled to serve, the Power which is seated upon the throne of their own soul. It is impossible to read the compositions of the most celebrated writers of the present day without being startled with the electric life which burns within their words. They measure the circumference and sound the depths of human nature with a comprehensive and all-penetrating spirit, and they are themselves perhaps the most sincerely astonished at its manifestations; for it is less their spirit than spirit of the age. Poets are the hierophants of an unapprehended inspiration; the mirrors of the gigantic shadows which futurity casts upon the present; the words which express what they understand not; the trumpets which sing to battle, and feel not what they inspire; the influence which is moved not, but moves. Poets are the unacknowledged legislators of the world.[17]

[17] The first and last parts of the *Defence* have been reprinted here complete, but a good deal of the central section, Shelley's version of a history of poetry to set against that offered by Peacock, has been omitted.

Thomas de Quincey
1785–1859

FROM "LETTERS TO A YOUNG MAN WHOSE EDUCATION HAS BEEN NEGLECTED" 1823

THOMAS DE QUINCEY (1785–1859) was more distinguished as a stylist than as an original thinker, but his miscellaneous critical essays offer some sharp insights into the nature of Romantic literature. He was much influenced by Wordsworth, and the short extract printed here contains his reworking, in terms which were to have wide currency, of the statement made in the Preface to *Lyrical Ballads* (see above, p. 33*n*.) that the proper antithesis to poetry is science. Wordsworth went on in the Preface to claim that "The knowledge both of the Poet and the Man of Science is pleasure" (see above p. 37, but later he found another term to distinguish modes of strengthening the mind and being which seemed unrelated to the acquisition of Knowledge, as *The Prelude* (1805) records:

> I sought not then
> Knowledge; but craved for power, and power I found
> In all things   (VIII, 753–5).

That nourishment of the moral being Wordsworth found in nature he calls "power" and he came later, in the "Essay, Supplementary to the Preface" (that is, supplementary to the Preface to the *Poems* of 1815), to argue that the great poet "has to call forth and to communicate *power*".[1] It was left to de Quincey to relate knowledge to science, and power to poetry, in what became a well known sentence, "All that is literature seeks to communicate power; all that is not literature, to communicate knowledge" (see p. 141).

In going on to define power as the conscious possession and organisation of hitherto unawakened modes of feeling, De Quincey was no doubt influenced by Hazlitt (see above, p. 111); but in spite of the derivative nature of his ideas, he provided a memorable and influential formulation of an important aspect of Romantic critical thinking.

[1] *Poetical Works*, edited E. de Selincourt, Volume II (1944), p. 428.

THE word *literature* is a perpetual source of confusion, because it is used in two senses, and those senses liable to be confounded with each other. In a philosophical use of the word, literature is the direct and adequate antithesis of books of knowledge. But, in a popular use, it is a mere term of convenience for expressing inclusively the total books in a language. In this latter sense, a dictionary, a grammar, a spelling-book, an almanac, a pharmacopoeia, a Parliamentary report, a system of farriery, a treatise on billiards, the Court Calendar, etc., belong to the literature. But, in the philosophical sense, not only would it be ludicrous to reckon these as parts of the literature, but even books of much higher pretensions must be excluded—as, for instance, books of voyages and travels, and generally all books in which the matter to be communicated is paramount to the manner or form of its communication ("ornari res ipsa negat, contenta doceri").[2] It is difficult to construct the idea of "literature" with severe accuracy; for it is a fine art—the supreme fine art, and liable to the difficulties which attend such a subtle notion; in fact a severe construction of the idea must be the *result* of a philosophical investigation into this subject, and cannot precede it. But, for the sake of obtaining some expression for literature that may answer our present purpose, let us throw the question into another form. I have said that the antithesis of literature is books of knowledge. Now, what is that antithesis to *knowledge*, which is here implicitly latent in the word literature? The vulgar antithesis is *pleasure* ("aut prodesse volunt, aut delectare poetae").[3] Books, we are told, propose to *instruct* or to *amuse*. Indeed! However, not to spend any words upon it, I suppose you will admit that this wretched antithesis will be of no service to us. And, by the way, let me remark to you, in this, as in other cases, how men by their own errors of understanding, by feeble thinking, and inadequate distinctions, forge chains of meanness and servility for themselves. For, this miserable alternative being once admitted, observe what follows. In which class of books does the *Paradise Lost* stand? Among those which instruct, or those which *amuse*! Now, if a man answers among those which instruct, he lies; for there is no

[2] Manilius, III. 39: "The subject itself defies embellishment, and is content to serve for instruction".

[3] Horace, *Ars Poetica*, line 333.

instruction in it, nor could be in any great poem, according to the meaning which the word must bear in this distinction, unless it is meant that it should involve its own antithesis. But if he says, "No; amongst those which amuse," then what a beast must he be to degrade, and in this way, what has done the most of any human work to raise and dignify human nature. But the truth is, you see that the idiot does not wish to degrade it; on the contrary, he would willingly tell a lie in its favour, if that would be admitted; but such is the miserable state of slavery to which he has reduced himself by his own puny distinction; for, as soon as he hops out of one of his little cells, he is under a necessity of hopping into the other. The true antithesis★ to knowledge, in this case, is not *pleasure*, but power. All that is literature seeks to communicate power; all that is not literature, to communicate knowledge. Now, if it be asked what is meant by communicating power, I, in my turn, would ask by what name a man would designate the case in which I should be made to feel vividly, and with a vital consciousness, emotions which ordinary life rarely or never supplies occasions for exciting, and which had previously lain unwakened, and hardly within the dawn of consciousness—as myriads of modes of feelings are at this moment in every human mind for want of a poet to organise them? I say, when these inert and sleeping forms *are* organised, when these

★ For which distinction, as for most of the sound criticism on poetry, or any subject connected with it that I have ever met with, I must acknowledge my obligations to many years' conversation with Mr. Wordsworth. Upon this occasion it may be useful to notice that there is a rhetorical use of the word "power", very different from the analytic one here introduced, which, also, is due originally to Mr. Wordsworth, and will be found in no book before 1798; this is now become a regular slang term in London conversation. In reference to which, it is worth notice that a critic, speaking of the late Mr. Shelley, a year or two ago, in the most popular literary journal of the day, said, "It is alleged that there is power in Mr. Shelley's poetry; now, there can be no power shown in poetry, except by writing good poems" (or words to that effect). Waiving, however, the question of Mr. Shelley's merits, so far is this remark from being true, that the word was originally introduced expressly to provide for the case where, though the poem was *not* good from defect in *composition*, or from other causes, the stamina and *matériel* of good poetry as fine thinking and passionate conceptions, could not be denied to exist.

possibilities *are* actualized, is this conscious and living possession of mine *power*, or what is it?

When, in *King Lear*, the height and depth, and breadth, of human passion is revealed to us, and, for the purpose of a sublime antagonism, is revealed in the weakness of an old man's nature and in one night two worlds of storm are brought face to face—the human world, and the world of physical nature—mirrors of each other, semi-choral antiphonies, strophe and antistrophe heaving with rival convulsions, and with the double darkness of night and madness, when I am thus suddenly startled into a feeling of the infinity of the world within me, is this power, or what may I call it? Space, again, what is it in most men's minds? The lifeless form of the world without us, a postulate of the geometrician, with no more vitality or real existence to their feelings than the square root of two. But, if Milton has been able to *inform* this empty theatre, peopling it with Titanic shadows, forms that sat at the eldest counsels of the infant world, chaos and original night,—

> "Ghostly shapes,
> To meet at noontide, Fear and trembling Hope,
> Death the Skeleton,
> And Time the Shadow,"—[4]

so that, from being a thing to inscribe with diagrams, it has become under his hands a vital agent on the human mind,—I presume that I may justly express the tendency of the *Paradise Lost*, by saying that it communicates power; a pretension far above all communication of knowledge. Henceforth, therefore, I shall use the antithesis power and knowledge as the most philosophical expression for literature (that is, Literae Humaniores) and anti-literature (that is, Literae didacticae—παιδεια).[5]

[4] Inaccurately quoted from Wordsworth, "Yew-trees", lines 25–8.

[5] That is, literature as art, or polite literature, as opposed to didactic or educational literature.

Thomas Carlyle

1795–1881

FROM "CHARACTERISTICS" 1831

THOMAS CARLYLE (1795–1881) published his essay "Characteristics",
from which the following extracts are taken, in 1831. He was very well read
in German criticism, and brought out a commentary on "The State of
German Literature" in 1827, in which he reviewed the critical thinking of,
among others, Kant, Schiller, Jean Paul Richter and Schlegel. His own
opinions on literature grew out of his study of German writers, and the
title "Characteristics", echoing *Characteristiken und Kritiken* (1801) by A. W.
von Schlegel, sufficiently illustrates the degree to which he acted as a trans-
mitter of German ideas. In this essay, Carlyle puts forward vigorously the
notion that in human activity "the true force is an unconscious one" (p. 145).
He thus exposes simply and without qualifications what is indeed latent in
much Romantic critical writing, namely that "the characteristic of right
performance is a certain spontaneity, an unconsciousness" (p. 147). His vision
is of the poet as seer, divinely inspired, and the notion of a careful artist
shaping his work disappears in this extreme view of the artist as one who does
not know what he does, or how he does it. Carlyle's emphasis on the unconscious foreshadows what has been a major theme in some important
twentieth-century criticism, namely the belief, stimulated by the writings of
Carl Jung, that "a synthetic or creative function does pertain to the unconscious" (a quotation from Maud Bodkin, *Archetypal Patterns in Poetry*, 1934,
p. 73).

BOUNDLESS as is the domain of man, it is but a small fractional
proportion of it that he rules with Consciousness and by Fore-
thought: what he can contrive, nay, what he can altogether know
and comprehend, is essentially the mechanical, small; the great is
ever, in one sense or other, the vital; it is essentially the mysterious,
and only the surface of it can be understood. But Nature, it might
seem, strives, like a kind mother, to hide from us even this, that she
is a mystery: she will have us rest on her beautiful and awful bosom

as if it were our secure home; on the bottomless boundless Deep, whereon all human things fearfully and wonderfully swim, she will have us walk and build, as if the film which supported us there (which any scratch of a bare bodkin will rend asunder, any sputter of a pistol-shot instantaneously burn up) were no film, but a solid rock-foundation. Forever in the neighbourhood of an inevitable Death, man can forget that he is born to die; of his Life, which, strictly meditated, contains in it an Immensity and an Eternity, he can conceive lightly, as of a simple implement wherewith to do day-labour and earn wages. So cunningly does Nature, the mother of all highest Art, which only apes her from afar, "body forth the Finite from the Infinite"; and guide man safe on his wondrous path, not more by endowing him with vision, than, at the right place, with blindness! Under all her works, chiefly under her noblest work, Life, lies a basis of Darkness, which she benignantly conceals; in Life, too, the roots and inward circulations which stretch down fearfully to the regions of Death and Night, shall not hint of their existence, and only the fair stem with its leaves and flowers, shone on by the fair sun, shall disclose itself and joyfully grow.

However, without venturing into the abstruse, or too eagerly asking Why and How, in things where our answer must needs prove, in great part, an echo of the question, let us be content to remark farther, in the merely historical way, how that Aphorism of the bodily Physician holds good in quite other departments. Of the Soul, with her activities, we shall find it not less true than of the Body: nay, cry the Spiritualists, is not that very division of the unity Man, into a dualism of Soul and Body, itself the symptom of disease; as, perhaps, your frightful theory of Materialism, of his being but a Body, and therefore, at least, once more a unity, may be the paroxysm which was critical, and the beginning of cure! But omitting this, we observe, with confidence enough, that the truly strong mind, view it as Intellect, as Morality, or under any other aspect, is nowise the mind acquainted with its strength; that here as before the sign of health is Unconsciousness. In our inward, as in our outward world, what is mechanical lies open to us: not what is dynamical and has vitality. Of our Thinking, we might say, it is but the mere upper surface that we shape into articulate Thoughts; —underneath the region of argument and conscious discourse, lies the region of meditation; here, in its quiet mysterious depths, dwells what vital force is in us; here, if aught is to be created, and not merely manufactured and communicated, must the work go on. Manufacture is intelligible, but trivial; Creation is great, and cannot be understood. Thus if the Debater and Demonstrator, whom we may rank as the lowest of true thinkers, knows what he has done, and how he did it, the Artist, whom we rank as the highest, knows not; must speak of Inspiration, and in one or the other dialect, call his work the gift of a divinity.

But on the whole, "genius is ever a secret to itself"; of this old truth we have, on all sides, daily evidence. The Shakespeare takes no airs for writing *Hamlet* and the *Tempest*, understands not that it is anything surprising: Milton, again, is more conscious of his faculty, which accordingly is an inferior one. On the other hand, what cackling and strutting must we not often hear and see, when, in some shape of academical prolusion, maiden speech, review article, this or the other well-fledged goose has produced its goose-egg, of quite measurable value, were it the pink of its whole kind; and wonders why all mortals do not wonder!

Foolish enough, too, was the College Tutor's surprise at Walter Shandy: how, though unread in Aristotle, he could nevertheless argue; and not knowng the name of any dialectic tool, handled them all to perfection.[1] Is it the skilfulest anatomist that cuts the best figure at Sadler's Wells?[2] or does the boxer hit better for knowing that he has a *flexor longus* and a *flexor brevis*?[3] But indeed, as in the higher case of the Poet, so here in that of the Speaker and Inquirer, the true force is an unconscious one. The healthy Understanding, we should say, is not the Logical, argumentative, but the Intuitive; for the end of Understanding is not to prove and find reasons, but to know and believe. Of logic, and its limits, and uses and abuses, there were much to be said and examined; one fact, however, which chiefly concerns us here, has long been familiar: that the man of

[1] Alluding to Laurence Sterne's *Tristram Shandy* (1759–67) Book I, Chapter XIX.

[2] *Anatomist . . . Sadler's Wells:* perhaps alluding to the famous acrobat, dancer and clown, Joseph Grimaldi, who ran Sadler's Wells theatre from 1818 to 1828.

[3] "Flexor" muscles bend, as opposed to "extensor" muscles that stretch.

logic and the man of insight; the Reasoner and the Discoverer, or even Knower, are quite separable,—indeed, for most part, quite separate characters. In practical matters, for example, has it not become almost proverbial that the man of logic cannot prosper? This is he whom business-people call Systematic and Theoriser and Word-monger; his *vital* intellectual force lies dormant or extinct, his whole force is mechanical, conscious: of such a one it is foreseen that, when once confronted with the infinite complexities of the real world, his little compact theorem of the world will be found wanting; that unless he can throw it overboard and become a new creature, he will necessarily founder. Nay, in mere Speculation itself, the most ineffectual of all characters, generally speaking, is your dialectic man-at-arms; were he armed cap-a-pie in syllogistic mail of proof, and perfect master of logic-fence, how little does it avail him! Consider the old Schoolmen, and their pilgrimage towards Truth: the faithfulest endeavour, incessant unwearied motion, often great natural vigour; only no progress: nothing but antic feats of one limb poised against the other; there they balanced, somersetted, and made postures; at best gyrated swiftly, with some pleasure, like Spinning Dervishes, and ended where they began. So is it, so will it always be, with all System-makers and builders of logical card-castles; of which class a certain remnant must, in every age, as they do in our own, survive and build. Logic is good, but it is not the best. The Irrefragable Doctor,[4] with his chains of induction, his corollaries, dilemmas and other cunning logical diagrams and apparatus, will cast you a beautiful horoscope, and speak reasonable things; nevertheless your stolen jewel, which you wanted him to find you, is not forthcoming. Often by some winged word, winged as the thunderbolt is, of a Luther, a Napoleon, a Goethe, shall we see the difficulty split asunder, and its secret laid bare; while the Irrefragable, with all his logical tools, hews at it, and hovers round it, and finds it on all hands too hard for him.

Again, in the difference between Oratory and Rhetoric, as indeed everywhere in that superiority of what is called the Natural over the Artificial, we find a similar illustration. The Orator persuades and carries all with him, he knows not how; the Rhetorician can prove

[4] *Irrefragable Doctor:* i.e. "irrefutable authority", a title originally given to Alexander of Hales (died 1245), a learned theologian.

that he ought to have persuaded and carried all with him: the one is in a state of healthy unconsciousness, as if he "had no system"; the other, in virtue of regimen and dietetic punctuality, feels at best that "his system is in high order." So stands it, in short, with all the forms of Intellect, whether as directed to the finding of truth, or to the fit imparting thereof; to Poetry, to Eloquence, to depth of Insight, which is the basis of both these; always the characteristic of right performance is a certain spontaneity, an unconsciousness; "the healthy know not of their health, but only the sick."[5] So that the old precept of the critic, as crabbed as it looked to his ambitious disciple, might contain in it a most fundamental truth, applicable to us all, and in much else than Literature: Whenever you have written any sentence that looks particularly excellent, be sure to blot it out. . . .[6]

To begin with our highest Spiritual function, with Religion, we might ask, Whither has Religion now fled? Of Churches and their establishments we here say nothing; nor of the unhappy domains of Unbelief, and how innumerable men, blinded in their minds, have grown to "live without God in the world";[7] but, taking the fairest side of the matter, we ask, What is the nature of that same Religion, which still lingers in the hearts of the few who are called, and call themselves, specially the Religious? Is it a healthy religion, vital, unconscious of itself; that shines forth spontaneously in doing of the Work, or even in preaching of the Word? Unhappily, no. Instead of heroic martyr Conduct, and inspired and soul-inspiring Eloquence, whereby Religion itself were brought home to our living bosoms, to live and reign there, we have "Discourses on the Evidences,"[8] endeavouring, with smallest result, to make it probable that such a thing as Religion exists. The most enthusiastic Evangelicals do not preach a Gospel, but keep describing how it should and might be preached: to awaken the sacred fire of faith, as by a sacred contagion,

[5] "the healthy . . . sick": a variant of an old proverb, "Health is not valued till sickness come".

[6] Whenever . . . blot it out: quoted from Boswell's Life of Samuel Johnson, entry for 30 April, 1773 (edited G. Birkbeck Hill, 1887, II. 237).

[7] live without God in the world: source untraced.

[8] Discourses on the Evidences: alluding perhaps to William Paley's Evidences of Christianity (1794).

is not their endeavour; but, at most, to describe how Faith shows and acts, and scientifically distinguish true Faith from false. Religion, like all else, is conscious of itself, listens to itself; it becomes less and less creative, vital; more and more mechanical. Considered as a whole, the Christian Religion of late ages has been continually dissipating itself into Metaphysics; and threatens now to disappear, as some rivers do, in deserts of barren sand.

Of Literature, and its deep-seated, wide-spread maladies, why speak? Literature is but a branch of Religion, and always participates in its character: however, in our time, it is the only branch that still shows any greenness; and, as some think, must one day become the main stem. Now, apart from the subterranean and tartarean regions of Literature;—leaving out of view the frightful, scandalous statistics of Puffing, the mystery of Slander, Falsehood, Hatred and other convulsion-work of rabid Imbecility, and all that has rendered Literature on that side a perfect "Babylon the mother of Abominations," in very deed making the world "drunk" with the wine of her iniquity;[9]—forgetting all this, let us look only to the regions of the upper air; to such Literature as can be said to have some attempt towards truth in it, some tone of music, and if it be not poetical, to hold of the poetical. Among other characteristics, is not this manifest enough: that it knows itself? Spontaneous devotedness to the object, being wholly possessed by the object, what we can call Inspiration, has well-nigh ceased to appear in Literature. Which melodious Singer forgets that he is singing melodiously? We have not the love of greatness, but the love of the love of greatness. Hence infinite Affectations, Distractions; in every case inevitable Error. Consider, for one example, this peculiarity of Modern Literature, the sin that has been named View-hunting. In our elder writers, there are no paintings of scenery for its own sake; no euphuistic gallantries with Nature, but a constant heartlove for her, a constant dwelling in communion with her. View-hunting, with so much else that is of kin to it, first came decisively into action through the *Sorrows of Werter*;[10] which wonderful Performance, indeed, may in many senses be regarded as the progenitor of

[9] *Babylon . . . wine of her iniquity:* alluding to *Revelation*, xviii, 2 and 5.

[10] *Sorrows of Werter:* The novel by J. W. von Goethe (1749–1832); published in 1774, it was revised in 1787.

all that has since become popular in Literature; whereof, in so far as concerns spirit and tendency, it still offers the most instructive image; for nowhere, except in its own country, above all in the mind of its illustrious Author, has it yet fallen wholly obsolete. Scarcely ever, till that late epoch, did any worshipper of Nature become entirely aware that he was worshipping, much to his own credit; and think of saying to himself: Come, let us make a description! Intolerable enough: when every puny whipster plucks out his pencil, and insists on painting you a scene; so that the instant you discern such a thing as "wavy outline," "mirror of the lake," "stern head-land," or the like, in any Book, you tremulously hasten on; and scarcely the Author of Waverley himself[11] can tempt you not to skip.

Nay, is not the diseased self-conscious state of Literature disclosed in this one fact, which lies so near us here, the prevalence of Reviewing! Sterne's wish[12] for a reader "that would give-up the reins of his imagination into his author's hands, and be pleased he knew not why, and cared not wherefore," might lead him a long journey now. Indeed, for our best class of readers, the chief pleasure, a very stinted one, is this same knowing of the Why; which many a Kames and Bossu[13] has been, ineffectually enough, endeavouring to teach us: till at last these also have laid down their trade; and now your Reviewer is a mere *taster*; who tastes, and says, by the evidence of such palate, such tongue, as he has got, It is good, It is bad. Was it thus that the French carried out certain inferior creatures on their Algerine Expedition,[14] to taste the wells for them, and try whether they were poisoned? Far be it from us to disparage our own craft, whereby we have our living! Only we must note these things: that Reviewing spreads with strange vigour; that such a man as Byron

---

[11] *Author:* Sir Walter Scott.

[12] *Sterne's wish:* cited inaccurately from *Tristram Shandy*, Book 3, Chapter XII.

[13] *Kames and Bossu:* Henry Home, Lord Kames (1696–1782), published his *Elements of Criticism* in 1762. René le Bossu (1631–80) was a French critic, author of an *Essay on Epic Poetry*.

[14] *Algerine Expedition:* After trouble arising out of a dispute over interest on debts, the French sent an expedition against Algiers in June 1830, and captured the city a month later.

reckons the Reviewer and the Poet equal; that at the last Leipzig Fair,[15] there was advertised a Review of Reviews. By and by it will be found that all Literature has become one boundless self-devouring Review; and, as in London routs, we have to *do* nothing, but only to *see* others do nothing—Thus does Literature also, like a sick thing, superabundantly "listen to itself."

[15] *Leipzig Fair:* the great annual convention of booksellers and publishers held in Leipzig.

John Stuart Mill

1806–1873

FROM "WHAT IS POETRY" AND "TWO KINDS OF POETRY" OR "THOUGHTS ON POETRY AND ITS VARIETIES" 1833; REVISED 1859

THE rigorous analytical training to which John Stuart Mill (1806–73) was subjected by his father, James Mill (1773–1836), philosopher and associate of Jeremy Bentham, made him initially a utilitarian. In his *Autobiography* (1873), he describes the great crisis of mind he suffered as a young man, when his philosophy proved inadequate to rescue him from a state of wretchedness brought on by unremitting study. He records that the poems of Wordsworth restored for him a capacity for joy, and his account of his passage through the crisis to recovery dramatises a larger transition from mechanistic to organic theories about the activity of the mind (see the headnote on S. T. Coleridge above, p. 72), or, one might say, from reason to romanticism.

Mill published two essays on poetry in a journal called *The Monthly Repository;* the first, "What is Poetry?" appeared in January 1833, the second, "Two Kinds of Poetry" in October of the same year, over the pen-name "Antiquus". The two essays were later revised and amalgamated by him under the title "Thoughts on Poetry and its Varieties", and issued in his *Dissertations and Discussions* (1859). Here are reprinted part of the first and the whole of the second essay, from the 1833 text, as presented in *Early Essays by John Stuart Mill*, edited by J. M. W. Gibbs (1897), pp. 201–14 and 221–36; passages omitted in 1859 are printed in square brackets.

Mill takes off from Wordsworth's placing of the poet as opposed to the "Man of Science" (Preface to the *Lyrical Ballads*; see above, p. 37), and develops an extreme formulation of the expressive theory of poetry. To him poetry "is feeling, confessing itself to itself in moments of solitude" (p. 158), and looks inward; the poet need have no concern with the world outside himself. In the second essay, Mill turns the proposition round, and claims that the expression of feeling is poetry, that "One may write genuine poetry, and not be a poet" (p. 163). Poetry is thus the natural expression of the strongly emotional man, who is opposed to the man of science or business;

and this leads him to distinguish two kinds of poet, one in whom "feeling waits upon thought", like Wordsworth, and the other who "merely pours forth the overflowing of his feelings" (p. 165), like Shelley. The second kind is more essentially poetical as more impassioned; and although Mill recognises the value of a trained intellect for the poet, he has to allow that the poet "whose feeling has been his sole teacher" may be superior (p. 173). He thus elevates the lyric above all other kinds of poetry, as "more eminently and peculiarly poetry than any other" (p. 167), and as spontaneity becomes a principal criterion, he treats narrative as at best a necessary evil; so, the end of the first essay, "What is Poetry?"—a long section on painting, music and architecture in relation to poetry, most of which is omitted here—contains one notable paragraph in which we are told that an epic poem, "in so far as it is epic (*i.e.* narrative), . . . is not poetry at all". (In this connection, compare the more extreme view of Edgar Allan Poe, p. 200 below.)

In defining poetry, Mill distinguishes it from eloquence; poetry for him does not require an audience, whereas eloquence does. This distinction was developed differently by Alexander Smith; see below p. 186. Another notable feature of Mill's discussion is his attempt to differentiate poetry from fiction, and establish the superiority of the poem over the novel; in general critical writings at this time the novel received comparatively little attention.

WHAT IS POETRY?

I T has often been asked, What is Poetry? And many and various are the answers which have been returned. The vulgarest of all—one with which no person possessed of the faculties to which Poetry addresses itself can ever have been satisfied—is that which confounds poetry with metrical composition: yet to this wretched mockery of a definition, many have been led back, by the failure of all their attempts to find any other that would distinguish what they have been accustomed to call poetry, from much which they have known only under other names.

That, however, the word "poetry" *does* import something quite peculiar in its nature, something which may exist in what is called prose as well as in verse, something which does not even require the instrument of words, but can speak through those other audible symbols called musical sounds, and even through the visible ones, which are the language of sculpture, painting, and architecture; all this, as we believe, is and must be felt, though perhaps indistinctly, by all upon whom poetry in any of its shapes produces any impression beyond that of tickling the ear. To the mind, poetry is either nothing, or it is the better part of all art whatever, and of real life too; and the distinction between poetry and what is not poetry, whether explained or not, is felt to be fundamental.

Where everyone feels a difference, a difference there must be. All other appearances may be fallacious, but the appearance of a difference is a real difference. Appearances too, like other things, must have a *cause*, and that which can *cause* anything, even an illusion, must be a reality. And hence, while a half-philosophy disdains the classifications and distinctions indicated by popular language, philosophy carried to its highest point may frame new ones, but never sets aside the old, content with correcting and regularizing them. It cuts fresh channels for thought, but it does not fill up such as it finds ready-made, but it traces, on the contrary, more deeply, broadly, and distinctly, those into which the current has spontaneously flowed.

Let us then attempt, in the way of modest inquiry, not to coerce and confine nature within the bounds of an arbitrary definition, but rather to find the boundaries which she herself has set, and erect a barrier round them; not calling mankind to account for having mis-applied the word "poetry," but attempting to clear up the conception which they already attach to it, and to bring before their minds as a distinct *principle* that which, as a vague *feeling*, has really guided them in their actual employment of the term.

The object of poetry is confessedly to act upon the emotions; and therein is poetry sufficiently distinguished from what Wordsworth affirms to be its logical opposite, namely, not prose, but matter of fact or science. The one addresses itself to the belief, the other to the feelings. The one does its work by convincing or persuading, the other by moving. The one acts by presenting a proposition to the understanding, the other by offering interesting objects of con-templation to the sensibilities.

This, however, leaves us very far from a definition of poetry. We have distinguished it from one thing, but we are bound to dis-tinguish it from everything. To bring thoughts or images to the mind for the purpose of acting upon the emotions, does not belong to poetry alone. It is equally the province (for example) of the novelist: and yet the faculty of the poet and that of the novelist are as distinct as any other two faculties; and the faculty of the novelist and of the orator, or of the poet and the metaphysician. The two characters may be united, as characters the most disparate may; but they have no natural connection.

Many of the finest poems are in the form of novels, and in almost all good novels there is true poetry. But there is a radical distinction between the interest felt in a novel as such, and the interest excited by poetry; for the one is derived from incident, the other from the representation of feeling. In one, the source of the emotion excited is the exhibition of a state or states of human sensibility; in the other, of a series of states of mere outward circumstances. Now, all minds are capable of being affected more or less by representations of the latter kind, and all, or almost all, by those of the former; yet the two sources of interest correspond to two distinct, and (*as respects their greatest development*) mutually exclusive, characters of mind. [So much is the nature of poetry dissimilar to the nature of fictitious narrative, that to have a really strong passion for either of the two, seems to presuppose or to superinduce a comparative indifference to the other.]

At what age is the passion for a story, for almost any kind of story, merely as a story, the most intense?—in childhood. But that also is the age at which poetry, even of the simplest description, is least relished and least understood; because the feelings with which it is especially conversant are yet undeveloped, and not having been even in the slightest degree experienced, cannot be sympathized with. In what stage of the progress of society, again, is story-telling most valued, and the story-teller in greatest request and honour?— in a rude state; like that of the Tartars and Arabs at this day, and of almost all nations in the earliest ages. But in this state of society there is little poetry except ballads, which are mostly narrative, that is, essentially *stories*, and derive their principal interest from the *incidents*. Considered as poetry, they are of the lowest and most elementary kind: the feelings depicted, or rather indicated, are the simplest our nature has; such joys and griefs as the immediate pressure of some outward event excites in rude minds, which live wholly immersed in outward things, and have never, either from choice or a force they could resist, turned themselves to the contemplation of the world within. Passing now from childhood, and from the childhood of society, to the grown-up men and women of this most grown-up and unchildlike age—the minds and hearts of greatest depth and elevation are commonly those which take greatest delight in poetry; the shallowest and emptiest, on the contrary, are by universal remark, the most addicted to novel-reading. This accords, too, with all analogous experience of human nature. The sort of persons whom not merely in books but in their lives, we find perpetually engaged in hunting for excitement from without, are invariably those who do not possess, either in the vigour of their intellectual powers or in the depth of their sensibilities, that which would enable them to find ample excitement nearer at home. The same persons whose time is divided between sight-seeing, gossip, and fashionable dissipation, take a natural delight in fictitious narrative; the excitement it affords is of the kind which comes from without. Such persons are rarely lovers of poetry, though they may fancy themselves so because they relish novels in verse. But poetry, which is the delineation of the deeper and more secret workings of the human heart, is interesting only to those to whom it recalls what they have felt, or whose imagination it stirs up to conceive what they could feel, or what they might have been able to feel had their outward circumstances been different.

Poetry, when it is really such, is truth; and fiction also, if it is good for anything, is truth: but they are different truths. The truth of poetry is to paint the human soul truly: the truth of fiction is to give a true picture *of life*. The two kinds of knowledge are different, and come by different ways, come mostly to different persons. Great poets are often proverbially ignorant of life. What they know has come by observation of themselves; they have found *there* one highly delicate, and sensitive, and refined specimen of human nature, on which the laws of emotion are written in large characters, such as can be read off without much study: and other knowledge of mankind, such as comes to men of the world by outward experience, is not indispensable to them as poets; but to the novelist such knowledge is all in all; he has to describe outward things, not the inward man; actions and events, not feelings; and it will not do for him to be numbered among those who, as Madame Roland said of Brissot,[1] know man but not men.

[1] *Madame Roland . . . Brissot:* Jeanne Roland (1754–93) played an important part in the political affairs of the moderates, the Girondists in the French

All this is no bar to the possibility of combining both elements, poetry and narrative or incident, in the same work, and calling it either a novel or a poem; but so may red and white combine on the same human features, or on the same canvas; [and so may oil and vinegar, though opposite natures, blend together in the same composite taste.] There is one order of composition which requires the union of poetry and incident, each in its highest kind—the dramatic. Even there the two elements are perfectly distinguishable, and may exist of unequal quality, and in the most various proportion. The incidents of a dramatic poem may be scanty and ineffective, though the delineation of passion and character may be of the highest order; as in Goethe's glorious "Torquato Tasso:"[2] or again, the story as a mere story may be well got up for effect, as in the case with some of the most trashy productions of the Minerva press:[3] it may even be, what those are not, a coherent and probable series of events, though there be scarcely a feeling exhibited which is not represented falsely, or in a manner absolutely commonplace. The combination of the two excellencies is what renders Shakespeare so generally acceptable, each sort of readers finding in him what is suitable to their faculties. To the many he is great as a story-teller, to the few as a poet.

In limiting poetry to the delineation of states of feeling, and denying the name where nothing is delineated but outward objects, we may be thought to have done what we promised to avoid—to have not *found*, but *made* a definition, in opposition to the usage of the English language, since it is established by common consent that there is a poetry called *descriptive*. We deny the charge. Description is not poetry because there is descriptive poetry, no more than science is poetry because there is such a thing as a didactic poem [; no more, we might almost say, than Greek or Latin is poetry because there are Greek and Latin poems]. But an object which admits of being described, or a truth which may fill a place in a

Revolution, and was in the end guillotined. Jacques Brissot (1754–93), leader of the Girondists, was also executed later in 1793.

[2] *Torquato Tasso:* a poetic drama on the subject of the epic poet, written in 1790.

[3] *Minerva press:* a printing firm which specialised in issuing sentimental novels.

scientific treatise, may *also* furnish an occasion for the generation of poetry, which we thereupon choose to call descriptive or didactic. The poetry is not in the object itself, nor in the scientific truth itself, but in the state of mind in which the one and the other may be contemplated. The mere delineation of the dimensions and colours of external objects is not poetry, no more than a geometrical ground-plan of St. Peter's or Westminster Abbey is painting. Descriptive poetry consists, no doubt, in description, but in description of things as they appear, not as they *are*; and it paints them not in their bare and natural lineaments, but arranged in the colours and seen through the medium of the imagination set in action by the feelings. If a poet is to describe a lion, he will not set about describing him as a naturalist would, nor even as a traveller would, who was intent upon stating the truth, the whole truth, and nothing but the truth. He describes him by *imagery*, that is, by suggesting the most striking likenesses and contrasts which might occur to a mind contemplating the lion, in the state of awe, wonder, or terror, which the spectacle naturally excites, or is, on the occasion, supposed to excite. Now this is describing the lion professedly, but the state of excitement of the spectator really. The lion may be described falsely or in exaggerated colours, and the poetry be all the better; but if the human emotion be not painted with the most scrupulous truth, the poetry is bad poetry, i.e. is not poetry at all, but a failure.

Thus far our progress towards a clear view of the essentials of poetry has brought us very close to the last two attempts at a definition of poetry which we happen to have seen in print, both of them by poets and men of genius. The one is by Ebenezer Elliott,[4] the author of "Corn-Law Rhymes," and other poems of still greater merit. "Poetry," says he, "is impassioned truth." The other is by a writer in Blackwood's Magazine, and comes, we think, still nearer the mark. He defines poetry, "man's thoughts tinged with his feelings."[5] There is in either definition a near approximation to what we are in search of. Every truth which man can announce, every thought, even every outward impression, which can enter into his consciousness, may become poetry when shewn through

[4] *Ebenezer Elliott* (1781–1849) was famous for his attack on the Bread Tax in his *Corn-Law Rhymes* (1831).

[5] I have not traced this quotation.

any impassioned medium, when invested with the colouring of joy, or grief, or pity, or affection, or admiration, or reverence, or awe, or even hatred or terror: and, unless so coloured, nothing, be it as interesting as it may, is poetry. But both these definitions fail to discriminate between poetry and eloquence. Eloquence, as well as poetry, is thoughts coloured by the feelings. Yet common apprehension and philosophic criticism alike recognize a distinction between the two: there is much that everyone would call eloquence, which no one would think of classing as poetry. A question will sometimes arise, whether some particular author is a poet; and those who maintain the negative commonly allow, that though not a poet, he is a highly *eloquent* writer. The distinction between poetry and eloquence appears to us to be equally fundamental with the distinction between poetry and narrative, or between poetry and description. It is still farther from having been satisfactorily cleared up than either of the others [, unless, which is highly probable, the German artists and critics have thrown some light upon it which has not yet reached us. Without a perfect knowledge of what they have written, it is something like presumption to write upon such subjects at all, and we shall be the foremost to urge that, whatever we may be about to submit, may be received, subject to correction from *them*].

Poetry and eloquence are both alike the expression or uttering forth of feeling. But if we may be excused the antithesis, we should say that eloquence is *heard*, poetry is *over*heard. Eloquence supposes an audience; the peculiarity of poetry appears to us to lie in the poet's utter unconsciousness of a listener. Poetry is feeling, confessing itself to itself in moments of solitude, and embodying itself in symbols, which are the nearest possible representations of the feeling in the exact shape in which it exists in the poet's mind. Eloquence is feeling pouring itself out to other minds, courting their sympathy, or endeavouring to influence their belief, or move them to passion or to action.[6]

All poetry is of the nature of soliloquy. It may be said that poetry which is printed on hot-pressed paper and sold at a bookseller's

[6] T. S. Eliot's essay, "The Three Voices of Poetry" (1953), in *On Poetry and Poets* (1957), pp. 89–102, makes no reference to Mill, but considers further the issues discussed here, with special reference to poetic drama.

shop, is a soliloquy in full dress, and on the stage. But there is nothing absurd in the idea of such a mode of soliloquizing. What we have said to ourselves, we may tell to others afterwards; what we have said or done in solitude, we may voluntarily reproduce when we know that other eyes are upon us. But no trace of consciousness that any eyes are upon us must be visible in the work itself. The actor knows that there is an audience present; but if he act as though he knew it, he acts ill. A poet may write poetry with the intention of publishing it; he may write it even for the express purpose of being paid for it; that it should *be* poetry, being written under such influences, is far less probable; not, however, impossible; but no otherwise possible than if he can succeed in excluding from his work every vestige of such lookings-forth into the outward and every-day world, and can express his feelings exactly as he has felt them in solitude, or as he feels that he should feel them, though they were to remain for ever unuttered. But when he turns round and addresses himself to another person; when the act of utterance is not itself the end, but a means to an end—viz. by the feelings he himself expresses, to work upon the feelings, or upon the belief, or the will, of another,—when the expression of his emotions, or of his thoughts tinged by his emotions, is tinged also by that purpose, by that desire of making an impression upon another mind, then it ceases to be poetry, and becomes eloquence.

Poetry, accordingly, is the natural fruit of solitude and meditation; eloquence, of intercourse with the world. The persons who have most feeling of their own, if intellectual culture have given them a language in which to express it, have the highest faculty of poetry; those who best understand the feelings of others, are the most eloquent. The persons, and the nations, who commonly excel in poetry, are those whose character and tastes render them least dependent for their happiness upon the applause, *or* sympathy, or concurrence of the world in general. Those to whom that applause, that sympathy, that concurrence are most necessary, generally excel most in eloquence. And hence, perhaps, the French, who are the *least* poetical of all great and refined nations, are among the most eloquent: the French, also, being the most sociable, the vainest, and the least self-dependent.

If the above be, as we believe, the true theory of the distinction commonly admitted between eloquence and poetry; or though it be not *that*, yet if, as we cannot doubt, the distinction above stated be a real *bonâ fide* distinction, it will be found to hold, not merely in the language of words, but in all other language, and to intersect the whole domain of art.

Take, for example, music: we shall find in that art, so peculiarly the expression of passion, two perfectly distinct styles; one of which may be called the poetry, the other the oratory of music. This difference, being seized, would put an end to much musical sectarianism. There has been much contention whether the character of Rossini's music—the music, we mean, which is characteristic of that composer—is compatible with the expression of passion. Without doubt, the passion it expresses is not the musing, meditative tenderness, or pathos, or grief of Mozart, the great poet of his art. Yet it is passion, but *garrulous* passion—the passion which pours itself into other ears; and therein the better calculated for *dramatic* effect, having a natural adaptation for dialogue. Mozart is also great in musical oratory; but his most touching compositions are in the opposite style—that of soliloquy. Who can imagine "Dove sono" heard?[7] We imagine it *over*heard. . . .

The narrative style answers to what is called historical painting, which it is the fashion among connoisseurs to treat as the climax of the pictorial art. That it is the most difficult branch of the art we do not doubt, because, in its perfection, it includes, in a manner, the perfection of all the other branches. As an epic poem, though in so far as it is epic (i.e. narrative), it is not poetry at all, is yet esteemed the greatest effort of poetic genius, because there is no kind whatever of poetry which may not appropriately find a place in it. But a historical picture as such, that is, as the representation of an incident, must necessarily, as it seems to us, be poor and ineffective. The narrative powers of painting are extremely limited. Scarcely any picture, scarcely any series even of pictures, tells its own story without the aid of an interpreter; [you must know the story beforehand; *then*, indeed, you may see great beauty and appropriateness in the painting.] But it is the single figures which, to us, are the great

[7] *Dove sono:* "Dove sono i bei momenti" ("Where have the glorious times gone?"), an aria sung in Act III of Mozart's *The Marriage of Figaro* (1786) by Countess Almaviva.

charm even of a historical picture. It is in these that the power of the art is really seen: in the attempt to *narrate*, visible and permanent signs are far behind the fugitive audible ones, which follow so fast one after another, while the faces and figures in a narrative picture, even though they be Titian's, stand still. Who would not prefer one Virgin and Child by Raphael to all the pictures which Rubens, with his fat, frouzy Dutch Venuses, ever painted? Though Rubens, besides excelling almost everyone in his mastery over the mechanical parts of his art, often shows real genius in *grouping* his figures, the peculiar problem of historical painting. But then, who, except a mere student of drawing and colouring, ever cared to look twice at any of the figure themselves? The power of painting lies in poetry, of which Rubens had not the slightest tincture—not in narrative, where he might have excelled.

TWO KINDS OF POETRY

NASCITUR POETA[8] is a maxim of classical antiquity, which has passed to these latter days with less questioning than most of the doctrines of that early age. When it originated, the human faculties were occupied, fortunately for posterity, less in examining how the works of genius are created, than in creating them: and the adage, probably, had no higher source than the tendency common among mankind to consider all power which is not visibly the effect of practice, all skill which is not capable of being reduced to mechanical rules, as the result of a peculiar gift. Yet this aphorism, born in the infancy of psychology, will perhaps be found, now when that science is in its adolescence, to be as true as an epigram ever is, that is, to contain some truth: truth, however, which has been so compressed and bent out of shape, in order to tie it up into so small a knot of only two words, that it requires an almost infinite amount of unrolling and laying straight, before it will resume its just proportions.

We are not now intending to remark upon the grosser misapplications of this ancient maxim, which have engendered so

---

[8] *Nascitur poeta:* in full, "Poeta nascitur, non fit" ("A man is born, not made, a poet"). A version of this phrase was cited as an "old proverb" by Sir Philip Sidney in his *Apology for Poetry* (printed 1595), but it has not been traced further back than the late fifteenth century.

many races of poetasters. The days are gone by, when every raw youth whose borrowed phantasies have set themselves to a borrowed tune, mistaking, as Coleridge says,[9] an ardent desire of poetic reputation for poetic genius, while unable to disguise from himself that he had taken no means whereby he might *become* a poet, could fancy himself a born one. Those who would reap without sowing, and gain the victory without fighting the battle, are ambitious now of another sort of distinction, and are born novelists, or public speakers, not poets. And the wiser thinkers begin to understand and acknowledge that poetic excellence is subject to the same necessary conditions with any other mental endowment; and that to no one of the spiritual benefactors of mankind is a higher or a more assiduous intellectual culture needful than to the poet. It is true, he possesses this advantage over others who use the "instrument of words," that, of the truths which he utters, a larger proportion are derived from personal consciousness, and a smaller from philosophic investigation. But the power itself of discriminating between what really is consciousness, and what is only a process of inference completed in a single instant; and the capacity of distinguishing whether that of which the mind is conscious be an eternal truth, or but a dream— are among the last results of the most matured and perfect intellect. Not to mention that the poet, no more than any other person who writes, confines himself altogether to intuitive truths, nor has any means of communicating even these but by words, every one of which derives all its power of conveying a meaning from a whole host of acquired notions, and facts learnt by study and experience.

Nevertheless, it seems undeniable in point of fact, and consistent with the principles of a sound metaphysics, that there are poetic *natures*. There is a mental and physical constitution or temperament, peculiarly fitted for poetry. This temperament will not of itself make a poet, no more than the soil will the fruit; and as good fruit may be raised by culture from indifferent soils, so may good poetry from naturally unpoetical minds. But the poetry of one who is a poet by nature, will be clearly and broadly distinguishable from the poetry of mere culture. It may not be truer; it may not be more

[9] *Coleridge says:* in *Biographia Literaria* (1817), Chapter II (ed. J. Shawcross, 1907, Vol. I, p.25).

useful; but it will be different: fewer will appreciate it, even though many should affect to do so; but in those few it will find a keener sympathy, and will yield them a deeper enjoyment.

One may write genuine poetry, and not be a poet; for whosover writes out truly any one human feeling, writes poetry. All persons, even the most unimaginative, in moments of strong emotion, speak poetry; and hence the drama is poetry, which else were always prose, except when a poet is one of the characters. What *is* poetry, but the thoughts and words in which emotion spontaneously embodies itself? As there are few who are not, at least for *some* moments and in *some* situations, capable of *some* strong feeling, poetry is natural to most persons at some period of their lives. And anyone whose feelings are genuine, though but of the average strength,—if he be not diverted by uncongenial thoughts or occupations from the indulgence of them, and if he acquire by culture, as all persons may, the faculty of delineating them correctly, —has it in his power to be a poet, so far as a life passed in writing unquestionable poetry may be considered to confer that title. But *ought* it to do so? Yes, perhaps, in the table of contents of a collection of "British Poets." But "poet" is the name also of a variety of *man*, not solely of the author of a particular variety of *book*: now, to have written whole volumes of real poetry, is possible to almost all kinds of characters, and implies no greater peculiarity of mental construction than to be the author of a history or a novel.

Whom, then, shall we call poets? Those who are so constituted, that emotions are the links of association by which their ideas, both sensuous and spiritual, are connected together. This constitution belongs (with certain limits) to all in whom poetry is a pervading principle. In all others, poetry is something extraneous and superinduced: something out of themselves, foreign to the habitual course of their everyday lives and characters; a quite other world, to which they may make occasional visits, but where they are sojourners, not dwellers, and which, when out of it, or even in it, they think of, peradventure, but as a phantom-world, a place of *ignes fatui*[10] and spectral illusions. Those who only have the peculiarity of association which we have mentioned, and which is one of the

[10] *ignes fatui*: literally "foolish fires", phosphorescent effects seen over marshes, or will-o'-the-wisps.

consequences of intense sensibility, instead of seeming not themselves when they are uttering poetry, scarcely seem themselves when uttering anything to which poetry is foreign. Whatever be the thing which they are contemplating, the aspect under which it first and most naturally paints itself to them, is its poetic aspect. The poet of culture sees his object in prose, and describes it in poetry; the poet of nature actually sees it in poetry.

This point is perhaps worth some little illustration; the rather, as metaphysicians (the ultimate arbiters of all philosophical criticism), while they have busied themselves for two thousand years, more or less, about the few *universal* laws of human nature, have strangely neglected the analysis of its *diversities*. Of these, none lie deeper or reach further than the varieties which difference of nature and of education makes in what may be termed the habitual bond of association. In a mind entirely uncultivated, which is also without any strong feelings, objects, whether of sense or of intellect, arrange themselves in the mere casual order in which they have been seen, heard, or otherwise perceived. Persons of this sort may be said to think chronologically. If they remember a fact, it is by reason of a fortuitous coincidence with some trifling incident or circumstance which took place at the very time. If they have a story to tell, or testimony to deliver in a witness-box, their narrative must follow the exact order in which the events took place: *dodge* them, and the thread of association is broken; they cannot go on. Their associations, to use the language of philosophers, are chiefly of the successive, not the synchronous kind, and whether successive or synchronous, are mostly *casual*.

To the man of science, again, or of business, objects group themselves according to the artificial classifications which the understanding has voluntarily made for the convenience of thought or of practice. But where any of the impressions are vivid and intense, the associations into which these enter are the ruling ones: it being a well-known law of association, that the stronger a feeling is, the more quickly and strongly it associates itself with any other object or feeling. Where, therefore, nature has given strong feelings, and education has not created factitious tendencies stronger than the natural ones, the prevailing associations will be those which connect objects and ideas with emotions, and with each other through the intervention of emotions. Thoughts and images will be linked together, according to the similarity of the feelings which cling to them. A thought will introduce a thought by first introducing a feeling which is allied with it. At the centre of each group of thoughts or images will be found a feeling; and the thoughts or images are only there because the feeling was there. All the combinations which the mind puts together, all the pictures which it paints, the wholes which Imagination constructs out of the materials supplied by Fancy, will be indebted to some dominant *feeling*, not as in other natures to a dominant *thought*, for their unity and consistency of character—for what distinguishes them from incoherences.

The difference, then, between the poetry of a poet, and the poetry of a cultivated but not naturally poetic mind, is, that in the latter, with however bright a halo of feeling the thought may be surrounded and glorified, the thought itself is still the conspicuous object; while the poetry of a poet is Feeling itself, employing Thought only as the medium of its utterance. In the one, feeling waits upon thought; in the other, thought upon feeling. The one writer has a distinct aim, common to him with any other didactic author; he desires to convey the thought, and he conveys it clothed in the feelings which it excites in himself, or which he deems most appropriate to it. The other merely pours forth the overflowing of his feelings; and all the thoughts which those feelings suggest are floated promiscuously along the stream.

It may assist in rendering our meaning intelligible, if we illustrate it by a parallel between the two English authors of our own day who have produced the greatest quantity of true and enduring poetry, Wordsworth and Shelley. Apter instances could not be wished for; the one might be cited as the type, the *exemplar*, of what the poetry of culture may accomplish; the other as perhaps the most striking example ever known of the poetic temperament. How different, accordingly, is the poetry of these two great writers! In Wordsworth, the poetry is almost always the mere setting of a thought. The thought may be more valuable than the setting, or it may be less valuable, but there can be no question as to which was first in his mind: what he is impressed with, and what he is anxious to impress, is some proposition, more or less distinctly conceived;

some truth, or something which he deems such. He lets the thought dwell in his mind, till it excites, as is the nature of thought, other thoughts, and also such feelings as the measure of his sensibility is adequate to supply. Among these thoughts and feelings, had he chosen a different walk of authorship (and there are many in which he might equally have excelled), he would probably have made a different selection of media for enforcing the parent-thought: his habits, however, being those of poetic composition, he selects in preference the strongest feelings, and the thoughts with which most of feeling is naturally or habitually connected. His poetry, therefore, may be defined to be, his thoughts, coloured by, and impressing themselves by means of, emotions. Such poetry, Wordsworth has occupied a long life in producing. And well and wisely has he done. Criticisms, no doubt, may be made occasionally both upon the thoughts themselves, and upon the skill he has demonstrated in the choice of his *media*: for, an affair of skill and study, in the most rigorous sense, it evidently was. But he has not laboured in vain: he has exercised, and continues to exercise, a powerful, and mostly a highly beneficial influence over the formation and growth of not a few of the most cultivated and vigorous of the youthful minds of our time, over whose heads poetry of the opposite description would have flown, for want of an original organization, physical and mental, in sympathy with it.

On the other hand, Wordsworth's poetry is never bounding, never ebullient: has little even of the appearance of spontaneousness: the well is never so full that it overflows. There is an air of calm deliberateness about all he writes, which is not characteristic of the poetic temperament: his poetry seems one thing, himself another; he seems to be poetical because he wills to be so, not because he cannot help it: did he will to dismiss poetry, he needs never again, it might almost seem, have a poetical thought. He never seems *possessed* by any feeling; no emotion seems ever so strong as to have entire sway, for the time being, over the current of his thoughts. He never, even for the space of a few stanzas, appears entirely *given up* to exultation, or grief, or pity, or love, or admiration, or devotion, or even animal spirits. He now and then, though seldom, *attempts* to write as if he were; and never, we think, without leaving an impression of poverty: as the brook which on nearly level ground quite fills its banks, appears but a thread when running rapidly down a precipitous declivity. He has feeling enough to form a decent, graceful, even beautiful decoration to a thought which is in itself interesting and moving; but not so much as suffices to stir up the soul by mere sympathy with itself in its simplest manifestation, nor enough to summon up that array of "thoughts of power" which in a richly stored mind always attends the call of really intense feeling. It is for this reason, doubtless, that the genius of Wordsworth is essentially unlyrical. Lyric poetry, as it was the earliest kind, is also, if the view we are now taking of poetry be correct, more eminently and peculiarly poetry than any other: it is the poetry most natural to a really poetic temperament, and least capable of being successfully imitated by one not so endowed by nature. [Wordsworth's attempts in that strain, if we may venture to say so much of a man whom we so exceedingly admire, appear to us cold and spiritless.]

Shelley is the very reverse of all this. Where Wordsworth is strong, he is weak; where Wordsworth is weak, he is strong. Culture, that culture by which Wordsworth has reared from his own inward nature the richest harvest ever brought forth by a soil of so little depth, is precisely what was wanting to Shelley: or let us rather say, he had not, at the period of his deplorably early death, reached sufficiently far in that intellectual progression of which he was capable, and which, if it has done so much for far inferior natures, might have made of him the greatest of our poets. For him, intentional mental discipline had done little; the vividness of his emotions and of his sensations had done all. He seldom follows up an idea; it starts into life, summons from the fairy-land of his inexhaustible fancy some three or four bold images, then vanishes, and straight he is off on the wings of some casual association into quite another sphere. He had not yet acquired the consecutiveness of thought necessary for a long poem; his more ambitious compositions too often resemble the scattered fragments of a mirror; colours brilliant as life, single images without end, but no picture. It is only when under the overruling influence of some one state of feeling, either actually experienced, or summoned up in almost the vividness of reality by a fervid imagination, that he writes as a great poet; unity of feeling being to him the harmonizing principle which a central idea is to minds of another class, and supplying the coherency and consistency which would else have been wanting. Thus it is in many of his smaller, and especially his lyrical poems. They are obviously written to exhale, perhaps to relieve, a state of feeling, or of conception of feeling, almost oppressive from its vividness. The thoughts and imagery are suggested by the feeling, and are such as it finds unsought. The state of feeling may be either of soul or of sense, or oftener (might we not say invariably?) of both; for the poetic temperament is usually, perhaps always, accompanied by exquisite senses. The exciting cause may be either an object or an idea. But whatever of sensation enters into the feeling, must not be local, or consciously bodily; it is a state of the whole frame, not of a part only; like the state of sensation produced by a fine climate, or indeed like all strongly pleasurable or painful sensations in an impassioned nature, it pervades the entire nervous system. States of feeling, whether sensuous or spiritual, which thus possess the whole being, are the fountains of that poetry, which we have called the poetry of poets; and which is little else than the utterance of the thoughts and images that pass across the mind while some permanent state of feeling is occupying it.

To the same original fineness of organization, Shelley was doubtless indebted for another of his rarest gifts, that exuberance of imagery, which when unrepressed, as in many of his poems it is, amounts even to a vice. The susceptibility of his nervous system, which made his emotions intense, made also the impressions of his external senses deep and clear: and agreeably to the law of association by which, as already remarked, the strongest impressions are those which associate themselves the most easily and strongly, these vivid sensations were readily recalled to mind by all objects or thoughts which had co-existed with them, by all feelings which in any degree resembled them. Never did a fancy so teem with sensuous imagery as Shelley's. Wordsworth economizes an image, and detains it until he has distilled all the poetry out of it, and it will not yield a drop more: Shelley lavishes his with a profusion which is unconscious because it is inexhaustible. [The one, like a thrifty housewife, uses all his materials and wastes none: the other scatters them with a reckless prodigality of wealth of which there is perhaps no similar instance.]

If, then, the maxim *nascitur poeta*, mean, either that the power of producing poetical compositions is a peculiar faculty which the poet brings into the world with him, which grows with his growth like any of his bodily powers, and is as independent of culture as his height, and his complexion; or that any natural peculiarity *whatever* is implied in producing poetry, real poetry, and in any quantity— such poetry too, as, to the majority of educated and intelligent readers, shall appear quite as good as, or even better than, any other; in either sense the doctrine is false. And nevertheless, there *is* poetry which could not emanate but from a mental and physical constitution peculiar, not in the *kind*, but in the *degree* of its susceptibility: a constitution which makes its possessor capable of greater happiness than mankind in general, and also of greater unhappiness; and because greater, so also more various. And such poetry, to all who know enough of nature to own it as being *in* nature, is much *more* poetry, is poetry in a far higher sense, than any other; since the common element of all poetry, that which constitutes poetry, human feeling, enters far more largely into this than into the poetry of culture. Not only because the natures which we have called poetical, really feel more, and consequently have more feeling to express; but because, the capacity of feeling being so great, feeling, when excited and not voluntarily resisted, seizes the helm of their thoughts, and the succession of ideas and images becomes the mere utterance of an emotion; not, as in other natures, the emotion a mere ornamental colouring of the thought.

Ordinary education and the ordinary course of life are constantly at work counteracting this quality of mind, and substituting habits more suitable to their own end: if instead of *substituting*, they were content to *superadd*, then there were nothing to complain of. But when will education consist, not in repressing any mental faculty or power, from the uncontrolled action of which danger is apprehended, but in training up to its proper strength the corrective and antagonist power?

In whomsoever the quality which we have described exists, and is not stifled, that person is a poet. Doubtless he is a *greater* poet in proportion as the fineness of his perceptions, whether of sense or of internal consciousness, furnishes him with an ampler supply of lovely images—the vigour and richness of his intellect with a greater abundance of moving thoughts. For it is through these thoughts and images that the feeling speaks, and through their impressiveness that it impresses itself, and finds response in other hearts; and from these media of transmitting it (contrary to the laws of physical nature) increase of intensity is reflected back upon the feeling itself. But all these it is possible to have, and not be a poet; they are mere materials, which the poet shares in common with other people. What constitutes the poet is not the imagery nor the thoughts, nor even the feelings, but the law according to which they are called up. He is a poet, not because he has ideas of any particular kind, but because the succession of his ideas is subordinate to the course of his emotions.

Many who have never acknowledged this in theory, bear testimony to it in their particular judgments. In listening to an oration, or reading a written discourse not professedly poetical, when do we begin to feel that the speaker or author is putting off the character of the orator or the prose writer, and is passing into the poet? Not when he begins to show strong feeling; *then* we merely say, he seems to feel what he says; still less when he expresses himself in imagery; *then*, unless illustration be manifestly his sole object, we are apt to say, This is affection. It is when the feeling (instead of passing away, or, if it continue, letting the train of thoughts run on exactly as they would have done if there were no influence at work but the mere intellect) becomes itself the originator of another train of association, which expels, or blends, with the former; as when (to take a simple example) the ideas or objects generally, of which the person has occasion to speak for the purposes of his discourse, are spoken of in words which we spontaneously use only when in a state of excitement, and which prove that the mind is at least as much occupied by a passive state of its own feelings, as by the desire of attaining the premeditated end which the discourse has in view.*

* And this, we may remark by the way seems to point to the true theory of poetic diction, and to suggest the true answer to as much as is erroneous of Mr. Wordsworth's celebrated doctrine on that subject. For on the one hand, *all* language which is the natural expression of feeling, is really poetical, and will always be felt as such, apart from conventional associations; but on the other, whenever intellectual culture has afforded a choice between several modes of expressing the same emotion, the stronger the feeling is, the more

Our judgments of authors who lay actual claim to the title of poets, follow the same principle. We believe that whenever, after a writer's meaning is fully understood, it is still matter of reasoning and discussion whether he is a poet or not, he will be found to be wanting in the characteristic peculiarity of association which we have so often adverted to. When, on the contrary, after reading or hearing one or two passages, the mind instinctively and without hesitation cries out, This is a poet, the probability is, that the passages are strongly marked with this peculiar quality. And we may add that in such case, a critic who, not having sufficient feeling to respond to the poetry, is also without sufficient philosophy to understand it though he feel it not, will be apt to pronounce, not "this is prose," but this is "exaggeration," "this is mysticism", or "this is nonsense."

Although a philosopher cannot, by culture, make himself, in the peculiar sense in which we now use the term, a poet, unless at least he have that peculiarity of nature which would probably have made poetry his earliest pursuit; a poet may always, by culture, make himself a philosopher. The poetic laws of association are by no means incompatible with the more ordinary laws; are by no means such as *must* have their course, even though a deliberate purpose require their suspension. If the peculiarities of the poetic temperament were uncontrollable in any poet, they might be supposed so in Shelley; yet how powerfully, in the Cenci,[11] does he coerce and restrain all the characteristic qualities of his genius! what severe simplicity, in place of his usual barbaric splendour! how rigidly does he keep the feelings and the imagery in subordination to the thought!

The investigation of nature requires no habits or qualities of mind, but such as may always be acquired by industry and mental activity. Because in one state the mind may be so given up to a state of feeling, that the succession of its ideas is determined by the present enjoyment or suffering which pervades it, that is no reason but that in the calm retirement of study, when under no peculiar excitement

naturally and certainly will it prefer the language which is most peculiarly appropriated to itself, and kept sacred from the contact of all more vulgar and familiar objects of contemplation.

---

[11] *Cenci:* a poetic tragedy, published in 1819.

either of the outward or of the inward sense, it may form any combinations, or pursue any trains of ideas, which are most conducive to the purposes of philosophic inquiry; and may, while in that state, form deliberate convictions, from which no excitement will afterwards make it swerve. Might we not go even further than this? We shall not pause to ask whether it be not a misunderstanding of the nature of passionate feeling to imagine that it is inconsistent with calmness, and whether they who so deem of it, do not confound the state of *desire* which unfortunately is possible to all, with the state of *fruition* which is granted only to the few. But without entering into this deeper investigation; that capacity of strong feeling, which is supposed necessarily to disturb the judgment, is also the material out of which all *motives* are made; the motives, consequently which lead human beings to the pursuit of truth. The greater the individual's capability of happiness and of misery, the stronger interest has that individual in arriving at truth; and when once that interest is felt, an impassioned nature is sure to pursue this, as to pursue any other object, with greater ardour; for energy of character is always the offspring of strong feeling. If, therefore, the most impassioned natures do not ripen into the most powerful intellects, it is always from defect of culture, or something wrong in the circumstances by which the being has originally or successively been surrounded. Undoubtedly strong feelings *require* a strong intellect to carry them, as more sail requires more ballast: and when, from neglect, or bad education, that strength is wanting, no wonder if the grandest and swiftest vessels make the most utter wreck.

Where, as in Milton, or to descend to our own times, in Coleridge, a poetic nature has been united with logical and scientific culture, the peculiarity of association arising from the finer nature so perpetually alternates with the associations attainable by commoner natures trained to high perfection, that its own particular law is not so conspicuously characteristic of the result produced, as in a poet like Shelley, to whom systematic intellectual culture, in a measure proportioned to the intensity of his own nature, has been wanting. Whether the superiority will naturally be on the side of the logician-poet or of the mere poet—whether the writings of the one ought, as a whole, to be truer, and their influence more beneficent, than those of the other—is too obvious in principle to need statement: it would be absurd to doubt whether two endowments are better than one: whether truth is more certainly arrived at by two processes, verifying and correcting each other, than by one alone. Unfortunately, in practice the matter is not quite so simple; there the question often is, which is least prejudicial to the intellect, uncultivation or malcultivation. For, as long as so much of education is made up of artificialities and conventionalisms, and the so-called training of the intellect—consists chiefly of the mere inculcation of traditional opinions, many of which, from the mere fact that the human intellect has not yet reached perfection, must necessarily be false; it is not always clear that the poet of acquired ideas has the advantage over him whose feeling has been his sole teacher. For the depth and durability of wrong as well as of right impressions, is proportional to the fineness of the material; and they who have the greatest capacity of natural feeling are generally those whose artificial feelings are the strongest. Hence, doubtless, among other reasons, it is, that in an age of revolutions in opinion, the contemporary poets, those at least who deserve the name, those who have any individuality of character, if they are not before their age, are almost sure to be behind it. An observation curiously verified all over Europe in the present century. Nor let it be thought disparaging. However urgent may be the necessity for a breaking up of old modes of belief, the most strong-minded and discerning, next to those who head the movement, are generally those who bring up the rear of it. A text on which to dilate would lead us too far from the present subject.

Alexander Smith

died 1851

FROM "THE PHILOSOPHY OF POETRY" 1835

THE author of this essay, which was printed over the initial "S" in *Blackwood's Magazine*, December 1835, has been identified recently as Alexander Smith of Banff, who was Postmaster there from 1827 until he died in 1851.[1] It may have been his only venture into the discussion of literary questions, but he published other philosophical essays. In "The Philosophy of Poetry" he seems to be very much abreast of his time in his account of poetry as the expression of emotion, and this part of his essay can be linked with what Wordsworth, Hazlitt and Mill have to say; but as Mill goes beyond Wordsworth in "limiting poetry to the delineation of states of feeling" (see p. 156), so Alexander Smith goes further than Mill in conceiving poetry in terms of language. This is seen in the difference between their ideas concerning eloquence; for Mill, "eloquence is *heard*, poetry is *overheard*" (p. 158), and the distinction between them lies in the effect sought; for Smith, "the sole object of poetry is to transmit the *feelings* of the speaker or writer, that of eloquence is to convey the *persuasion* of some *truth*" (pp. 186–7), and the distinction lies rather in their nature and function. His more rigorous identifications of poetry as the expression of emotion leads him to analyse the language of poetry as the "language in which that emotion vents itself" (p. 177), and so sets up a sharp distinction between prose and poetry; "prose is the language of intelligence, poetry of emotion. In prose we communicate our *knowledge* of the objects of sense or thought—in poetry we express how these objects *affect* us" (p. 176). In this way, Alexander Smith proposed an antithesis which has since, with numerous variations, formed the basis of much modern theorising. Perhaps its most notable formulation in the twentieth century has been in the critical books of I. A. Richards based on distinguishing "scientific" from "emotive" language (see especially *The Principles of Literary Criticism*, 1924). Coleridge had already attacked Wordsworth's argument that there is no essential difference between the language

[1] See M. H. Abrams, *The Mirror and the Lamp* (1953, reissued 1958), p. 149.

of poetry and the language of prose (see p. 14); Alexander Smith looked further into what an expressive theory of poetry implies in terms of language, and his foreshadowing of the distinctions proposed by such writers as I. A. Richards illustrates how deeply rooted in Romantic positions modern attitudes to poetry are. Smith's essay is notable for its lucidity and rigour of argument at a time when much criticism prefers a blaze of enthusiasm to a hard line of reasoning.

FEW questions have more frequently been asked, than that—"wherein does *poetry* differ from *prose*?" and few questions have been less satisfactorily answered. Those who have little taste for poetry, have seldom troubled themselves about this matter at all, while those who regard the art with enthusiasm, have seemed to shrink from too narrow an examination of the object of their adoration, as if they felt that they might thereby dissipate a charming illusion, and increase their knowledge at the expense of their enjoyment. For my own part, I confess myself one of those who are not so much dazzled with the charms of poetry, as to be unable to examine them steadily, or describe them coolly. My interest in it is such as to incline me to speculate upon the nature of its attractions, while I am yet sufficiently *insensible* to those attractions to be able to pursue my speculations with the most philosophical composure.

The term *prose*, is used in two significations; in one of which it stands opposed to *poetry*—in the other, to *verse*. It being admitted, however, that verse is not essential to poetry, it follows that *prose*, in the sense in which it is merely opposed to *verse*, may be *poetry*— and, in the sense in which it is merely opposed to *poetry*, may be *verse*. What is to be inquired here, is, what is the nature, not of *verse*, but of *poetry*, as opposed to prose. So strong, however, is the connexion between poetry and verse, that this subject would be but very indifferently treated should that connexion fail to be properly accounted for; and I shall, in the sequel, have occasion to point out how it happens that *verse* must, generally speaking, always be *poetry*.

It seems to me that a clear line of demarcation exists between poetry and prose, and one which admits of being plainly and accurately pointed out.

No distinction is more familiarly apprehended by those who have considered the different states in which the mind exists, or acts which it performs, than that which subsists between acts or states of *intelligence*, and acts or states of *emotion*. Acts or states of intelligence are those in which the mind perceives, believes, comprehends, infers, remembers. Acts or states of emotion are those in which it hopes, fears, rejoices, sorrows, loves, hates, admires, or dislikes. The essential distinction between poetry and prose is this:—prose is the language of *intelligence*, poetry of *emotion*. In prose, we communicate our *knowledge* of the objects of sense or thought—in poetry, we express how these objects *affect* us.

In order, however, to appreciate the justice of the definition of poetry now given, the term *feeling*, or *emotion*, must be taken in a somewhat wider, but more logical or philosophical, sense, than its ordinary acceptation warrants. In common discourse, if I mistake not, we apply the word *emotion* more exclusively to mental affections of a more violent kind, or at least only to high degrees of mental affection in general. Except in philosophical writings, the perception of the *beautiful* is not designated as a state of emotion. A man who is tranquilly admiring a soft and pleasing landscape, is not, in common language, said to be in a state of emotion; neither are curiosity, cheerfulness, elation, reckoned emotions. A man is said to be under emotion, who is strongly agitated with grief, anger, fear. At present, however, we include, in the term *emotion*, every species of mental (as distinct from bodily) pleasure or pain, desire or aversion, and all degrees of these states.

It will be asked, does every expression of emotion then constitute poetry? I answer it does, as regards the specific character of poetry, and that which distinguishes it from prose. Every expression of emotion is poetry, in the same way, but only in the same way, as every succession of sounds, at musical intervals, every single chord, is *music*. In one sense, we call such successions or harmonies *music*, only when they are combined into rhythmical pieces of a certain length; so we only call the expression of emotion *poetry*, when it expands itself to a certain extent, and assumes a peculiar defined form—of which more afterwards. But as even two or three notes, succeeding one another, or struck together at certain intervals, are *music*, as distinct from any other succession or combinations of sounds—such as the noise of machinery, of water, of fire-arms, so is the shortest exclamation expressive of emotion *poetry*, as distinct from the expression of any intellectual act, such as that of belief, comprehension, knowledge. To which it is to be added, that though looking to the specific essence of poetry, every expression of feeling is poetry, yet that expression may always be more or less true and successful; and, as we sometimes say of a dull or insipid air, that there is *no music* in it—so we say, that a composition, in its essential character poetical, is not *poetry*—as meaning, that it is not good poetry— i.e. though an expression of feeling, yet not of a refined feeling, or not a faithful, an affecting, or a striking expression of it.

By the *language of emotion*, however, I mean the language in which that emotion vents itself—not the description of the emotion, or the affirmation that it is felt. Such description or affirmation is the mere communication of a fact—the affirmation that I feel something. This is prose. Between such and the expression of emotion, there is much the same difference as that which exists between the information a person might give us of his feeling bodily pain, and the exclamations or groans which his suffering might extort from him.

But by expressions of feeling or emotion, it is not, of course, to be supposed that I mean mere *exclamation*. Feeling can only be expressed so as to excite the sympathy of others—(being the end for which it is expressed)—with reference to a cause or object moving that feeling. Such cause or object, in order to be comprehended, may require to be stated in the form of a proposition or propositions (whether general or particular), as in a narrative, a description or a series of moral truths. The essential character, however, of a poetical narrative or description, and that which distinguishes it from a merely prosaic one, is this—that its direct object is not to convey information, but to intimate a subject of feeling, and transmit that feeling from one mind to another. In prose, the main purpose of the writer or speaker is to inform, or exhibit truth. The information may excite emotion, but this is only an accidental effect. In poetry, on the other hand, the information furnished is merely subsidiary to the conveyance of the emotion. The particulars of the information are not so properly stated or told, as appealed or referred to by the speaker for the purpose of discovering and justifying his emotion, and creating a sympathetic participation of it in the mind of the hearer.

The description of a scene or an incident may be highly picturesque, striking, or even affecting, and yet not in the slightest degree poetical, merely because it is communicated as information, not referred to as an object creating emotion; because the writer states the fact accurately and distinctly as it is, but does not exhibit himself as affected or moved by it. Take the following extract, for instance:—

The Torch was lying at anchor in Bluefields' Bay. It was between eight and nine in the morning. The land wind had died away, and the sea breeze had not set in—there was not a breath stirring. The pennant from the masthead fell sluggishly down, and clung amongst the rigging like a dead snake; whilst the folds of the St. George's ensign that hung from the mizen peak were as motionless, as if they had been carved in marble.

The anchorage was one unbroken mirror, except where its glass-like surface was shivered into sparkling ripples by the gambols of a skip jack, or the flashing stoop of his enemy the pelican; and the reflection of the vessel was so clear and steady, that at the distance of a cable's length you could not distinguish the water line, nor tell where the substance ended and shadow began, until the casual dashing of a bucket overboard for a few moments broke up the phantom ship; but the wavering fragments soon re-united, and she again floated double, like the swan of the poet. The heat was so intense, that the iron stancheons of the awning could not be grasped with the hand; and where the decks were not screened by it, the pitch boiled out from the seams. The swell rolled in from the offing, in long shining undulations, like a sea of quicksilver, whilst every now and then a flying fish would spark out from the unruffled bosom of the heaving water, and shoot away like a silver arrow, until it dropped with a flash into the sea again. There was not a cloud in the heavens; but a quivering blue haze hung over the land, through which the white sugar works and overseers' houses on the distant estates appeared to twinkle like objects seen through a thin smoke, whilst each of the tall stems of the cocoa-nut trees on the beach, when looked at steadfastly, seemed to be turning round with a small spiral motion, like so many endless screws. There was a dreamy indistinctness about the outlines of the hills, even in the immediate vicinity, which increased as they receded, until the blue mountains in the horizon melted into sky.*

It would seem to me impossible for words to convey a more vivid picture than is here presented; yet there is not, I think, more *poetry* in it than in the specification of a patent.

* From "Heat and Thirst—A Scene in Jamaica", *Blackwood's Magazine*, XXVII (1830), 861.

To illustrate the distinction between poetry and prose, we may remark, that words of precisely the same grammatical and verbal import, nay, the *same words*, may be either prose or poetry, according as they are pronounced without, or with *feeling*; according as they are uttered, merely to inform or to express and communicate emotion. "The sun is set," merely taken as stating a fact, and uttered with the enunciation, and in the tone in which we communicate a fact, is just as truly prose, as "it is a quarter past nine o'clock." "The sun is set," uttered as an expression of the emotions which the contemplation of that event excites in a mind of sensibility, is poetry; and, simple as are the words, would, with unexceptionable propriety, find place in a poetical composition. "My son Absalom"[2] is an expression of precisely similar import to "my brother Dick," or "my uncle Toby," not a whit more poetical than either of these, in which there is assuredly no poetry. It would be difficult to say that "oh! Absalom, my son, my son," is not poetry; yet the grammatical and verbal import of the words is exactly the same in both cases. The interjection "oh," and the repetition of the words "my son," add nothing whatever to the meaning; but they have the effect of making words which are otherwise but the intimation of a fact, the expression of an *emotion* of exceeding depth and interest, and thus render them eminently poetical.*

The poem of *Unimore*,[3] published sometime ago by Professor Wilson in Blackwood's Magazine, commences with these words:

"Morven, and morn, and spring, and solitude."

Suppose those to be the explanatory words at the beginning of a dramatic piece, and stated thus: "Scene, Morven, a solitary tract in the Highlands—season, spring—time, the morning," it would be

* See an instance of a singular effect produced by the passionate repetition of a name in the ballad of "Oriana", by Alfred Tennyson ["Oriana" appeared in *Poems, Chiefly Lyrical*, 1830].

---

[2] Alluding to 2 *Samuel*, xix. 4.

[3] *Unimore*: Subtitled "A Dream of the Highlands", this blank verse poem in nine "visions" appeared in *Blackwood's Magazine*, XXX (1831), 137–91. The author, John Wilson (or "Christopher North"), wrote much for *Blackwood's*, and became Professor of Moral Philosophy at Edinburgh University.

absurd to say that the import conveyed is not precisely the same. Why is the second mode of expression prose? Simply because it informs. Why is the first poetry? (and who, in entering on the perusal of the composition, the commencement of which it forms, would deny it to be poetry?) because it conveys not information, but emotion; or at least what information it contains is not offered as such, being only an indirect intimation of the objects in regard to which the emotion is felt. The words, pronounced in a certain rhythm and tone, are those of a person placed in the situation described, and in the state of feeling which that situation would excite, the feeling, namely, of *sublimity*, inspired by solitude and mountainous or romantic scenery; of *beauty*,* by the brilliant hues of the morning sky, the splendour of the rising sun, and the bright green of the new leaves yet sparkling with dew; the feeling of *tenderness*, which we experience in regard to the infancy, not less of the vegetable, than of the animal world; the feeling, lastly, of complacent delight with which we compare the now passed desolation and coldness of winter, with the warmth and animation of the present and the approaching period. These are the feelings, joined perhaps with various legendary associations connected with the scene, that would be conveyed by the words we are considering. Pronouncing these words in the tone and manner which disposes us to sympathize with the feelings with which they were uttered, and exerting our imagination to promote that sympathy, we experience a peculiar delight which no words, conveying mere information, could create; we attribute that delight to the poetical character of the composition.

So much for what may be called the soul of poetry. Let us next consider the peculiarities of its bodily form, and outward appearance.

It is well known that emotions express themselves in different

* The philosophical reader will sufficiently understand what I mean by the *feeling* of sublimity and beauty, taken as distinct from certain *qualities* in outward objects supposed to be the cause of those feelings; to which qualities, however, and not the feelings, the terms *sublimity* and *beauty* are, in common discourse, more exclusively applied. The word *heat* either means something in the fire, or something in the sentient body affected by the fire. It is in a sense resembling the latter, that I here use sublimity and beauty.

tones and *inflections* of voice from those that are used to communicate mere processes of thought, properly so called; and also that, in the former case, the words of the speaker fall into more smooth and rhythmical combinations than in the latter. Our feelings are conveyed in a melodious succession of tones, and in a measured flow of words; our thoughts (and in a greater degree the less they are accompanied with feeling) are conveyed in irregular periods, and at harsh intervals of tone. Blank verse and rhyme are *but more artificial dispositions of the natural expressions of feeling*. They are adapted to the expression of feeling, i.e., suitable for poetry—but not necessary to it. They do not constitute poetry when they do not express feeling. The propositions of Euclid, the laws of Justinian,[4] the narratives of Hume, might be thrown into as elaborate verse as ever Pope or Darwin[5] composed; but they would never, even in that shape, be taken for poetry, unless so far as a certain structure of words is a natural indication of *feeling*. Indeed, when there is a possibility, from the nature of the subject, that feeling may be excited, the use of a measured structure of words, and a harmonious inflection of tones, implies that the speaker is in a *state of feeling;* and hence what he utters we should denominate poetry.

And in this behold the true reason why verse and poetry pass in common discourse for synonymous terms—verse, especially when recited in the modulations of voice requisite to give it its proper effect, possessing *necessarily* the peculiar qualities which distinguish an *expression of feeling*. Hence it may perhaps be truly said, that though all poetry is not verse, all serious verse is poetry—poetry in its kind, at least, if not of the degree of excellence to which we may choose to limit the designation. I say, all *serious* verse—because a great part of the amusement we find in humorous and burlesque poetry, arises from the incongruity observed between the language —that of feeling—and the subject, which may not only have no tendency to excite such feeling, but to excite a feeling of an opposite kind. But that—although verse, generally speaking, is poetry— poetry may exist without verse (although never without rhythmical

[4] *Justinian:* Byzantine Emperor, 527–65, who codified Roman law in his *Corpus Juris Civilis.*

[5] *Darwin:* Erasmus Darwin (1731–1802), grandfather of Charles Darwin, and author of the poem *The Botanic Garden* (1789–91).

language), is evident from a reference, for example, to the compositions ascribed to Ossian,[6] which none would deny to be poetry. . . .

But farther—the language of *emotion* is generally *figurative* or *imaginative* language. It is of the nature of emotion to express itself in the most forcible manner—in the manner most adapted to justify itself, and light up a kindred flame in the breast of the auditor. Hence the poet flies from the use of literal phraseology as unfit for his purpose; and the eye of his fancy darts hither and thither, until it lights on the figures or images that will most vividly and rapidly convey the sentiment that fills his soul. The mind, anxious to convey not the truth or fact with regard to the object of its contemplation, but its own feelings as excited by the object, pours forth the stream of its associations as they rise from their source. Our perceptions of external events and objects are distinct, fixed, and particular. The feelings which such subjects excite are dim, fluctuating, general. Our language is correspondent in each case. Hence many expressions highly poetical, that is, eminently fitted for conveying a *feeling* from one mind to another, would be, if taken in reference to the object, and considered in their grammatical meaning, absolutely nonsensical. Washington Irving speaks of the "dusty splendour"[7] of Westminster Abbey—an expression deservedly admired for the vividness of the impression it conveys. Taken as conveying a specific matter of information, it is absolute nonsense. *Splendour* is not a subject of which *dusty* could be an attribute; a space or a body might be dusty; but the splendour of an object might, in strict propriety of language, as well be spoken of as long, or loud, or square. So in the line,

"The starry Galileo and his woes,"[8]

the literal inapplicability of the epithet "starry" to an astronomer is obvious. The expression is one, not of a truth that is *perceived*, but of an association that is *felt*. No epithet, signifying the mere addiction

6 *Ossian:* James McPherson (1736–96), who published in 1762–3 prose versions of what he claimed were Gaelic epics. These tales in poetic prose were welcomed throughout Europe as splendid examples of genuine folk poetry, and had considerable influence on the Romantic movement.

7 *dusty splendour:* in the essay on Westminster Abbey in *The Sketch-Book of Geoffrey Crayon, Gent* (1820).

8 Byron, *Childe Harold's Pilgrimage*, Canto IV, Stanza 54.

of Galileo to astronomical pursuits, could have struck us like that which thus suggests the visible glories that belong to the field of his speculations. From the consideration now illustrated, it results also, that the imagery, having often no essential connexion with the object, but merely an accidental connexion in the mind of the poet, strikes one class of readers in the most forcible manner, and fails of all effect with others. The expression of Milton—"smoothing the raven plume of darkness till it smiled,"[9] is greatly admired, or at least often quoted. I must confess, that, to my mind, it is like a parcel of words set down at random. I may observe, indeed, that many persons of an imaginative frame of mind and who, in consequence, take a great delight in the mere exercise of imagination (and who at the same time possess a delicate ear for verse), find any poetry exquisite, however destitute of meaning, which merely suggests ideas or images that may serve as the germs of fancy in their own minds. There are many passages in Byron—Wordsworth—Young[10] —and these enthusiastically admired, which, I must confess, are to me utterly unintelligible; or at least, the understanding of which (where that is possible) I find to require as great an exercise of thought as would be required by so much of Butler's Analogy,[11] or Euclid's Demonstrations.

Lastly—as regards the peculiar character of the *language* of poetry —it is important to observe, that a principal cause of the boldness and variety that may be remarked to belong to poetical expression, is one which would, at first sight, seem to produce an effect directly the reverse; this is—*the fetters imposed by the verse*. The expression which would be the most obvious, and even the most exact (if exactitude were what was most required), is often not the one that will suit the verse. The consequence is, that a new one must be coined for the purpose; and I believe every poet would admit that some of his happiest epithets and most adorned expressions have been lighted upon in the course of a search for terms of a certain *metrical dimension*. The necessity of obeying the laws of the verse,

[9] Milton, *Comus*, lines 251–2 ("raven plume" should read "raven down").

[10] *Young:* Edward Young (1683–1765), author of *The Complaint, or Night-Thoughts* (1742–5).

[11] *Butler's Analogy:* Joseph Butler (1692–1752), Bishop of Durham, published his *Analogy of Religion* in 1736.

leads also to a peculiar latitude in the application of terms; and as the impression of this necessity is also present to the mind of the reader, he readily grants the poetical license to the composer, and admits of verbal combinations, which, in prose, would seem far-fetched and affected. Thus the verse, then, instead of contracting, extends the choice of expression. The aptitude of a term or an epithet to fill the verse, becomes part of its aptitude in general; and what is first tolerated from its necessity, is next applauded for its novelty.

Behold now the whole character of poetry. It is *essentially* the *expression of emotion*; but the expression of emotion *takes place* by measured language (it may be verse, or it may not)—harmonious tones—and figurative phraseology. And it will, I think, invariably be found, that wherever a passage, line, or phrase of a poetical composition, is censured as being of a *prosaic* character, it is from its conveying some matter of mere *information*, not subsidiary to the prevailing emotion, and breaking the continuity of that emotion.

It might perhaps be thought a more accurate statement, if, instead of defining poetry to be in its essence the *language of emotion*, and representing the imaginative character of poetry as merely resulting from its essential nature as thus defined, I had included its imaginative character in the definition, and made that character part of the essence of poetry. It will seem that the "language of imagination" would be to the full as just a definition of poetry as the "*language of emotion;*" or, at least, that these are respectively the definitions of two different species of poetry, each alike entitled to the denomination. I shall assign the reasons why I consider the statement I have adopted to be a more true and philosophical one than that now supposed.

In the first place, the conveyance, by language, of an imaginative mental process, needs not be in the slightest degree poetical. A novel is entirely a work of imagination—it is not therefore a poem. The description of an imagined scene or event, needs not indeed differ in the least from that of a real one; it may therefore be purely prosaical. It is not the imaginative process by itself, and merely as such, but the feelings that attend it, the expression of which constitutes poetry. So much as regards the subject of a composition. As regards style, in like manner, there may be a great deal of imagery or figurative phraseology in a composition, without entitling it to be reckoned poetical; or, so far as entitled to be called poetical, it will be found to be expressive of emotion. On the other hand, the expression of emotion, even in relation to an actual scene or event (if it is merely the language of emotion and not that of persuasion—which, as elsewhere remarked, is the definition of eloquence) is, in every case, poetical, and notwithstanding that the style may be perfectly free from imagery or figure; nor again, without implying emotion on the part of the writer or speaker, will any language, or any subject, be poetical. It is then essential to poetry to be of an emotive—not essential to it to be of an imaginative character. But this imaginative character, though not of the essence of poetry, results from that essence. It is in a moved or excited state of mind, and only, I might say, in a moved or excited state, that we resort to the use of figure or imagery. The exercise of imagination is pleasurable chiefly as an indulgence of emotion. Do we usually exercise imagination on uninteresting subjects?—or what does *interesting* or *uninteresting* mean, but exciting or not exciting emotion? What else is it but our craving desire to admire—to be awed—to sympathize—to love—to regret— to hope; in one word, to feel or to be moved, that leads us to picture in the mind, scenes, or forms, or characters of beauty or grandeur; or states of enjoyment or distress; or situations of agony or rapture; or incidents of horror or delight; or deeds of heroism, or tenderness, or mercy, or cruelty? Why do we recall the joys or the sorrows that are past? why do we dwell on hopes that have been blighted—affections that have been crushed—delusions that have been dispelled? Why do we summon up the scenes and the companions of our childhood and youth? It is because such images or pictures *move* us—and poetry is the expression of our emotions. . . .

And here I may distinguish two different exercises of the imagination in poetry. The first of these is where a figure of speech—a trope or metaphor—is used for the mere purpose of giving strength or illustration to some expression of feeling.* The other—and what is more properly called imagery in poetry—is where the recollection or imagination of a sensible impression is that itself which moves the feeling. In many cases—as in the instance just quoted—the two

* and it is because a figure may also be used to strengthen or illustrate a mere truth or the expression of an intellectual process, that figurative language is not necessarily *poetical*.

operations are blended. And as sensible objects are so often the exciting causes of feeling, the happy conveyance of the impressions they create is one of the chief arts of the poet. Hence the *picturesque* character of poetical language—its aptitude to present a picture or image of an actual object calculated to affect us.

We may now see that a poetical genius—a poetical taste—may be said to consist essentially of *sensibility* (or aptitude to feel emotion), and, by consequence, or *imagination* (or aptitude to place ourselves in situations exciting emotion). The poet—the reader of poetry—seeks not to know truth as distinct from falsehood or error—to reason or draw inferences—to generalize—to classify—to distinguish; he seeks for what may move his awe—admiration—pity—tenderness; scenes of sublimity and beauty; incidents exciting fear, suspense, grief—joy—surprise—cheerfulness—regret. Whether these scenes or these incidents are real or fictitious, he cares not. It is enough to him that he can imagine them. Behold the compressed lips—the knitted brows—the fixed and sharpened eye of the philosophical enquirer, whose aim it is to *know*—to discover and communicate truth. The character of his countenance is that of keen penetration, as if he would dart his glances into the innermost recesses of science. Compare with this the open forehead—the rolling eye—the flexible mouth—the changing features of the poet, whose aim it is to feel, and convey his feeling. His countenance has been moulded to the expression of feeling, and is a constant record of that succession of emotions which passes through his breast.

Let us not suppose, however, that the pleasure derived from poetical composition is simply a pleasure arising from being in a state of emotion. Many emotions are themselves far from pleasant; but we take pleasure in the skilful expression of these emotions, for the same reason that we are often delighted with the picture of an object which would itself attract no notice, or be positively offensive or painful.

A survey of the different species of poetical composition will serve to illustrate and strengthen the preceding statements. . . .

The difference between *eloquence* and *poetry* seems to me to consist in this, that, while the sole object of poetry is to transmit the *feelings* of the speaker or writer, that of eloquence is to convey the *persuasion* of some *truth*—whether with a view to excite to action or not. And in proportion as the writer, in enforcing any particular truth, exhibits himself as affected by such truth, i.e. as feeling emotion at the contemplation of it; or, which is the index of emotion, expresses himself in a figurative or imaginative style—in such proportion the composition, though in a prose form, becomes in reality, and is felt to be, poetical. Hence poetry may be eloquent, and eloquence poetical—which is only saying, in other words, that the expression of emotion may contain an impressive statement of some truth which excites the emotion; or, *vice versa*, that the enforcement of a truth may be attended with a striking display of emotion excited by the contemplation of that truth. The line that separates poetry and eloquence, then, is sometimes altogether imperceptible. Indeed, for reasons which we have seen, the same proposition which *not* in verse, will be *prose*—*in* verse will be *poetry*.

The reasons already assigned to show why verse must generally possess the poetical character, have occasioned the term poetry to be almost exclusively confined to verse: so that though a composition, not in verse, may be essentially poetical, as being the expression of emotion, we do not call it poetical unless eminently so—that is, distinguished by a peculiarly imaginative and refined cast of thought.*

And now, having attempted to assign the *essential distinction* that subsists between poetical and prosaic composition, I cannot help expressing my opinion that compositions in *verse* are, *as such*, and as distinct from the degree of merit they may individually possess, usually rated at a value far disproportionate to their real importance.

The expression of an *emotive* does not seem to possess any intrinsic superiority over that of an *intellectual* mental process. The interest attending it is different, but not necessarily greater. In one important respect it is inferior. Feelings associate among themselves, and are

* A prayer to the Deity is essentially poetical, as being the expression of awe, admiration, gratitude, contrition, entreaty. Hence good taste, as well as just religious feeling, is shocked by the introduction, in a prayer, of any mere *proposition* (such as the affirmation of a doctrine) not in its nature exciting emotion. But *verse*, however generally suitable to the expression of emotion, would be inconsistent with the simplicity that ought to belong to prayer.

capable of being presented in connexion; but they will generally connect in one order as well, or nearly so, as in another. Hence the want in poetry (that is, in what is *nothing but poetry*)★ of progressive interest—of that sort of interest which belongs to chains of fact or reasoning—interest kept alive by the expectation of, and gratified by the arrival at, a result. The mathematician's famous query[12] in regard to the Æneid, "What does all this prove?" is more faulty in regard to its applicability to the particular case, and to the narrowness of the idea it expresses, than as being destitute of a general foundation in truth. Take up any sentimental poem, that is, a composition which is poetry alone, poetry left to its own resources, "the Seasons,"[13] "the Pleasures of Hope"[14]—your enjoyment in reading will be much the same whether you dip into a page here and there, or go directly on from the commencement. Here then is one essential inferiority attaching to the poetical as compared with the prosaic character—to the expression of *emotive*, as compared with that of *intellectual* processes. But, waving this comparison, *verse* is not indispensable to the expression of feeling. What is prose in form, is often poetry in substance. Our question regards the value generally attached to verse, as verse. Is verse then never employed but in the conveyance of sentiments of a *more valuable* kind than are ever to be found in the prose form? In answer, I take upon me to affirm, that in any ordinary book of serious or tasteful reflection, there are sentiments to be found, which, extracted from the connexion in which they are presented, no one would think of looking at twice, which are to the full as important, as striking, as touching, as vividly and elegantly expressed, as any thing which one may please to

★ I say *what is nothing but poetry*, because the interest derived from story, incident, and character, can be equally well conveyed in prose composition, nay, infinitely better, from a variety of causes, and chiefly from the inadmissibility, in poetry, of the mention of any fact not calculated to be spoken of *with emotion*. Hence, at once, the comparative meagreness and obscurity of poetical narratives.

---

[12] *famous query:* source untraced.

[13] *The Seasons:* a blank verse poem in four books, published 1726–30 by James Thomson (1700–48).

[14] *The Pleasures of Hope:* a poem by Thomas Campbell (1777–1844), published in 1799.

signify the value of a sentiment by, as are the subjects of many a "sonnet," or set of "stanzas," or "verses" which will yet be copied, translated, criticised, and the date and occasion of its composition settled with as much precision as if it were the commencement of an era. Is it the mere versification then that confers the value? Now without doubt there is a peculiar pleasure in verse as such, a pleasure which is the effect of positive constitution, and about which, therefore, there can be no dispute. But the pleasure arising from versification merely, will only, I think, be ranked among the more insignificant of our gratifications. It is not an enjoyment of a vivid, considerable kind. It is at most agreeable. But so is elegant penmanship—so may be the pattern of a carpet, a room paper, or a chimney ornament. There is that trifling sort of gratification which one will rather meet than the contrary, but not what we should go far out of our way to find. Then, again, the perception of ingenuity and contrivance, is no doubt pleasing; but a pleasure of that kind which inevitably loses its value as we become familiarized to it. We give our tribute to the talent and ingenuity of the workman, but we derive little pleasure from the work. It is trite to observe that many things which cost a vast deal of skill and labour to do, are felt of very little value when done. But farther, I must allow, in addition to the sort of pleasure which we take in verse, as such, the additional intensity which it is capable of giving to the expression of the sentiment. But here the difference between verse and prose is but in degree, and the degree sometimes but very slight. *A sentiment, which expressed in prose would be of little value, cannot be of much when expressed in verse*. Is there not, then, I again ask, a degree of interest and importance generally attached to "verses," "lines," "stanzas," utterly disproportionate to what is in justice due?

One will be apt to say here, all this is disputing about a matter of *taste*, which is universally allowed to be idle. To a person destitute of a taste for poetry, it is as impossible to prove its value, as to prove the value of music to one who has no musical ear. Now all this would be very well if verse were something essentially different from anything else, and, in its distinctive nature, the object of a *specific taste*, distinguishable from other tastes. This cannot be pretended to be the case. The difference between a thought expressed in prose, and the same thought expressed in verse, is obviously too trifling to make the former the object of a distinct constitutional faculty. The musician can, with *mathematical precision*, state the intervals, and the chords, and the succession of sounds, which, and which alone, delight his ear. Musical successions or harmonies can never be mixed, or confounded with other species of sounds, nor with any thing else whatever, as poetry may be mixed or confounded with prose. Again, there is no one who fails of receiving a strong delight from music who has the mere organic perception of musical intervals (who has an ear). To every man who can merely take up or remember an air—who can hum, whistle, or sing it, *in tune*, music is not merely pleasing, but a substantial, material enjoyment. The love of music, then, is universal among those who have merely a certain physical capacity, and who-ever does not relish it, can be shown to want a physical capacity. Not so with poetry. A man who is extremely callous to its charms shall detect a flaw in versification as accurately as the keenest poetical enthusiast—shall do verse as much justice in the reading (in proportion to what he could do to prose composition)—shall even (I do not say he could do so without difficulty) compose faultless verses. He shall be—with the reservation we are supposing, if a reservation it must be—a man of sense, feeling, taste; nay, generally addicted to literary pursuits. Here, then, is one having all the physical and mental requisites for enjoying poetry, and who, though without in any con-siderable degree enjoying, may even be able to distinguish its beauties. If such a person fails in deriving any lively enjoyment from poetry—and numerous cases of this kind I believe exist—must not the fair inference be, not that he wants a peculiar faculty, but that, to the object of this supposed faculty there is attached a somewhat fictitious and imaginary value?

The comparison now made between poetry and music may not, it is true, seem a fair one, inasmuch as a love of music is so indisputably dependent on a certain physical organization. There are many cases, it will be urged, in which *taste* is allowed to be the *sole arbiter* without appeal to any other tribunal, where yet there is no particular inde-pendent faculty such as an ear for music, and where yet the degree of taste for particular species of beauty differs remarkably in different individuals—as taste for painting, sculpture, architecture, natural scenery. Now I say, in the first place, that each of these objects of taste differ from every other thing in a way that *poetry* does not differ from *prose*, and may claim to be amenable to taste in a way that poetry, *simply as distinguished from prose*, cannot; and, next, that I believe there is no person of cultivated mind who is so indifferent to the objects of taste now enumerated, as many persons of cultivated mind are to poetry.

What then do I aim at showing? That all poetry is worthless? that the pleasure derived from poetry is altogether factitious and imaginary? no more than I should aim at showing that prose is worthless; that the pleasure derived from prose is factitious and imaginary. But I contend that poetry, *as poetry*, has no more claim to have value attached to it than prose has *as prose*. I object not to the estimation that is made of numerous individuals of the species, but to that mode of the species itself. I complain, not that many compositions that are poetical are placed in the highest rank of literary merit; not even that their being poetical is conceived greatly to heighten their value, and to display a peculiar and additional talent in the authors of them; but that many others have this value assigned to them, *simply because they are poetical, and for nothing else*. But, after all, what is there here, it will be asked, that any body disputes? Who desires, on the one hand, that worthless poetry should be preserved or valued? Who would deny, on the other, that worthless poetry is, in fact, despised and allowed to perish?

Now I acknowledge the difficulty, without specific proofs, which my present limits would not admit, of satisfying any one who should object to the justice of the opinions now offered. These opinions undoubtedly relate to a question of degree. I do not affirm that all poetry is rated above its value. I do not deny that some poetry is rejected. But I affirm, that much of what is allowed a place as poetry *of value*, poetry worth preserving and reading, is intrinsically worthless at least as regards any *pleasure to be derived from the perusal of it*. The truth of this position, with merely the general reasons on which it is founded, I must leave to be determined by the experience and reflection of individual readers.

John Keble

1792–1866

FROM *LECTURES ON POETRY* 1832–41;
PUBLISHED 1844

JOHN KEBLE (1792–1866) is perhaps best known now as the founder of the
Oxford Movement in 1833, and for the college in Oxford which com-
memorates his name. In his lifetime he was famous as the author of several
volumes of religious verse, beginning with *The Christian Year* (1827), and
although his poems now appear generally undistinguished, and he himself
set no great value on them, a few still adorn the hymn-books, like "Blest are
the pure in heart", and "New every morning is the love". In 1832 he was
elected Professor of Poetry at Oxford, an office which demanded of him no
more than a lecture each term, to be delivered in Latin. Keble held the office
for the full term possible under the regulations, ten years, and the lectures he
delivered were published in Latin in 1844 with a complimentary dedication
to William Wordsworth. They had earned him some reputation for originality and power among the learned, and the translation by E. K. Francis,
from which the following extracts are taken, has revealed for a wider
audience in the twentieth century the importance of what Keble had to say.

He begins from an expressive theory of poetry as having its essence in
feeling, in "the depths of the heart", but modifies this by emphasising the
degree of restraint and control over the simple utterance of passionate outcry
which civilisation has imposed. Poetry is seen as disguised, not direct,
expression of emotion, as a means of giving relief to the overburdened heart
without revealing its secrets, and as maintaining a proper reserve through
"those indirect methods best known to poets" (p. 195). Its harmonies have a
kind of healing power, and Keble's general idea of poetry links it closely
with music as "of all arts . . . nearest to Poetry" (p. 196). He goes on to find
in all poetry, not only that of the Christian era, a foreshadowing of "Revealed Truth itself", as poetry fosters piety; he thus assimilates to a Christian
view Wordsworth's more general conception of the "divine spirit" of the
poet (see above, p. 38).

Keble's lofty idea of the "almost religious" function of poetry is given strength by his recognition of what many adherents of the theory that poetry expresses feelings neglect altogether (see, for instance, the selections from Wordsworth, Coleridge and Mill in this volume), namely, the need for art; success in poetry depends upon a thorough skill in obeying "the technical laws of art" (p. 195). Another important aspect of his argument is his emphasis on the therapeutic value of poetry as a "kind of medicine divinely bestowed upon man" (p. 195). This was no idle claim, as Matthew Arnold was to testify to Wordsworth's "healing power" in his "Memorial Verses" (1850), and John Stuart Mill found Wordsworth's poems a "medicine for my state of mind" during the crisis in his mental history recorded in Chapter 5 of his *Autobiography* (1873).

To begin with, then, we are all so framed by nature that we experience great relief, when carried away by any strong current of thought or feeling, if we are at last able, whether by speech or gesture or in any other way, to find an expression for it. This is most clearly seen in the case of those who, even when alone, mutter and croon to themselves, under the influence of strong emotion. Illustrations are to be found again and again in Tragedy: where nothing is commoner than to represent the most important characters detailing their deeds and their schemes aloud to themselves. And such freedom (though too often abused) would assuredly not be tolerated on any terms, were not the audience conscious from their own experience of a certain natural propriety therein.

What need to spend time on this? In all languages, those common forms of lament, of exclamation, even of cursing, do not they all point the same way? Such curses are indeed impious and profane, the utterance of depraved and wicked men, but at least they serve to demonstrate how relevant to the stay of passion are speech and expression, yielding outlet as it were to the spirit.

But such utterance was suitable only in men uncivilized and scarcely removed from savagery: they would, almost like wild beasts, shout out aloud with uncouth outcry, at once and in any way, whatever came into their minds. Yet there lingers, I believe, even in the most abandoned a higher and better instinct, which counsels silence as to many things: and, if they are willing to obey the instinct, they will rather die than declare openly what is in their mind. We may note too that men so wrought upon—I mean, for instance, by vanity, grief, and other like human emotions—very often exhibit

G

excessive shamefacedness, being overquick and sensitive in their sense of shame as in everything else: especially such as "live the lives of freeborn citizens in a happy country, conditions which", as Cicero justly notes of the citizens of Rome, "give men's minds a more delicate sensibility."[1]

Thus it comes about that those to whom, most of all, utterance would be the relief from a burden are altogether restrained by a sort of shame, far from discreditable, nay rather, noble and natural, from any such relief. What must they do? they are ashamed and reluctant to speak out, yet, if silent, they can scarcely keep their mental balance; some are said even to have become insane.

Not very far removed from these, yet not exactly the same, appears clearly to be the case of lofty souls in whom, as in the youthful Nisus of Virgil,

> The restless mind is bent on some great emprise.[2]

Some great emprise—something that is great, yet still vague and undecided, of which the outline and the details have yet to be filled in. All recognise this experience whose minds have at any time been overwhelmed in pondering, more closely than of wont, on the vicissitudes of human affairs, on the marvellous ordered symmetry of the universe, or last of all, on the holy vision of true and divine goodness.

The mind indeed, oppressed and overcome by a crowd of great thoughts, pressing in upon it at one and the same time, knew not where to turn, and sought for some such relief and solace for itself as tears give to the worn-out body. And this is to feel the same craving as I ascribed to men torn by violent passion; but there was this difference, the latter shrunk, through shame, from any speech: the former feeling is higher and nobler, and therefore is neither able nor willing to be expressed in the speech of daily life.

I say therefore that that Almighty Power, which governs and harmonizes, not heaven and earth only, but also the hearts of men, has furnished amplest comfort for sufferers of either kind in the gift of Poetry. . . .

[1] A free rendering of a sentence in Cicero, *Epistolae ad Familiares* (Letters to his Friends), V. xxi.

[2] *Aeneid*, IX. 186.

But how can the needs of modest reserve, and that becoming shrinking from publicity before noticed, be better served than if a troubled or enthusiastic spirit is able to express its wishes by those indirect methods best known to poets? At all events, it is remarkable how felicitous are the outlets which minds moved by strong excitement, and aspiring by a kind of blind impulse to high ideals, have sometimes found for themselves, by following the leadings of measure and rhythm, as they first offered, like a labyrinthine clue. They needed, in fact, some clue to guide them amid a thousand paths to take the right, and this clue, as every one can see, scansion and measure, simply in themselves, are well able to supply.

Let us therefore deem the glorious art of Poetry a kind of medicine divinely bestowed upon man: which gives healing relief to secret mental emotion, yet without detriment to modest reserve: and, while giving scope to enthusiasm, yet rules it with order and due control. . . .

We need not spend much time in considering how far Poetry enters into Music: for it is universally allowed that they are twin sisters, and just as an echo reproduces and returns from afar the human voice, so Poetry and Music alike give back the subtle turns and changes of the mind. Indeed, I often wonder how it happens that, in this art beyond all others, untrained minds are conscious of the differences between composers; so that, while the numbers and measures of one linger long in the popular mind, those of another cannot even win the ear of any but cultured hearers. My conclusion is something like this: the mere sequence and progression of sound, which I suppose would be termed Melody, somehow appeals more easily and effectively to ear and mind than those other qualities associated with what is styled Harmony: which is a subtly woven blend of sound ordered after fixed rules, many elements being combined at one and the same time. The popular favourites, I apprehend, please by the sequence rather than by the combination of sounds. Only a few highly trained experts can appreciate the masters of intricate Harmony.

Moreover, their appreciation in this case is only appreciation of the musician's conformity to technical rules of art; though they themselves, even in dealing with simpler compositions, do not hesitate to borrow their phrases from any quarter, so long as they find words fit to express the emotions excited by Music. It is indeed true that, like the blind man who, endeavouring to give his idea of the colour of scarlet, said that it seemed to him like the blare of a trumpet,[3] just so men's language, whether they be cultured or uncultured, is always hard put to it to find expedients by which to describe alike the softer or severer kinds of Music. What is this but a confession that, even in harmonies, success implies not only conformity to and delicate and skilful variations of the technical laws of art, but also the power of giving faithful and felicitous expression to the deepest secrets of the human spirit? this is indeed the final crown of the most perfect harmony, yet it is also often attained, even where harmony is absent, by means of the simple order and sequence of sounds. This is, I apprehend, the reason why vocal music has most in common with Poetry: the works being generally so blended with musical measure that it is hard to say, taking the whole total impression of pleasure, what part of it is due to Poetry, what to Music.

In short, it is the common verdict that Music of all arts approaches nearest to Poetry, and moreover approaches it on that side of its effect which is concerned in piercing into, and drawing out to the light, the secrets of the soul: and in this verdict some such function is assigned to Poetry itself as we have all along been feeling after. . . .

The central point of our theory is that the essence of all poetry is to be found, not in high-wrought subtlety of thought, nor in pointed cleverness of phrase, but in the depths of the heart and the most sacred feelings of the men who write. . . .

"But," it is urged, "there have been distinguished Christian writers who have anathematized secular literature, and banished Poetry as being 'wine of devils' from the pure confines of the Church and who even ascribe the works of Homer and Pindar to evil spirits."* I grant this is so; but you will also find that most of these very men have quoted many passages from heathen writers when it

---

* See Bacon, *Advancement of Learning*, II, xxii. 13. Augustine speaks of some lines of the *Eunuchus* alluding to Jupiter and Danae as "vessels" containing the "wine of error", Jerome also calls the works of poets the "food of demons". Elsewhere Bacon says "one of the fathers in great severity called poesy *vinum daemonum*."

---

3 I have not traced the source of this allusion.

suited their own purpose: that they have sometimes recommended the study of them to the clergy: and that, while ascribing such works to Demons, they yet allow that the whole range of fictions of this kind has been providentially framed to foreshadow and resemble the facts of sacred truth. In short, the Fathers of the Church proscribe, it seems to me, this class of literature, much in the same spirit which long ago led the most devoted of Homer's admirers to banish all poetry from his Republic. They, like Plato, felt the immense influence which the divine art of Poetry must wield in any society: and so they strove with might and main to prevent this influence from doing harm, and to make sure that the Gentiles might not be misled, as they saw the Jews had been, and their minds distracted from truth by care for what was only a type and a shadow of it. There is, then, nothing in their teaching inconsistent with the belief that all that array of poets and poetry, upon which Greeks and Romans prided themselves, pointed forward in God's Providence to a coming order of things, even though the writers themselves were unconscious of it.

And, if they truly possess this quality, we may heartily approve the policy of our forefathers in assigning so great a share and influence in the education of youth to the ancient Greek and Latin poets. In this they do no more than follow in the footsteps of the Providence which, so many ages ago, saw fit to train the opening minds of God's own people in studies of the same kind: and, just as it gave to the Jews the oracles of the prophets, so to the rest of the world, though under a different dispensation, accorded Homer, Plato, and Virgil as first elements of wisdom and truth. Finally, let us be well assured of this: it vitally concerns the interests of sacred truth to maintain the usage which has survived in our Universities up to the present time, of requiring from our students a close and constant study of the writings of the classic poets, philosophers, and historians: who may all be considered poets, so far at least as they are wont to elevate the mind by the clear light either of memory or lofty speculation.

One word more: some may feel surprised that we ascribe a serious and almost religious function to a literature in which there is so much that is degrading, so much that is trivial; but I would ask such to remember that (if I may be pardoned for saying so) there are many things found in the Scriptures strikingly out of accord with what we weak men should have antecedently expected. Let us rest in the assurance that on such a question human anticipations are almost worthless, all being ordered by the will of Him who alone knows and directs the secret cause of all things.

But, to return to my argument: since it is clear, or at least a probable hypothesis, that in the highest of all interests, on which alone depends the final happiness of the race of man, poetry was providentially destined to prepare the way for Revealed Truth itself, and to guide and shape men's minds for reception of still nobler teaching, it is consistent to see the same principle at work in what I may call less important departments of its influence. I cling to the belief that, in each several age of the world, in each several region of the earth, true and genuine Poetry has, by its silent influence, fostered sincere and grave piety. We shall not readily find an instance of any state, provided indeed it enjoy the advantage of stable law and morality, which has changed its existing religious belief for a more serious and holier creed, unless the tone of its favourite poets has first undergone a change. And assuredly, wherever religion has been weakened, there men fall back into the condition in which our ancestors were before embracing Christianity. There is no reason then, why they should not be raised gradually to a better life by the same means and method, namely, by a new order of Poetry.

Edgar Allan Poe

1809–1849

FROM "THE POETIC PRINCIPLE";
PUBLISHED 1850

THE essay from which substantial selections are here printed was delivered as a lecture a number of times by the author in the last years of his life, and was first published after his death in the *New York Home Journal*, August 31, 1850. It sums up much of Poe's own thinking about the nature of poetry, and brings some lines of romantic critical theorising to a culminating point; after Poe came Matthew Arnold with his appeal to Aristotle in the Preface to his *Poems* of 1853, and Baudelaire and the symbolist poets in France. It is reasonable to put Poe thus in relation to European writers, for he had studied Wordsworth, Coleridge and Shelley, and attacks the "heresy of *The Didactic*" (p. 202) to which his fellow Americans, above all Ralph Waldo Emerson (1803–82), were prone.

The implications of the Wordsworthian phrase "the spontaneous over-flow of powerful feelings" (see above, p. 27) were developed by Shelley and by J. S. Mill, who rejects the idea of narrative poetry and puts a supreme value on the lyric (see above, p. 167). Poe goes further, in maintaining that a long poem cannot exist, because excitement cannot be sustained through-out the reading of it; *Paradise Lost* and the *Iliad* can only be seen as a 'series of minor poems" or lyrics (p. 201). What had been a cherished ideal for Wordsworth and Keats, the composing of a long poem on an epic scale, thus goes by the board. The best length for a poem he defined elsewhere, in *The Philosophy of Composition* (1846), as about 100 lines, and the main criterion for judging it becomes its intensity, its sustaining of a pitch of excitement.

The poem is valued also as it is the rhythmical creation of Beauty (p. 205); it has nothing directly to do with truth or morality, except in so far as untruths and vice are ugly, and the "sole arbiter is Taste" (p. 205). Since the ultimate pleasure in poetry is derived from the "contemplation of the Beau-tiful" (p. 205), then excellence in a poem should be self-evident, and "It is *not* excellence if it require to be demonstrated as such" (p. 206). Poe fittingly ends by citing a lyric from Alfred Tennyson's "The Princess" (1847), for Tennyson was to exemplify Poe's idea of a long poem as a collection of lyrics in *In Memoriam*, which, like *The Poetic Principle*, first appeared in print in 1850.

IN speaking of the Poetic Principle, I have no design to be either thorough or profound. While discussing, very much at random, the essentiality of what we call Poetry, my principal purpose will be to cite for consideration, some few of those minor English or American poems which best suit my own taste, or which, upon my own fancy, have left the most definite impression. By "minor poems" I mean, of course, poems of little length. And here, in the beginning, permit me to say a few words in regard to a somewhat peculiar principle, which, whether rightfully or wrongfully, has always had its influence in my own critical estimate of the poem. I hold that a long poem does not exist. I maintain that the phrase, "a long poem," is simply a flat contradiction in terms.

I need scarcely observe that a poem deserves its title only inasmuch as it excites, by elevating the soul. The value of the poem is in the ratio of this elevating excitement. But all excitements are, through a psychal[1] necessity, transient. That degree of excitement which would entitle a poem to be so called at all, cannot be sustained throughout a composition of any great length. After the lapse of half an hour, at the very utmost, it flags—fails—a revulsion ensues—and then the poem is, in effect, and in fact, no longer such.

There are, no doubt, many who have found difficulty in reconciling the critical dictum that the "Paradise Lost" is to be devoutly admired throughout, with the absolute impossibility of maintaining for it, during perusal, the amount of enthusiasm which that critical dictum would demand. This great work, in fact, is to be regarded as poetical, only when, losing sight of that vital requisite in all works of Art, Unity, we view it merely as a series of minor poems. If, to preserve its Unity—its totality of effect or impression—we read it (as would be necessary) at a single sitting, the result is but a constant alternation of excitement and depression. After a passage of what we feel to be true poetry, there follows, inevitably, a passage of platitude which no critical pre-judgment can force us to admire; but if, upon completing the work, we read it again; omitting the first book—that is to say, commencing with the second—we shall be surprised

[1] *Psychal:* spiritual.

at now finding that admirable which we before condemned—that damnable which we had previously so much admired. It follows from all this that the ultimate, aggregate, or absolute effect of even the best epic under the sun, is a nullity:—and this is precisely the fact.

In regard to the Iliad, we have, if not positive proof, at least very good reason, for believing it intended as a series of lyrics; but, granting the epic intention, I can say only that the work is based in an imperfect sense of art. The modern epic is, of the supposititious ancient model, but an inconsiderate and blindfold imitation. But the day of these artistic anomalies is over. If, at any time, any very long poem *were* popular in reality, which I doubt, it is at least clear that no very long poem will ever be popular again.

That the extent of a poetical work is, *ceteris paribus*, the measure of its merit, seems undoubtedly, when we thus state it, a proposition sufficiently absurd—yet we are indebted for it to the Quarterly Reviews. Surely there can be nothing in mere *size*, abstractly considered—there can be nothing in mere *bulk*, so far as a volume is concerned, which has so continuously elicited admiration from these saturnine pamphlets! A mountain, to be sure, by the mere sentiment of physical magnitude which it conveys, *does* impress us with a sense of the sublime—but no man is impressed after *this* fashion by the material grandeur of even "The Columbiad."[2] Even the Quarterlies have not instructed us to be so impressed by it. *As yet*, they have not *insisted* on our estimating Lamartine[3] by the cubic foot, or Pollok[4] by the pound—but what else are we to *infer* from their continual prating about "sustained effort"? If by "sustained effort," any little gentleman has accomplished an epic, let us frankly commend him for the effort—if this indeed be a thing commendable—but let us forbear praising the epic on the effort's account. It is to be hoped that common sense, in the time to come, will prefer deciding upon a work of art, rather by the impression it makes, by the effect it produces, than by the time it took to impress the effect or by the

[2] *The Columbiad:* an epic poem written in 1807 by Joel Barlow (1754–1812), a New England poet, on the history of America as seen by Columbus.

[3] *Lamartine:* Alphonse-Marie-Louis de Lamartine (1790–1869), French Romantic poet.

[4] *Pollok:* Robert Pollok (1798–1827), Scottish poet, author of a once popular blank verse poem in ten books called *The Course of Time*.

amount of "sustained effort" which had been found necessary in effecting the impression. The fact is, that perseverance is one thing, and genius quite another—nor can all the Quarterlies in Christendom confound them. By-and-by, this proposition, with many which I have been just urging, will be received as self-evident. In the meantime, by being generally condemned as falsities, they will not be essentially damaged as truths.

On the other hand, it is clear that a poem may be improperly brief. Undue brevity degenerates into mere epigrammatism. A *very* short poem, while now and then producing a brilliant or vivid, never produces a profound or enduring effect. There must be the steady pressing down of the stamp upon the wax. De Béranger[5] has wrought innumerable things, pungent and spirit-stirring; but, in general, they have been too imponderous to stamp themselves deeply into the public attention; and thus, as so many feathers of fancy, have been blown aloft only to be whistled down the wind. . . .

While the epic mania—while the idea that, to merit in poetry, prolixity is indispensable—has, for some years past, been gradually dying out of the public mind, by mere dint of its own absurdity— we find it succeeded by a heresy too palpably false to be long tolerated, but one which, in the brief period it has already endured, may be said to have accomplished more in the corruption of our Poetical Literature than all its other enemies combined. I allude to the heresy of *The Didactic*. It has been assumed, tacitly and avowedly, directly and indirectly, that the ultimate object of all Poetry is Truth. Every poem, it is said, should inculcate a moral; and by this moral is the poetical merit of the work to be adjudged. We Americans especially have patronised this happy idea; and we Bostonians,[6] very especially, have developed it in full. We have taken it into our heads that to write a poem simply for the poem's sake, and to acknowledge such to have been our design, would be to confess ourselves radically wanting in the true Poetic dignity and force:—but the simple fact is,

[5] *De Béranger:* Pierre-Jean Béranger (1780–1857), a prolific French writer of popular light verse.

[6] *We Bostonians:* alluding to the influential group of writers whose activities centred on Boston, and especially perhaps to R. W. Emerson; see above p. 199.

that, would we but permit ourselves to look into our own souls, we should immediately there discover that under the sun there neither exists nor *can* exist any work more thoroughly dignified—more supremely noble than this very poem—this poem *per se*—this poem which is a poem and nothing more—this poem written solely for the poem's sake.

With as deep a reverence for the True as ever inspired the bosom of man, I would, nevertheless, limit, in some measure, its modes of inculcation. I would limit to enforce them. I would not enfeeble them by dissipation. The demands of Truth are severe. She has no sympathy with the myrtles. All *that* which is so indispensable in Song, is precisely all *that* with which *she* has nothing whatever to do. It is but making her a flaunting paradox, to wreathe her in gems and flowers. In enforcing a truth, we need severity rather than efflorescence of language. We must be simple, precise, terse. We must be cool, calm, unimpassioned. In a word, we must be in that mood which, as nearly as possible, is the exact converse of the poetical. *He* must be blind, indeed, who does not perceive the radical and chasmal differences between the truthful and the poetical modes of inculcation. He must be theory-mad beyond redemption who, in spite of these differences, shall still persist in attempting to reconcile the obstinate oils and waters of Poetry and Truth.

Dividing the world of mind into its three most immediately obvious distinctions, we have the Pure Intellect, Taste, and the Moral Sense. I place Taste in the middle, because it is just this position which, in the mind, it occupies. It holds intimate relations with either extreme; but from the Moral Sense is separated by so faint a difference that Aristotle has not hesitated to place some of its operations among the virtues themselves. Nevertheless, we find the *offices* of the trio marked with a sufficient distinction. Just as the Intellect concerns itself with Truth, so Taste informs us of the Beautiful while the Moral Sense is regardful of Duty. Of this latter, while Conscience teaches the obligation, and Reason the expediency, Taste contents herself with displaying the charms:—waging war upon Vice solely on the ground of her deformity—her disproportion—her animosity to the fitting, to the appropriate, to the harmonious—in a word, to Beauty.

An immortal instinct, deep within the spirit of man, is thus, plainly, a sense of the Beautiful. This it is which administers to his delight in the manifold forms, and sounds, and odours, and sentiments amid which he exists. And just as the lily is repeated in the lake, or the eyes of Amaryllis in the mirror, so is the mere oral or written repetition of these forms, and sounds, and colours, and odours, and sentiments, a duplicate source of delight. But this mere repetition is not poetry. He who shall simply sing, with however glowing enthusiasm, or with however vivid a truth of description, of the sights, and sounds, and odours, and colours, and sentiments, which greet *him* in common with all mankind—he, I say, has yet failed to prove his divine title. There is still a something in the distance which he has been unable to attain. We have still a thirst unquenchable, to allay which he has not shown us the crystal springs. This thirst belongs to the immortality of Man. It is at once a consequence and an indication of his perennial existence. It is the desire of the moth for the star.[7] It is no mere appreciation of the Beauty before us—but a wild effort to reach the Beauty above. Inspired by an ecstatic prescience of the glories beyond the grave, we struggle, by multi-form combinations among the things and thoughts of Time, to attain a portion of that Loveliness whose very elements, perhaps, appertain to eternity alone. And thus when by Poetry—or when by Music, the most entrancing of the Poetic moods—we find ourselves melted into tears—we weep them—not as the Abbate Gravina[8] supposes—through excess of pleasure, but through a certain, petulant, impatient sorrow at our inability to grasp *now*, wholly, here on earth, at once and for ever, those divine and rapturous joys, of which *through* the poem, or *through* the music, we attain to but brief and indeterminate glimpses.

The struggle to apprehend the supernal Loveliness—this struggle, on the part of souls fittingly constituted—has given to the world all *that* which it (the world) has ever been enabled at once to understand and *to feel* as poetic.

The Poetic Sentiment, of course, may develop itself in various modes—in Painting, in Sculpture, in Architecture, in the Dance—

[7] *desire of the moth for the star:* quoting Shelley, "To—" ("One word is too oft profaned"), line 13.

[8] *Abbate Gravina:* Gian Vincenza Gravina (1664–1718), author of several critical essays, and founder of an Academy of Arcadians in Rome.

very especially in Music—and very peculiarly, and with a wide field, in the composition of the Landscape Garden. Our present theme, however, has regard only to its manifestation in words. And here let me speak briefly on the topic of rhythm. Contenting myself with the certainty that Music, in its various modes of metre, rhythm, and rhyme, is of so vast a moment in Poetry as never to be wisely rejected—is so vitally important an adjunct, that he is simply silly who declines its assistance, I will not now pause to maintain its absolute essentiality. It is in Music, perhaps, that the soul most nearly attains the great end for which, when inspired by the Poetic Sentiment, it struggles—the creation of supernal Beauty. It *may* be, indeed, that here this sublime end is, now and again, attained *in fact*. We are often made to feel, with a shivering delight, that from an earthly harp are stricken notes which *cannot* have been unfamiliar to the angels. And thus there can be little doubt that in the union of Poetry with Music in its popular sense, we shall find the widest field for the Poetic development. The old Bards and Minnesingers had advantages which we do not possess—and Thomas Moore,[9] singing his own songs, was, in the most legitimate manner, perfecting them as poems.

To recapitulate, then:—I would define, in brief, the Poetry of words as *The Rhythmical Creation of Beauty*. Its sole arbiter is Taste. With the Intellect or with the Conscience, it has only collateral relations. Unless incidentally, it has no concern whatever either with Duty or with Truth.

A few words, however, on explanation. *That* pleasure which is at once the most pure, the most elevating, and the most intense, is derived, I maintain, from the contemplation of the Beautiful. In the contemplation of Beauty we alone find it possible to attain that pleasurable elevation, or excitement, *of the soul*, which we recognise as the Poetic Sentiment, and which is so easily distinguished from Truth, which is the satisfaction of the Reason, or from Passion, which is the excitement of the heart. I make Beauty, therefore—using the word as inclusive of the sublime—I make Beauty the province of the poem, simply because it is an obvious rule of Art that effects should be made to spring as directly as possible from their

[9] *Thomas Moore:* the Irish poet (1779–1852), who achieved fame with his "Irish Melodies", which he began to publish in 1807.

causes:—no one as yet having been weak enough to deny that the peculiar elevation in question is at least *most readily* attainable in the poem. It by no means follows, however, that the incitements of Passion, or the precepts of Duty, or even the lessons of Truth, may not be introduced into a poem, and with advantage; for they may subserve, incidentally, in various ways, the general purposes of the work:—but the true artist will always contrive to tone them down in proper subjection to that *Beauty* which is the atmosphere and the real essence of the poem. . . .

It was by no means my design, however, to expatiate upon the *merits* of what I should read you. These will necessarily speak for themselves. Boccalini,[10] in his "Advertisements from Parnassus," tells us that Zoilus[11] once presented Apollo a very caustic criticism upon a very admirable book:—whereupon the god asked him for the beauties of the work. He replied that he only busied himself about the errors. On hearing this, Apollo, handing him a sack of unwinnowed wheat, bade him pick out *all the chaff* for his reward.

Now this fable answers very well as a hit at the critics—but I am by no means sure that the god was in the right. I am by no means certain that the true limits of the critical duty are not grossly misunderstood. Excellence in a poem especially, may be considered in the light of an axiom, which need only be properly *put*, to become self-evident. It is *not* excellence if it require to be demonstrated as such:—and thus, to point out too particularly the merits of a work of Art, is to admit that they are *not* merits altogether. . . .

From Alfred Tennyson—although in perfect sincerity I regard him as the noblest poet that ever lived—I have left myself time to cite only a very brief specimen. I call him, and *think* him the noblest of poets—*not* because the impressions he produces are, at *all* times, the most profound—*not* because the poetical excitement which he

[10] *Boccalini:* Traiano Boccalini (1556–1613), best known for his satirical essay in literary criticism, *Ragguagli di Parnaso*, in which Apollo is imagined as receiving complaints from all who care to make them, and judging each case on its merits.

[11] *Zoilus:* a name for a severe critic, after the historical Zoilus, who lived in the third century B.C. His works are lost, but he became notorious for his censure of the poems of Homer.

induces is, at *all* times, the most intense—but because it *is*, at all times, the most ethereal—in other words, the most elevating and the most pure. No poet is so little of the earth, earthy. What I am about to read is from his last long poem, "The Princess":

Tears, idle tears, I know not what they mean,
Tears from the depth of some divine despair
Rise in the heart, and father to the eyes,
In looking on the happy Autumn-fields,
And thinking of the days that are no more.

Fresh as the first beam glittering on a sail,
That brings our friends up from the underworld,
Sad as the last which reddens over one
That sinks with all we love below the verge;
So sad, so fresh, the days that are no more.

Ah, sad and strange as in dark summer dawns
The earliest pipe of half-awaken'd birds
To dying ears, when unto dying eyes
The casement slowly grows a glimmering square;
So sad, so strange, the days that are no more.

Dear as remember'd kisses after death,
And sweet as those by hopeless fancy feign'd
On lips that are for others; deep as love,
Deep as first love, and wild with all regret;
O Death in Life, the days that are no more.

Thus, although in a very cursory and imperfect manner, I have endeavoured to convey to you my conception of the Poetic Principle. It has been my purpose to suggest that, while this Principle itself is, strictly and simply, the Human Aspiration for Supernal Beauty, the manifestation of the Principle is always found in *an elevating excitement of the Soul*—quite independent of that passion which is the intoxication of the heart—or of that Truth which is the satisfaction of the Reason. For, in regard to Passion, alas! its tendency is to degrade, rather than to elevate the Soul. Love, on the contrary—Love—the true, the divine Eros—the Uranian, as distinguished from the Dionæan Venus[12]—is unquestionably the purest and truest of all poetical themes. And in regard to Truth—if, to be sure, through the attainment of a truth, we are led to perceive a harmony where none was apparent before, we experience, at once, the true poetical effect—but this effect is referable to the harmony alone, and not in the least degree to the truth which merely served to render the harmony manifest.

We shall reach, however, more immediately a distinct conception of what the true Poetry is, by mere reference to a few of the simple elements which induce in the Poet himself the true poetical effect. He recognises the ambrosia which nourishes his soul, in the bright orbs that shine in Heaven—in the volutes of the flower—in the clustering of low shrubberies—in the waving of the grain-fields—in the slanting of tall, Eastern trees—in the blue distance of mountains—in the grouping of clouds—in the twinkling of half-hidden brooks—in the gleaming of silver rivers—in the repose of sequestered lakes—in the star-mirroring depths of lonely wells. He perceives it in the songs of birds—in the harp of Æolus—in the sighing of the night-wind—in the repining of the forest—in the surf that complains to the shore—in the fresh breath of the woods—in the scent of the violet—in the voluptuous perfume of the hyacinth—in the suggestive odour that comes to him, at eventide, from far-distant, undiscovered islands, over dim oceans, illimitable and unexplored. He owns it in all noble thoughts—in all unworldly motives—in all holy impulses—in all chivalrous, generous, and self-sacrificing deeds. He feels it in the beauty of woman—in the grace of her step—in the lustre of her eye—in the melody of her voice—in her soft laughter—in her sigh—in the harmony of the rustling of her robes. He deeply feels it in her winning endearments—in her burning enthusiasms—in her gentle charitites—in her meek and devotional endurances—but above all—ah, far above all—he kneels to it—he worships it in the faith, in the purity, in the strength, in the altogether divine majesty—of her *love*.

[12] *Uranian . . . Dionaean Venus:* meaning heavenly or pure love as opposed to earthly love. In some accounts of the origin of Venus, Goddess of Love and Beauty, she is associated with Uranus, personification of the sky, and ruler of the Titans, and in others with Dione, a sea-nymph, said to be her mother by Zeus (see Homer, *Iliad*, IV. 391).

Appendix

In this Appendix excerpts are reprinted from two influential works, one German, the other French, which both help to provide a European context for the critical essays produced by the English Romantic writers. Immanuel Kant's *Critique of Pure Reason* (1781) modified the view of English empirical philosophers like David Hume that knowledge should begin with an understanding of experience, and argued that an understanding of the mind must come first. He was concerned to explain the action of the mind in apprehending the necessary, *a priori*, conditions of experience, such as the categories of space and time, and the phenomenal world, the world of nature. The mind combines and synthesises a variety of elements of experience into a single act of knowledge, and the agency responsible for this Kant identified as the imagination. The passages reprinted here explain further Kant's idea of the imagination as the ground of perception, and as functioning on the one hand blindly and *a priori* in a transcendental or unknowable synthesis which is the "ground of the possibility of all knowledge", and, on the other hand, as an active faculty bringing into a synthesis the manifold perceptions which occur in the mind. Kant provided a theoretical basis for much Romantic critical thinking, and the extent of his influence on Coleridge may be seen by comparing these passages with the extracts from *Biographia Literaria* on pp. 71–93.

François René de Chateaubriand (1768–1848) lived in exile from France during much of the revolutionary period, from 1792 to 1800. These years he spent in England, under the stress of exile and of various family misfortunes, abandoned his early rationalism and, through a melancholy amounting to a sickness of the soul, he returned to the Christian faith, starting work on *The Genius of Christianity*, which was eventually published in Paris in 1802. Its publication soon after Chateaubriand's return to France coincided with Napoleon's re-establishment of Roman Catholicism in France, and the book was a great success. In it the Christian religion is given a Romantic colouring and associated especially with the feelings and the imagination. The passage translated here is headed "Du Vague des Passions", describing a condition of the spirit which can perhaps best be described as a confused yearning which nothing can satisfy; it forms the concluding section of a Book (Part 2, Book 3 of *Le Genié du Christianisme*) concerned with the impact of poetry on men, and the ways in which Christianity has influenced the sentiments expressed in poetry ("De la Poésie dans ses rapports avec les hommes—Passions").

Here is found at once a description of Romantic melancholy, an explanation of the appeal of Christianity to the Romantic spirit, and an illustration of the ease with which the Romantic emphasis on the primacy of feeling could be related historically to the rise of the Christian faith. The lectures of Schlegel from which extracts are printed above, pp. 50–59, echoed Chateaubriand, and in turn influenced Coleridge. The English Romantics continually suggest a religious colouring in the language they use to describe the act of imagination, the importance of the feelings, or the value of poetry, as when Coleridge speaks of the imagination as "a repetition in the finite mind of the eternal act of creation in the infinite I AM", Keats writes of the "holiness of the heart's affections", and Wordsworth refers to the "divine spirit" of the poet. They are careful to avoid the explicit association of poetic feeling with Christian faith, which is to be found in Chateaubriand, and later in Keble's lectures (see above, pp. 196–8), but it lies there, dormant or repressed, in much Romantic critical writing.

Immanuel Kant

1724–1804

FROM THE CRITIQUE OF PURE REASON 1781

BY *synthesis*, in its most general sense, I understand the act of putting different representations together, and of grasping what is manifold in them in one [act of] knowledge. Such a synthesis is *pure*, if the manifold is not empirical but is given *a priori*, as is the manifold in space and time. Before we can analyse our representations, the representations must themselves be given, and therefore as regards *content* no concepts can first arise by way of analysis. Synthesis of a manifold (be it given empirically or *a priori*) is what first gives rise to knowledge. This knowledge may, indeed, at first, be crude and confused, and therefore in need of analysis. Still the synthesis is that which gathers the elements for knowledge, and unites them to [form] a certain content. It is to synthesis, therefore, that we must first direct our attention, if we would determine the first origin of our knowledge.

Synthesis in general, as we shall hereafter see, is the mere result of the power of imagination, a blind but indispensable function of the soul, without which we should have no knowledge whatsoever, but of which we are scarcely ever conscious. To bring this synthesis *to concepts* is a function which belongs to the understanding, and it is through this function of the understanding that we first obtain knowledge properly so called. . . .

What we have expounded separately and singly in the preceding section, we shall now present in systematic inter-connection. There are three subjective sources of knowledge upon which rests the possibility of experience in general and of knowledge of its objects—*sense*, *imagination*, and *apperception*. Each of these can be viewed as empirical, namely, in its application to given appearances. But all of them are likewise *a priori* elements or foundations, which make this empirical employment itself possible. *Sense* represents appearances empirically in *perception*, *imagination* in *association* (and reproduction), *apperception* in the *empirical consciousness* of the identity of the reproduced representations with the appearances whereby they were given, that is, in recognition.

But all perceptions are grounded *a priori* in pure intuition (in time, the form of their inner intuition as representations), association in pure synthesis of imagination, and empirical consciousness in pure apperception, that is, in the thorough-going identity of the self in all possible representations.

If, now, we desire to follow up the inner ground of this connection of the representations to the point upon which they have all to converge in order that they may therein for the first time acquire the unity of knowledge necessary for a possible experience, we must begin with pure apperception. Intuitions are nothing to us, and do not in the least concern us if they cannot be taken up into consciousness, in which they may participate either directly or indirectly. In this way alone is any knowledge possible. We are conscious *a priori* of the complete identity of the self in respect of all representations which can ever belong to our knowledge, as being a necessary condition of the possibility of all representations. For in me they can represent something only in so far as they belong with all others to one consciousness, and therefore must be at least capable of being so connected. This principle holds *a priori*, and may be called the trans-cendental principle of the *unity* of all that is manifold in our represen-tations, and consequently also in intuition. Since this unity of the manifold in one subject is synthetic, pure apperception supplies a principle of the synthetic unity of the manifold in all possible intuition.*

This synthetic unity presupposes or includes a synthesis, and if the former is to be *a priori* necessary, the synthesis must also be *a priori*. The transcendental unity of apperception thus relates to the pure synthesis of imagination, as an *a priori* condition of the possibility of all combination of the manifold in one knowledge. But only the *productive* synthesis of the imagination can take place *a priori*; the reproductive rests upon empirical conditions. Thus the principle of the necessary unity of pure (productive) synthesis of imagination, prior to apperception, is the ground of the possibility of all know-ledge, especially of experience.

We entitle the synthesis of the manifold in imagination transcen-dental, if without distinction of intuitions it is directed exclusively to

---

* This proposition is of great importance and calls for careful considera-tion. All representations have a necessary relation to a *possible* empirical consciousness. For if they did not have this, and if it were altogether impos-sible to become conscious of them, this would practically amount to the admission of their non-existence. But all empirical consciousness has a necessary relation to a transcendental consciousness which precedes all special experience, namely, the consciousness of myself as original apper-ception. It is therefore absolutely necessary that in my knowledge all con-sciousness should belong to a single consciousness, that of myself. Here, then, is a synthetic unity of the manifold (of consciousness), which is known *a priori*, and so yields the ground for synthetic *a priori* propositions which concern pure thought, just as do space and time for the propositions which refer to the form of pure intuition. The synthetic proposition, that all the variety of *empirical consciousness* must be combined in one single self-consciousness, is the *absolutely* first and synthetic principle of our thought in general. But it must not be forgotten that the bare representation "I" in relation to all other representations (the collective unity of which it makes possible) is transcendental consciousness. Whether this representation is clear (empirical consciousness) or obscure, or even whether it ever actually occurs, does not here concern us. But the possibility of the logical form of all know-ledge is necessarily conditioned by relation to this apperception *as a faculty*.

the *a priori* combinations of the manifold; and the unity of this synthesis is called transcendental, if it is represented as *a priori* necessary in relation to the original unity of apperception. Since this unity of apperception underlies the possibility of all knowledge, the transcendental unity of the synthesis of imagination is the pure form of all possible knowledge; and by means of it all objects of possible experience must be represented *a priori*.

The unity of apperception in relation to the synthesis of imagination is the *understanding*; and this same unity, with reference to the *transcendental synthesis* of the imagination, the *pure understanding*. In the understanding there are then pure *a priori* modes of knowledge which contain the necessary unity of the pure synthesis of imagination in respect of all possible appearances. These are the *categories*, that is, the pure concepts of understanding. The empirical faculty of knowledge in man must therefore contain an understanding which relates to all objects of the senses, although only by means of intuition and of its synthesis through imagination. All appearances, as data for a possible experience, are subject to this understanding. This relation of appearances to possible experience is indeed necessary, for otherwise they would yield no knowledge and would not in any way concern us. We have, therefore, to recognise that pure understanding, by means of the categories, is a formal and synthetic principle of all experiences, and that appearances have *a necessary relation to the understanding*.

We will now, starting from below, namely, with the empirical, strive to make clear the necessary connection in which understanding, by means of the categories, stands to appearances. What is first given to us is appearance. When combined with consciousness, it is called perception. (Save through its relation to a consciousness that is at least possible, appearance could never be for us an object of knowledge, and so would be nothing to us; and since it has in itself no objective reality, but exists only in being known, it would be nothing at all.) Now, since every appearance contains a manifold, and since different perceptions therefore occur in the mind separately and singly, a combination of them, such as they cannot have in sense itself, is demanded. There must therefore exist in us an active faculty for the synthesis of this manifold. To this faculty I give the title, imagination. Its action, when immediately directed upon perceptions, I entitle apprehension.* Since imagination has to bring the manifold of intuition into the form of an image, it must previously have taken the impressions up into its activity, that is, have apprehended them.

But it is clear that even this apprehension of the manifold would not by itself produce an image and a connection of the impressions, were it not that there exists a subjective ground which leads the mind to reinstate a preceding perception alongside the subsequent perception to which it has passed, and so to form whole series of perceptions. This is the reproductive faculty of imagination, which is merely empirical.

If, however, representations reproduced one another in any order, just as they happened to come together, this would not lead to any determinate connection of them, but only to accidental collocations; and so would not give rise to any knowledge. Their reproduction must, therefore, conform to a rule, in accordance with which a representation connects in the imagination with some one representation in preference to another. This subjective and *empirical* ground of reproduction according to rules is what is called the *association* of representations.

Now if this unity of association had not also an objective ground which makes it possible that appearances should be apprehended by the imagination otherwise than under the condition of a possible synthetic unity of this apprehension, it would be entirely accidental that appearances should fit into a connected whole of human knowledge. For even though we should have the power of associating perceptions, it would remain entirely undetermined and accidental whether they would themselves be associable; and should they not be associable, there might exist a multitude of perceptions, and indeed an entire sensibility, in which much empirical consciousness would arise in my mind, but in a state of separation, and without

---

* Psychologists have hitherto failed to realise that imagination is a necessary ingredient of perception itself. This is due partly to the fact that that faculty has been limited to reproduction, partly to the belief that the senses not only supply impressions but also combine them so as to generate images of objects. For that purpose something more than the mere receptivity of impressions is undoubtedly required, namely, a function for the synthesis of them.

belonging to a consciousness of myself. This, however, is impossible. For it is only because I ascribe all perceptions to one consciousness (original apperception) that I can say of all perceptions that I am conscious of them. There must, therefore, be an objective ground (that is, one that can be comprehended *a priori*, antecedently to all empirical laws of the imagination) upon which rests the possibility, nay, the necessity, of a law that extends to all appearances—a ground, namely, which constrains us to regard all appearances as data of the senses that must be associable in themselves and subject to universal rules of a thoroughgoing connection in their reproduction. This objective ground of all association of appearances I entitle their *affinity*. It is nowhere to be found save in the principle of the unity of apperception, in respect of all knowledge which is to belong to me. According to this principle all appearances without exception, must so enter the mind or be apprehended, that they conform to the unity of apperception. Without synthetic unity in their connection, this would be impossible; and such synthetic unity is itself, therefore, objectively necessary.

The objective unity of all empirical consciousness in one consciousness, that of original apperception, is thus the necessary condition of all possible perception; and [this being recognised we can prove that] the affinity of all appearances, near or remote, is a necessary consequence of a synthesis in imagination which is grounded *a priori* on rules.

Since the imagination is itself a faculty of *a priori* synthesis, we assign to it the title, productive imagination. In so far as it aims at nothing but necessary unity in the synthesis of what is manifold in appearance, it may be entitled the transcendental function of imagination. That the affinity of appearances, and with it their association, and through this, in turn, their reproduction according to laws, and so [as involving these various factors] experience itself, should only be possible by means of this transcendental function of imagination, is indeed strange, but it is none the less an obvious consequence of the preceding argument. For without this transcendental function no concepts of objects would together make up a unitary experience.

The abiding and unchanging "I" (pure apperception) forms the correlate of all our representations in so far as it is to be at all possible that we should become conscious of them. All consciousness as truly belongs to an all-comprehensive pure apperception, as all sensible intuition, as representation, does to a pure inner intuition, namely, to time. It is this apperception which must be added to pure imagination, in order to render its function intellectual. For since the synthesis of imagination connects the manifold only as it *appears* in intuition, as, for instance, in the shape of a triangle, it is, though exercised *a priori*, always in itself sensible. And while concepts, which belong to the understanding, are brought into play through relation of the manifold to the unity of apperception, it is only by means of the imagination that they can be brought into relation to sensible intuition.

A pure imagination, which conditions all *a priori* knowledge, is thus one of the fundamental faculties of the human soul. By its means we bring the manifold of intuition on the one side, into connection with the condition of the necessary unity of pure apperception on the other. The two extremes, namely sensibility and understanding, must stand in necessary connection with each other through the mediation of this transcendental function of imagination, because otherwise the former, though indeed yielding appearances, would supply no objects of empirical knowledge, and consequently no experience. Actual experience, which is constituted by apprehension, association (reproduction), and finally recognition of appearances, contains in recognition, the last and highest of these merely empirical elements of experience, certain concepts which render possible the formal unity of experience, and therewith all objective validity (truth) of empirical knowledge. These grounds of the recognition of the manifold, so far as they concern *solely the form of an experience in general*, are the *categories*. Upon them is based not only all formal unity in the [transcendental] synthesis of imagination, but also, thanks to that synthesis, all its empirical employment (in recognition, reproduction, association, apprehension) in connection with the appearances. For only by means of these fundamental concepts can appearances belong to knowledge or even to our consciousness, and so to ourselves.

François-René de Chateaubriand

1768–1848

FROM *THE GENIUS OF CHRISTIANITY* 1802

THERE remains to be described that condition of the spirit which, as it seems to me, has not yet been properly noticed; it is that which precedes the development of passions, when our faculties, young, vigorous, complete, but under restraint, work only upon themselves, without aim or purpose. The further human beings progress in civilisation, the more this condition of aimlessness in the feelings grows. The outcome is most unfortunate, and the large number of examples we see before our eyes, together with the multitude of books which treat of man and his feelings, make us expert without experience: we are disenchanted without having known delight; there remain desires, and yet we have no more illusions. The imagination is rich, fertile and full of wonders, while life is poor, barren and disillusioned. We live with full hearts in an empty world; and, without having practised anything, we are undeceived about everything.

The bitterness which this state of mind infuses through life is unbelievable; the heart winds and turns in all directions seeking to use powers it feels to be unavailing. The ancients were hardly aware of this secret malaise, this souring of repressed passions which work upon one another; a splendid political life, the sports of the gymnasium or of the parade-ground, the affairs of the Forum and the public square filled their idle moments, and left no place for the troubles of the heart.

In addition to this, they were not given to exaggerations, to longings, to fears without an object, to a flux of ideas and sentiments, to a constant changeability, steady only in disgust, tendencies which we acquire in the society of women. Setting aside the direct passion which they arouse in the contemporary world, women have an influence also on other feelings. In their nature they have a certain lack of restraint which they communicate to us; they make our nature as men less positive, and our passions, softened by the effect of them, are coloured simultaneously with an uncertainty and a tenderness.

Finally, the Greeks and the Romans, scarcely extending their vision beyond this life, and not in the least guessing at pleasures more perfect than this world offers, were not driven, as we are, to musings and to longings by the very nature of their worship. Designed to provide for our sufferings and our needs, the Christian religion displays to us the double image of the afflictions of earthly life and the joys of heaven, and, by this means, it becomes in the mind a main-spring of present evils and of distant hopes, from which flow endless musings. The Christian sees himself always as a traveller who passes here through a vale of tears, and who will find rest only in the tomb. The world is not the object of his desires, for he knows that man lives but a few days, and that the world will soon be lost to him.

The persecutions suffered by the first Christians increased in them this disgust with the things of this life. The invasion by barbarians brought it to its highest pitch, and the human spirit took from this an imprint of sadness and even a tincture of melancholy which has never since been obliterated. On all sides rose monasteries, where unhappy men deceived by the world sought retirement, and those who preferred to abstain from certain of life's feelings rather than reveal them only to see them cruelly betrayed. But in our time these ardent spirits, lacking both monasteries and the virtue which might take them into one, find themselves strangers in the midst of men. Disgusted by their age, appalled by their religion, they endure the world without yielding themselves to it; so they become prey to a million wild fancies; so we have seen arise this vicious melancholy which is engendered among passions when these passions, lacking an object, feed upon themselves in the lonely heart. [Ed. trans.]

Index

The index is in two sections: firstly, critical terms; secondly, the names of authors mentioned in the text. The index of critical terms is necessarily selective, but should provide references to the main discussions of the significant vocabulary of Romantic critical theory.

1. INDEX OF CRITICAL TERMS

2. INDEX OF AUTHORS MENTIONED IN THE TEXT